Structural Change and Convergence

**European University Studies**

Europäische Hochschulschriften

Publications Universitaires Européennes


**Series V**        **Economics and Management**

Reihe V          Volks- und Betriebswirtschaft

Série V          Sciences économiques


Volume/Band  **3433**

Nicole Palan

# Structural Change and Convergence

An Empirical Analysis of Production Structures in Europe

Bibliographic Information published by the Deutsche Nationalbibliothek
The Deutsche Nationalbibliothek lists this publication in the Deutsche Nationalbibliografie;
detailed bibliographic data is available in the internet at http://dnb.d-nb.de.

ISSN 0721-7339
ISBN 978-3-631-62743-3 (Print)
E-ISBN 978-3-653-02614-6 (E-Book)
DOI 10.3726/ 978-3-653-02614-6

© Peter Lang GmbH
Internationaler Verlag der Wissenschaften
Frankfurt am Main 2013
All rights reserved.
PL Academic Research is an Imprint of Peter Lang GmbH.
Peter Lang – Frankfurt am Main · Bern · Bruxelles · New York · Oxford · Warszawa · Wien

www.peterlang.com

# Contents

# List of Abbreviations

| | |
|---|---|
| *aCDI* | Average Crude Diversification Index |
| AR | auto-regressive |
| AUT | Austria |
| *b* | employment share |
| BEL | Belgium |
| CC | Central European Club |
| cswSHE | country- and sector-weighted Heterogeneity Index |
| cwSHE | country-weighted Heterogeneity Index |
| CYP | Cyprus |
| CZ | Czech Republic |
| DE | Germany |
| DK | Denmark |
| *DIV* | Diversification Index |
| *E* | Employment |
| EC | European Community |
| EEC | European Economic Community |
| EFTA | European Free Trade Association |
| ESP | Spain |
| EST | Estonia |
| EU | European Union |
| FIN | Finland |
| FBT | Food, Beverages and Tobacco |
| FR | France |
| GATT | General Agreements on Tariffs and Trade |
| GRC | Greece |
| GVC | Global Value Chain |
| *HHI* | Hirschman-Herfindahl Index |
| HR | Human Resource |
| HUN | Hungary |
| *I* | Industries |
| ICT | Information and Communication Technologies |
| IRL | Ireland |
| IRS | increasing returns to scale |
| IT | Italy |
| $iSHE^{N}$ | Index of inter-industry Heterogeneity |
| *lCDI* | Index of Least Diversity |
| LVA | Latvia |

| | |
|---|---|
| LTU | Lithuania |
| MA | moving average |
| MLT | Malta |
| NEG | New Economic Geography |
| NC | Northern European Club |
| $N$ | Countries |
| NLD | Netherlands |
| $O$ | Ogive Index |
| OECD | Organization of Economic |
| POL | Poland |
| PRT | Portugal |
| $RDI$ | Refined Diversification Index |
| R&D | Research and Development |
| $S$ | Sectors |
| SC | Southern European Club |
| $SEI$ | Shannon Entropy Index |
| $SHE$ | Index of Structural Heterogeneity |
| $sSHE^{N}$ | Index of inter-sectoral Heterogeneity |
| SVK | Slovakia |
| SVN | Slovenia |
| SWE | Sweden |
| swSHE | sector-weighted Heterogeneity Index |
| UK | United Kingdom |
| US | United States |
| $T$ | Theil Index |
| WTO | World Trade Organization |

# Acknowledgements

I owe the greatest debt of gratitude to my beloved husband Stefan Palan. Without his endurance and uplifting words during all stages of my doctoral thesis, his time spent proof-reading papers and this text or his support on all kind of computer problems, this book would not have been realized. For his comments and valuable advice on early drafts of this book as well as his support in the steps necessary on the path to become the researcher I want to be, I thank Professor Heinz D. Kurz, who I have gratefully worked with for the last years. Special thanks go to Professor Henryk Gurgul whose knowledge and support on time series analysis helped to improve this text very much. I also wish to thank my co-author Claudia Schmiedeberg for the pleasant and fruitful collaboration. I benefited a lot from the lively discussions with her, from her competence and motivation.

Moreover, I wish to thank Wilhelm Pfähler for his warm welcome during my research visit to the Institute of International Economics at the University of Hamburg as well as for his interest in this topic. Special thanks also go to David Colander and Mike Dietrich for their input on Chapter 3 at the EAEPE Conference 2009 and to Ulrich Witt and Bart Verspagen for their comments on an early draft of Chapter 4. I also thank the participants of the Summer School on Evolutionary Economics in Graz 2007 and the Winter School on Evolutionary Economics at the Max Planck Institute in Jena 2008 for both their comments and help regarding my research as well as for the great time we spent together. I very much appreciated the moral support of my colleagues as well as the financial support of the Department of Social and Economic Sciences at the Karl-Franzens-University Graz. Without the generous support of the Anniversary Fund of the Oesterreichische Nationalbank (project 13372) this book would have probably been never written, so I also owe much of my current position and the ability to conduct independent, interesting research to this institution.[1] Moreover I would like to thank the University of Graz for entirely financing the publication costs of this book. Last but not least, I am grateful to my family and especially wish to thank my parents for their lively interest in my work, their support in all steps of my education and having shown me the importance and value of knowledge from an early age on. I'd be all the happier if I was able to present this book to my father in person. Instead, I wish to dedicate this work to him.

---

[1]   This research project was supported by funds of the Oesterreichische Nationalbank (Anniversary Fund, project number: 13372).

# 1 Objectives and Motivation

The starting point and main motivation to conduct this research project was the interest of effects of European integration on the economies of European countries. Therefore, this research project deals with research questions at the crossroad between structural change and international economics. In other words, it deals with changes of the location patterns of industries as well as with changes in the specialization patterns of countries due to economic integration. This topic is of particular interest with regard to the economic developments in Europe since economic integration via the Single Market and the adoption of a single currency has led to a gradual removal of trade and production barriers. The removal of these barriers is likely to have major effects on both the relocation of industries and the competitiveness of countries, causing changes in specialization patterns. Due to enhanced possibilities of international trade and the well-functioning of a common currency union, it seems to be highly relevant whether countries are economically drifting apart and whether markets are flexible enough to absorb growing specialization and concentration patterns. Moreover, the innovations in the information and communication technologies have altered the way goods are being produced, to which degree the production can be outsourced and fragmented between countries. The development of global value chains in this respect are likely to have altered not only the ways in which international trade is organized but also affected the specialization and concentration patterns of countries all over the world (Baldwin 2012).

The contribution of this research project is in a field of research that has evolved only recently. A sound economic analysis and understanding of the forces at hand are yet limited. Whereas the convergence of income levels has been widely studied in the literature (e.g. Easterlin 1960, Borts and Stein 1964, Williamson 1965 and Theil 1967), structural convergence has received far less attention, although studies indicate that income and productivity convergence do not necessarily imply structural convergence and even if so, the process of structural convergence is much slower than convergence of productivity levels due to agglomeration and path-dependent economic development (Fagerberg 2000 and Gugler and Pfaffermayr 2004).

Anderton et al. (1992) distinguish between three separate concepts of structural convergence. First, structural convergence can stand for the assimilation of economic institutions, legal practices and organizational frameworks in which firms operate. Second, structural convergence can be understood as the assimilation of costs and prices, inflation and exchange rates. Third, structural convergence can be understood as real convergence, i.e. the reduction of differences with regard to working conditions and living standards, but also with regard to employment shares, unemployment rates and labour productivity levels. In this research project, we focus on this third branch of structural heterogeneity only.

European economic integration has led to a gradual removal of trade and production barriers. According to economic theory this should result in global efficiency gains and an increase in the competitiveness of Europe, by allowing the exploitation of advantages steaming from economies of scale and differences with regard to factor endowments (Ohlin 1933, Krugman 1991a and Krugman 1991b). However, the welfare gains for each single country (and region respectively) depend crucially on the direction the reallocation of economic activities takes. Models of new economic geography and trade (Krugman 1980 and Helpman and Krugman 1985) have in recent years shown that in contrast to classical models, integration need not make all regions and countries involved gain, but could likely favour economic centers at the cost of periphery regions. Economic integration would thus increase economic concentration and increase the disparities within the European Union. This development would contradict one of the central pieces of European economic policy, which is the aim to achieve economic cohesion between the member states of the European Union and their regions (art. 158 and 160 of the treaty establishing the European Community). Moreover, the European Commission expected that the effect of European integration above all would be the rise of intra-industry trade but not a rise in specialization. This is the opposite proposition of Krugman's thesis, whereby economic integration would automatically increase specialization of countries and the concentration of industries (De Grauwe 2009).

The aim of this project is to study the forces leading to economic (de-)concentration of industries and (de-)specialization of countries. First, an extended literature review reports both theoretical and empirical findings with a special focus on developments regarding Western European Countries.

Second, we identify the most common indices used in the empirical specialization and concentration literature. We then compare their characteristics, advantages and shortcomings. We aim to evaluate to what extent these two factors drive the empirical results. In order to unravel the differences between the most common specialization indices, both absolute and relative indices are applied to European employment shares and then discuss the origins of different outcomes and analyze the important characteristics of individual indices.

Third, we give evidence whether European integration has so far led to more heterogeneity between the core and periphery regions, i.e. whether high-tech, high-skill industries have moved to the favourable core, with only traditional and local production remaining at the periphery as theory would predict (Krugman 1991 and Ottaviano and Thisse 1999). In this respect we are also interested whether clubs of countries that are characterized by similar economic structures emerged over time. Then, we assign individual countries to clubs, i.e. groups of countries which share common features, and analyze the development of clubs and their individual countries over time. By doing so, we can distinguish between economic late-comers and front-runners and reproduce the structural change which occurred in each sub-sample. Fourth, we examine whether economic integration has altered the location of industries and are above all interested in the development of service industries since empirical studies tend to focus on manufacturing industries only and since we should distinguish between traditional and tradable services. Furthermore, we study the interdependencies of industry characteristics such as increasing returns to scale the degree of inter- and intra-industry linkages on the concentration level. Last, we focus on the transition of formerly centrally planned economies and investigate the convergence towards the Western European Countries.

In particular, we address the following research questions:

1. What are the major driving forces of (de-)concentration and (de-)specialization patterns according to economic theory? Are these results in line with empirical findings? This is of special relevance, since a deep insight into the processes leading to concentration and specialization are needed in order to establish a successful economic policy for the European Union, especially for (structurally) lagging countries.
2. Which kind of statistical tools are available to study concentration and specialization developments? What are the characteristics of a good specialization measure? Having defined them, what kind of (dis-)advantages are connected with each of the single methods investigating concentration and specialization, respectively?
3. Has economic integration altered the location of industries in Western Europe? If so, which industries are affected the most and which characteristics do these industries share? Which countries are able to attract high-growth industries and thus are likely to grow better in the future, offering better job opportunities for workers?

We do thus not cope with changes in economic structure that are related to the changes in the distribution of production factors in different sectors or countries explicitly. Moreover, we are well aware of the impact of institutions and the change thereof on the development of economic systems – as Nelson (2005) put it institutions have to be understood as "an integral part of any structural changes in the economy". We do not deal with issues related to institutional changes or with the integration of formerly Eastern European Countries into the European Union, to name just two examples, in the book.

# 2 Literature on Concentration and Specialization Patterns

Before turning to the causes and consequences of concentration, agglomeration and specialization it is necessary to define these concepts: Agglomeration can exist at various levels of space and we can either study this phenomenon at the urban, regional, national or international level. Moreover, agglomeration can be found for single industries as well as for whole economies. Whereas industrial agglomeration is associated with the concentration of one industry, absolute agglomeration implies the concentration of overall production in limited space. One prominent example of industrial agglomeration at the city level is the textile industry around Prato, Italy or the automobile industry in Detroit, U.S.; its equivalent to the regional concentration of the computer industry in the Silicon Valley. At the national level, a good example is the exposure of Japan on high-tech gadgets. There are however also international agglomerations. In Europe, there exists the "hot banana", reaching from Milan to London, spanning from Northern Italy, through Southern Germany and South-east France, Belgium, the Netherlands towards South-East England (Krugman 1991a). In this book, we will mainly focus on the development of industries at the national level as well as the specialization of countries. Since we are also interested in the transition of economies from industrial to service societies, we will explore the reasons for inter-sectoral heterogeneity shortly.

For the discussion of structural convergence, we have to distinguish two types of structural change: inter-sectoral and inter-industry change. The former refers to variations of employment shares between the aggregate sectors of an economy. The latter relates to changes of production structures within one of the aggregate sectors, for instance a change in the share of the textile industry of total manufacturing employment. The nomenclature of this distinction is not consistent across the literature; in the remainder of this book we will speak of sectors in the sense of the three aggregate sectors agriculture, manufacturing, and services, in contrast to industries, such as machinery or financial intermediation services.

## 2.1 Inter-sectoral Heterogeneity

Arguments for inter-sectoral convergence can be derived from the three-sector-hypothesis (Fisher 1939, Fisher 1952, Clark 1940 or Fourastié 1949) and the convergence hypothesis of Chenery (1960). According to these hypotheses, all

European countries should have undergone similar paths of economic development and should have reached a stage at which the tertiary sector is the largest in the economy. This process is due to developments both on the supply side (technological progress) and the demand side (changes in consumer preferences): In countries which were still characterized by large shares of agriculture in the 1970s, technical progress (above all a higher degree of mechanization) ought to have increased productivity in the primary sector, making more and more workers redundant in agriculture such that people move to manufacturing. Simultaneously, demand is considered to have reached saturation in the primary sector[2], leading to a reduction of the agrarian workforce as well.

While the agricultural sector is characterized by the extensive use of natural resources and thus falling economies of scale (Clark 1940), production in the manufacturing sector is characterized by increasing economies of scale and the fact that goods are more easily transportable as they are not so easily perishable compared to many service goods. Therefore at some point in time, there is excessive labour supply in the manufacturing sector and due to cross-sectoral labour mobility workers then move to the service sector. Imitation, knowledge transfer and mechanization are also likely to destroy employment in the manufacturing sector while employment in the service sector rises until it reaches equal levels in all countries, as incomes converge. Due to lower labour productivity than in other parts of the economy, the service sector causes rising employment in the tertiary sector as income per capita increases (Baumol 1967 and Baumol 2001). As Stiroh (2002) showed, the productivity growth in distributional services is especially low compared to manufacturing industries since possibilities for rationalization (by making use of technological advances) are limited. According to Fuchs (1980) the growth rate in the service sector however lags behind because skill-upgrading has been more pronounced in the manufacturing than in the service sector. Moreover, some part of increasing employment in the service sector can be attributed to outsourcing processes in the manufacturing industries, such that the effect of an increasing service sector is overrated. Thus the proportion of the tertiary sector has increased over time due to the increased division of labour. As more and more manufacturing firms do not have departments for R&D, marketing and market research, advertising, financing, transportation or insurances but outsource these services to specialized firms (Görgens 1975), the importance of intermediate producer services has risen substantially (Gershuny and Miles 1983). These processes have also altered the

---

2    The income elasticity for agricultural goods is low – ranging for most goods in between 0.1 and 0.2 for EU countries, some goods are characterized by negative income elasticity (Hill and Ingersent 1982).

structures within the service sector, transferring employment opportunities from the provision of personal services such as the health and social work industry towards the production or the use of services associated with the production or use of manufacturing goods such as R&D or Business Services. To explain structural change by developments on the demand side, Kuznets (1972) argued in line with Engel's law that the share of the agricultural sector is inversely correlated with per capita income, whereas the other sectors' shares are positively correlated. Thus a shift of consumer preferences towards services makes employment in the tertiary sector grow. Consequently, the difference in per capita income is one of the major determinants of inter-sectoral heterogeneity in production structures between countries, and income convergence is expected to first drive inter-sectoral and at later stages also inter-industry convergence. The expansion of the tertiary sector has boundaries, however. Due to the cost-disease in service industries (Baumol 1967), prices for services rise relatively faster than commodity prices. Appelbaum and Schettkat (1997) point out that if consumers' demand is not inelastic to changes in these relative prices, it is likely that they will substitute the consumption of legally provided services and will move to consume services provided by the shadow economy thus driving down official employment rates in the service sector. The rising employment share of services does not result from shifts in real demand but from the lower productivity growth. In this line of argument, both Klodt (1995) as well a Rowthorn and Ramaswamy (1997) show that industries with highest productivity growth lose importance due to declines in both output and employment whereas structural change makes less productive industries grow. Therefore differences in the productivity levels of countries can lead to a quite heterogeneous development of employment structures over time.

Building on the three sector hypothesis, one has to be aware of several caveats: In recent years the impact of industries associated with information and communication technologies (ICT) has risen dramatically, and the degree of heterogeneity between "classical" services such as real estate and knowledge-producing branches within the service sector has increased. It has therefore been argued that the three-sector-hypothesis should be complemented by a forth sector (Porat 1976 and OECD 2005). Yet our data are too highly aggregated to allow for a forth sector. As a consequence, we decided to work with three aggregate sectors and included ICT branches in the manufacturing or service sector respectively throughout the whole book. For this reason, we study the impact of the diffusion of information and communication technologies in the economy only through inter-industry convergence.

A second caveat is the rigidity of the sector classification. Fourastié (1949) pleaded for a constant redefinition of sectors when labour changes occur in industries. Since service industries in the classic definition only contain industries with low labour productivity, industries such as business services - which have been characterized by a sharp increase of labour productivity - should no longer be considered part of the service sector but rather part of the manufacturing sector. Today's nomenclature of sectors is more in line with Clark (1940), however, since the service sector today comprises both high and low labour productive industries. Thus, in investigating the processes of tertiarization we also have to pay attention to the heterogeneity between service industries and distinguish between traditional services and standardized services with potential for rationalization and automation (Jones and Kierkowski 1990, Jones and Kierkowski 2001 and Wolff 2007). We therefore have to keep in mind, that the reliability of the three-sector-hypothesis is weakened as soon as service industries other than personal ones are investigated.

A third caveat is that according to Fourastié (1949), the low productivity growth in service industries would lead to a rise in employment possibilities more than offsetting the loss of jobs in the manufacturing sector. Baumol (1967 and 2011), however showed that the employment shift from manufacturing to service industries is not only driven by differential productivity growth but also by the cost disease associated with the service sector. Therefore, the output share of services in final demand remains constant over time if measured in constant prices. Thus, to some degree the increase in the output share of services thus is a pure price effect resulting from the fact that services are measured at current prices and that wages in the service sector tend to rise more than an economy's average rate even though services in general are more technologically stagnant than manufacturing industries. If measures in employment shares are used, the transition from the manufacturing to the service sector should appear smaller than measured with output data.

Moreover, studies have provided empirical evidence that the income elasticity of the entire service sector does not differ markedly from unity. This is due to the fact that only part of the service sector is highly sensitive to income increases (Summers 1985, Falvey and Gemmell 1996). Therefore important arguments undermine the unconditional validity of the three-sector-hypothesis: As soon as service industries exhibit significant increases in labour productivity or income elasticities, the reliability of the three-sector-hypothesis is weakened and the structural change towards the service sector is overestimated.

Last but not least, during recent times it has been repeatedly argued that two phenomena make the distinction between services and manufacturing obsolete anyhow: First, the tertiarization of manufactured products and second, the implementation of information technologies in service goods. Therefore, the competitiveness of manufacturing firms increasingly depends on the quality of services provided once a product is sold and thus firms in manufacturing more and more often produce services or sell services that are outsourced to specialized service firms providing more personalized intermediate services than traditional services in education, health and leisure associated fields (Grömling et al. 1998).

Information and communication technologies raise the productivity of production processes in service industries. Thus it is no longer true that there is generally only little potential for productivity growth in services – but that there are differences across industries within the service sector. Industries that use standardized inputs to produce standardized outputs can be characterized by economies of scale to almost the same degree as it is the case for manufacturing industries. It is especially industries that heavily rely on information as a source of commodity that can be characterized by economies of scale: whereas the production of the first unit entails high set-up costs, the costs of reproduction are very small such that information services can be delivered at virtually zero marginal costs to an almost infinite number of customers (Shapiro and Varian 1998). Moreover, the uno-actu principle no longer applies for many service industries, creating new possibilities to concentrate production in few places instead of providing them in every country. For other sorts of services, however, the proximity of supply and demand still is important and thus de-concentration processes remain prominent.

Hence, instead of assigning industries to manufacturing or services, it could be more adequate to group economic activities according to their input structure, even though this implies more detailed data requirements (Preissl 2007). In former days, the service sector used to comprise all industries that neither belonged to the agricultural nor to the manufacturing sector, thus the service sector constituted the rest of all industries. Another characterization of service industries was that services could neither be stored nor traded and thus supplier and customer of a service had to be at the same place at the same time in order to sell/consume a service.

For our investigation of European countries in chapter 5, we therefore expect to find inter-sectoral convergence processes has taken place since the 1970s. Countries like Greece, Portugal and Spain, which were characterized by a disproportionately high employment share in agriculture and relatively low labour productivity at the beginning of the investigation period in the 1970s, are expected to have undergone a period of extensive catch-up and transition towards industrialized and service economies. The convergence process is expected to slow down over time as catch-up potentials are exhausted. A certain degree of heterogeneity between countries will however remain due to differences in natural resources, country size, institutional frameworks, and cultural backgrounds (Chenery 1960 and Chenery and Syrquin 1975). Models of the

New Economic Geography (Krugman 1991a, Krugman 1991b and Puga 1999) especially suggest that the impact of differences in country size on divergence processes should not be underestimated. The degree to which manufacturing firms outsource services varies across countries. Whereas in Germany a major part of business services are still carried out within industrial firms, other Western European countries tend to buy the very same services from specialized firms, statistically located in the service sector. Thus, Germany ought to be more heavily specialized into the manufacturing sector than other countries of equivalent development.

## 2.2  Inter-Industry Heterogeneity

Regarding inter-industry heterogeneity the direction of development is less clear-cut, since there are many centrifugal and centripetal forces at work. Individual characteristics of industries and countries, as well as the initial distribution of the labour force, wage differentials, labour mobility and transportation costs determine the concentration of industries and the specialization of countries. In what follows, we therefore discuss the main forces of concentration and specialization, respectively.

First, however, it is necessary to clarify different concepts of concentration and specialization: Absolute industry concentration is defined as production (or employment) in one industry being clustered in one or a few countries (Aiginger and Davies 2004). The textiles industry for instance is heavily concentrated in Southern European Countries, whereas the wood industry is mainly located in Northern European Countries. Relative concentration refers to the deviation of a country's employment share in an industry from the average employment share of the reference group in that industry. Thus, industries that are characterized by a low degree of relative localization are more evenly distributed over space than industries showing high levels of relative concentration. Whereas industries that are absolutely concentrated also need to be relatively concentrated, the opposite does not need to be true[3].

The same applies to the concept of absolute and relative specialization: Absolute specialization implies that a small number of industries exhibit high shares of the overall employment of a single country. Absolute specialization thus addresses the differences with regard to the industry mix of individual countries. Relative specialization refers to the deviation of a country's industry structure from the average industry structure of the reference group of countries.

---

3    For more details see Chapter 3.

This kind of relative specialization reveals for instance comparative advantages of countries. Absolute concentration can also imply that the overall economic output, i.e. the entire economic activity, takes place in very few locations only implying that not only one single industry is clustered but many industries are clustered in the very same location as this location offers advantages in production.

Turning to the factors that influence the increase or decrease of concentration and specialization respectively, we can identify a number of important push and pull features. Already Hirschman (1958) pointed out the necessity to identify the *pull* and *push forces* that either lead to a core-periphery structure or to an even pattern of industrialization across space. Regarding inter-industry convergence and divergence, the direction of development is less clear-cut, since there are both centrifugal and centripetal forces at work, depending on the individual characteristics of industries and countries, as well as on the initial distribution of the labour force, wage differentials, labour mobility and the degree of transportation costs. Globalization has altered the competitive dynamics of nations, firms, and industries - above all those that are internationally tradable and where technological imitations, the fast adoption of new technologies is possible as it is the case for the textile industry.

In the following we explain forces of relative concentration and relative specialization respectively. This distinction is necessary since these two forms of heterogeneity may but need not necessarily go hand in hand (Aiginger and Davies 2004). The description is limited, however, since we do not discuss the agglomeration of cities as in Thünen (1826) nor the problems associated with urban agglomerations or firm agglomeration as in Hotelling (1929).

## 2.2.1 Comparative Advantages

Advantages due to productivity differences were the first sources to be identified leading to international concentration and specialization patterns. Economic integration allows for a better exploitation of comparative advantages due to labour productivity (Ricardo 1817), factor endowments (natural resources, skills) and factor intensity differences in production (Ohlin 1933 or Balassa 1963) thereby enhancing advantages from the division of labour across countries. In this context, Weber (1909) distinguished between universal factors of location that are abundant in all production places and therefore do not have to be transported on the one hand and industry- or country-specific production factors on the other hand. The more important both country- and industry-specific resources are for an industry and the more these factors are localized, the more the location of production is determined by these factors and concentrated in few locations. A good example for industry-specific concentration is the abundance with wood in Scandinavian countries that made this industry concentrate in these favourable countries. In recent decades, wage differences are likely to have determined the optimal location of labour-intensive industries such as the textile industry in low-wage regions in South-Asia. Changes in comparative advantages are thus likely to have effects on the location of industries, even more so if transportation costs are low and international competition between countries becomes fiercer. High wage countries are thus determined to specialize into high-productivity, high-tech and research-intensive industries in order to ensure further economic growth. Low wage countries on the contrary will tend to move into the production of labour- and probably resource-intensive industries. As both European and international integration processes take place at the same time, we have to distinguish between industries where competition comes from other high-wage countries such as the US and Japan or whether competition stems from South East Asian countries in order to be to able predict (de-) specialization patterns of individual countries according to comparative advantages. If the latter applies, then all Western European Countries are likely to be affected likewise and employment will drop in all countries. If competition stems from other highly industrialized countries however, we expect different effects on individual countries thus leading to increasing relative concentration and specialization. To give an example: As cost competitiveness in labour-intensive and low-skill industries of the Southern European Countries compared to extra-European low-cost countries decreased due to declining transport costs worldwide, the production of these industries is expected to have been transferred to extra-European countries. This implies that the ongoing globalization makes all European countries lose competitiveness in labour-intensive, low-skill, and low-technology industries in favour of low-cost countries outside Europe, and forces all European countries to shift production towards high-technology, high-skill and capital-intensive industries. Whether concentration or de-concentration processes prevail in such an environment, depends on two things: First, whether Western European countries specialize in the same high-skill and high-tech industries or whether they specialize in different industries. On the other hand, economic integration could lead to converging effects as well: While countries can have initial advantages due to different factor endowments, these benefits are expected to be arbitraged away either through capital, knowledge and technology flows to disadvantaged locations, where marginal returns are highest due to diminishing returns to economic activities. Second, the balance between concentration and de-concentration depends on whether all countries are affected by reallocation processes at the same time. It is possible that some countries come under pressure sooner than others. In this case, divergence processes should set in first and only at later stages – when all countries are equally affected – convergence takes place. This implies structural convergence between Western European countries in mature and shrinking industries such as textiles and leather especially since the 1990s as will be shown in chapter 4 and is discussed in Palan and Rainer (2013). In contrast, the employment in capital-intensive and high-skill industries should have become more concentrated, reflecting endowment differences (capital, labour and skills) between Western European countries, and the importance of forward and backward linkages - leading to one-country specialization and ongoing structural divergence. If migration of high-skill workers is greater than migration of low-skilled workers, economic integration in Europe should lead to even more economic concentration. The international division of labour thus contributes to the persistence of structural differences between countries and even amplifies them since comparative advantages can be better exploited the deeper the economic integration becomes. Moreover, industries which are highly dependent on one input factor which is locally concentrated are expected to exhibit high concentration both at the beginning of the period and thereafter. The abundance of the natural resource wood in Scandinavian countries for instance determined the concentration of this industry to a considerable extent.

If we wish to understand to understand to which degree comparative advantages can explain the location patterns of today's world it has to be noted that until the 1960s, comparative advantages might have been able to describe the majority of specialization and trade taking place between Western European countries, since it was mainly inter-industry trade that took place. This has changed over the last decades as intra-industry trade has become ever more important. Industries that are highly dependent on endowments of natural resources such as wood, pulp and paper in Finland and Sweden are still characterized by concentration patterns due to natural advantages. Moreover, the importance of comparative advantages with regard to lower labour costs in Greece, Portugal and Spain which make these countries specialized into labour-intensive industries and these industries concentrated in these countries compared with all other Western European countries, must not be underestimated.

## 2.2.2 Changes in Trade Barriers

New Economic Geography (NEG) models in particular focus on the role of distance and transportation costs for the location of industries. Economic integration (as for instance the creation of a custom union, a common market, a common currency or common legislation practices) in general leads to falling transaction costs and can have either centrifugal or centripetal forces. Transportation costs in international trade are often defined as all expenses to ship goods from their origin point to their destination point and therefore act as a major determinant in location choices. The standard way of modelling transportation costs in international trade models is the use of the so called iceberg cost function, which relates transportation costs linearly with distance (Samuelson 1952 and Samuelson 1954), i.e. the value of the transported good itself, is taken as a measure for transportation costs. This assumption implies that any price increase of a transported good leads to a proportional increase in transportation costs, which is rather unrealistic as pointed out by Ottaviano et al. (2002) and Ottaviano and Thisse (2004). Many empirical studies gave evidence that transportation costs tend to initially increase (even though at decreasing rates) as trade volume grows, but start decreasing at some point due to economies of scale. This inverse U-shape relationship cannot be easily captured in theoretical models and moreover, a change in transportation costs due to technological advantages, is not accounted for (McCann 2005). Being aware of the caveats of iceberg functions, we turn to the implications of changes in transportation costs for the concentration of industries and the specialization of countries:

According to Krugman (1980 and 1991a, b) both specialization and concentration exhibit an inverse U-shaped relationship with transportation and trade costs[4], such that for a decrease in transaction costs from very high to intermediate levels, concentration increases. When, however, transaction costs get very low, centripetal forces outweigh centrifugal forces and thereby drive de-concentration and de-specialization processes. The arguments in detail are the following:

High transportation costs make the shipping of components very costly such that production and labour division processes are slowed down, forcing economic agents to operate at many locations with good transport access. For high trade costs exporting products is also very expensive, and firms therefore locate according to demand, which depends on the closeness to a large number of consumers and other firms (which in 2.2.3 is described as the home market effect). For a change in transportation costs to affect the location of production, moreover industry characteristics such as inter- and intra-industry linkages, the degree

---

4    Keep in mind that trade costs do not only contain freight charges proper but that transportation takes time and incurs indirect costs. Estimates according to Hummels (2000) point out that trade costs as high as 0.5 per cent of the total value of products that are shipped per day occur.

of competition within the industry and the degree of scale economies is important.

If transportation costs are high, then neither the home market effect nor forward and backward linkages play a significant role such that all countries tend to have positive employment shares in all industries. Only when transportation costs fall below a critical value, Krugman (1991) and Krugman and Venables (1995) show that a core-periphery pattern can evolve according to industry characteristics. The concentration of industries becomes more favourable as the advantages of supplying markets locally diminish and it becomes more profitable to restrict production to few places which offer good access to input factors (capital, human capital and other resources) and large home markets[5] (Buigues et al. 1990, Krugman 1980, and Davis and Weinstein 1997). The better access to suppliers and other complementary activities thus ought to make it easier to exploit economies of scale and raise productivity. Thereby production in large countries in the center of custom unions is favoured over production in small, periphery countries (Venables 1996 and Fujita et al. 1999).

Turning to empirical figures, transportation costs (in particular freight and time costs) have fallen due to more intensive use of air transportation, containerization and bulk shipping (Bordo et al. 1999). Freight costs have about halved since the mid-1970s due to better transport infrastructure and a more efficient capacity use as well as by technological progress (World Bank 2009). Falling communication costs interacting with falling transport costs (road transportation costs decreased by 40 per cent over the last three decades according to World Bank (2009) fostered the fragmentation and outsourcing of production processes. Consequently, relative wage differences have become more important since production can be easier transferred to faraway countries. New communication technologies have accelerated the diffusion of knowledge and technology worldwide and have made many services international tradable. From 1970 to 2000, the costs for overseas phone calls declined by almost 90 per cent and the costs for air transportation dropped by 50 per cent (Busse 2001). As a consequence, international competition has risen and production patterns are likely to be affected by new international trade possibilities and increases in the variety of consumer choices. Additionally to trade costs proper, non-tariff trade barriers have been a major factor of transaction costs within Europe until the completion of the internal market. The reduction of these barriers is estimated to have an

---

5    It has to be noted that home market effects lead to concentration only for intermediate levels of transport costs. For very high and very low transportation costs, home market effects are negligible since either it is not cost-efficient to export goods to foreign places or transportation becomes so cheap that the distance between producer and consumer becomes irrelevant.

effect equal to a decline in tariffs between 2.5 and 13.5 per cent depending on individual industry characteristics (Moore 1999). Emerson et al. (1988) report that non-tariff barriers to have ambiguous effects on the level of concentration as they interact with scale intensity. If non-tariff barriers are high, concentration tends to decrease in scale intensity. For low levels of non-tariff barriers on the contrary, concentration seems to increase with scale intensity of production. Thus, the implementation of the Single Market ought to have varying effects on individual industries depending on both the importance of economies of scale and prior non-tariff barriers. Pratten (1988) gives a list which industries are likely to react most sensitively on the abolishment of non-tariff barriers: These are industries relying on natural resources such as wood and wine, but also industries where variable and wage costs are dominant such as in the textile and the leather and shoe industry as well as in the production of machinery.

In Europe, the completion of the Single Market was expected to rise trade, make exports cheaper to other European countries by two per cent due to the removal of trade barriers (Peikman and Winters 1988). A reduction in trade barriers thus puts uncompetitive firms and industries under pressure since consumers will substitute local for foreign products, leading to a rise in imports in these industries. Lower competitiveness can steam from a broad range of factors such as lower productivity of workers, less know-how, older products but also from the fact that firms on average are smaller such that economies of scale can't be sufficiently exhausted (Smith and Venables 1988).

On the international level, the World Trade Organization (WTO) and the General Agreement on Tariffs and Trade (GATT) have had enormous impact on trade liberalization, especially from the mid 1980s onwards. The guidelines provided by the GATT and the WTO have fostered the international division of labour. By lowering tariffs and customs below 4 per cent at the end of the 20th century, exports grew on average by 6% annually such that total trade in 2000 was 22-times higher than in 1950 (World Trade Organization, 2008). Moreover, many non-tariff barriers have been abolished too (Hoeckman and Kostecki 1996). In this respect, the rise of Chinese exports to the rest of the world has had enormous impact on low-wage industries, above all on the textile industry in Western Europe, where Portugal and Italy can hardly stand up to the increasing low-wage competition (Commission of European Communities, 1993). Trade liberalization can thus increase concentration and specialization processes since the division of labour becomes more advantageous. For the low-tech and low-wage industries such as the textile industry, the Commission of the European Union (2003) and European Union (2002) identify above all the following challenges due to changes in the economic environment: Major technological changes leading to shifts in competitiveness between highly industrialized and developing countries, differences in production costs; the emergence of major international competitors (such as China) since the WTO abolished exemptions for the protected textile industry in the 1990s as well as the de-location of production sites from Western to Eastern European Countries in the course of EU enlargement, changes in international trade. Firms in Western Europe can only stabilize employment if they are productive, innovative and are able to modernize their production. Relocation of mass production to third countries has taken place over the past decades since abolishing trade barriers and strengthening the integration of production markets is likely to affect the location and concentration patterns of this industry. Economic integration and trade liberalization consequently contribute to the persistence or even the broadening of structural differences between countries. These effects are of particular relevance for mature industries since the more standardized production becomes, the lower the necessity to produce close to consumers. In such cases production can be transferred to places offering cost-advantages while firms in high-wage countries will specialize into the production of new goods with higher value added. Only if the production requires specific skills and the market is nationally segmented, then production and thus employment will stick to the original place (Molle 2006). This could be especially true for the operation of multinational firms. Several studies show empirically that falling trade costs make horizontal multinational firms concentrate production where costs are lowest (Markusen and Venables 1998 and Markusen and Venables 2000).

Simultaneously, a decline in transportation costs could have fostered decentralization since foreign markets become more important in relation to the consumption possibilities in the home market. Thus, countries in the periphery have more opportunities to efficiently export their goods to other countries and are also likely to be more cost-efficient due to lower costs for rents and labour. Additionally, as countries harmonize their laws, rules and product standards, it is easier and less costly for foreign firms to set up affiliations in other countries also favouring the dispersion of production across countries. Thus, diversification processes could set in too at low costs of transaction. At medium-levels of transport costs however, agglomeration forces are likely to prevail. Moreover, to the extent that economic integration leads to increased mobility of input factors (natural resources, capital or human workers), the effect on concentration processes is expected to turn out ambivalent. Hence, in determining the location of specific industries, it is crucial to take into account the combination of transport costs and factor mobility (Norman and Venables 1995). Declining transportation costs can destabilize agglomerations, since competition for peripheral locations increases, which decreases the value of knowledge obtained in agglomerations (Gersbach and Schmutzler 2000).

It remains to be seen whether economic integration fosters intra- or inter-industry agglomeration tendencies. The fragmentation of production processes has led to increases in trade of intermediate goods and services. According to UNCTAD (2013), 80 per cent of total global trade annually currently occurs due to trade of multinational firms that have increasingly taking advantage of producing along global value chains. Simultaneously, the value added of developing countries in these global value chains (GVC) has been rising as the majority of developing countries are increasingly participating in GVCs. The share of this country groups in global value-added trade increased from 20 per cent in 1990 to 30 per cent in 2000 to over 40 per in 2012. The industries that are characterized by the most segmented value chains are office and accounting machinery, motor vehicles and communication equipment. For the competitiveness and further economic development of a country, the position within the global value chains is crucial since the value added is not equally distributed across the value chain.

The contrary hypothesis is that economic integration leads to intra-industry but not inter-industry specialization. The European Commission (1997) reported that intra-industry trade was rising but not inter-industry trade. If we assume intra-industry trade to be a good proxy for overall production and employment patterns, then this indicates structural dispersion of economic activity over time. At the aggregated level, countries become more similar if intra-industry trade as opposed to inter-industry trade gains importance. Jones and Kiezkowski (1990 and 2001) argue that this diversification within an industry as opposed to diversification across industries is a result of the international fragmentation of production. As trade costs decline, production chains are broken down into a growing set of small tasks, many of which are sequentially performed in different countries since fragmented production needs not necessarily to be carried out in close spatial proximity (Arndt and Kierzkowski 2000). A good example is the textile industries, where unskilled, labour-intensive parts of production are transferred to low-wage countries while only high-skill tasks remain in capital abundant Western European countries. As a consequence, specialization of countries should decrease over time, as industries become less and less concentrated.

## 2.2.3 Market Size Effect and Country Location

A central feature in NEG Models is the home market effect (Helpman and Krugman 1985), which is describes the phenomenon that there is a *"more than proportional relationship between a country's share of the world production of a good and its share of world demand for the same good"* (Crozet and Trionfetti

2008). Accordingly, Krugman-type models show that countries tend to export goods for which home demand is relatively large (Krugman 1980 and Krugman 1991a). The model by Krugman and Venables (1990) also implies that improved access might hurt countries in the periphery. They studied two countries that differ in size, and interpreted the large country as a central European country, such as Germany, which has easy access to many markets, and the small country as a peripheral economy, such as Portugal. At high trade costs each country's production of manufacturing is proportional to its size. However, at intermediate levels of trade costs a disproportionately large number of manufacturing firms locate in the large country owing to its better market access—another manifestation of the home-market effect. The reason is that as production moves to economic centers, on one hand the agglomeration effect becomes stronger but on the other hand the loss from being away from costumers increases because of transport costs. For small transport costs, the productivity gain from agglomeration may dominate the loss resulting from closer customers. For high transport costs, the productivity gain does not dominate at the center of the cluster, and so a new cluster of firms producing the other good appears. Hence, the theory suggests that lower transport costs imply a higher degree of specialization and more concentration.

That is, consumer-proximity considerations dominate firms' location decision, and lead to low concentration of industries and overall production alike. Krugman (1991a and 1991b) shows that this is the case even more so if economies of scale are weak and the share of production independent of specific factors (such as land) in production is small. Concentration levels are low as incentives to produce in many locations are predominant. If transport costs get low and economies of scale prevail, home market effects become more important (Krugman 1980 and Krugman and Helpman 1985) – even if the labour force is immobile. Under these circumstances, firms in larger countries gain competitiveness and overall production is likely to become concentrated at economic centers which offer better access to a large number of consumers and well-trained working force, making the periphery worse off. Since centers can pay higher wages, they attract even more workers such that people move to these favourable places (Krugman 1991). If trade costs are low, trade in intermediates and final goods becomes cheaper which implies that factor-market considerations dominate location. This again leads to low concentration since a concentration of increasing returns industries would drive up the relative price of the factor used intensively in this industry. Low transportation costs can lead also to a rise in economic concentration in increasing return industries since economies of scale can be exploited even more easily (Krugman 1991a and 1991b). On the other hand, the concentration of industries characterized by increasing returns to scale would drive up the relative prices for factors used in the production of these goods. This fact works against further concentration in the long run (Forslid 2002). Finally, for intermediate trade costs supplier-proximity considerations dominate the other two, leading to high concentration. The combination of product-market and factor market forces thus makes concentration of IRS industries non-monotonically dependent on trade costs, producing an inverted U-shape with maximum concentration for intermediate trade costs (Krugman 1991b, Krugman and Venables 1995 and Rossi-Hansberg 2005).

There are several caveats to be considered when studying the impact of home market effects in the real world as pointed out by Behrens et al. (2009): They show that that the influence of the home market effect is overestimated in standard NEG models since the advantage of large countries to some extent is due to the assumptions that there are only two countries, that there is factor price equalization across countries and that homogenous goods can be traded freely. All of these assumptions are problematic in the real world. Behrens et al. (2009) generate differing results from standard NEG models if three or more countries are considered. This new prediction takes into account important features of the real world such as comparative advantage due to cross-country technological differences and lack of factor price equalization.

Head et al. (2002) add to the criticism by giving evidence that home market effects can vanish if goods are differentiated according to the locations where production takes place rather than according to the firms that produce these goods. In their model, variety is rather linked to countries than to firms and consequently they show that the larger countries do not necessarily attract more than a proportional share of firms (production). They show the implications of an endogenous expenditure share for the international distribution of firms because, in addition to the relative market size, the different share of expenditures on differentiated goods across countries also affects the distribution of industries.

Yu (2005) also demonstrates that the demand conditions of consumers and their preferences play an important role whether home markets occur at all. Davis (1998) moreover shows that if the transportation costs for homogenous goods are equal to the transportation costs of differentiated goods, the larger country does not acquire more than a proportional share of manufacturing firms.

Baldwin et al. (2003), Fujita et al. (1999), Krugman (1991), Martin and Rogers (1995), and Ottaviano and van Ypersele (2005) all point to the importance of relative market size between two countries for explaining agglomeration. According to these models, the market size effect is stronger the lower the transportation costs and in extreme cases leads to full agglomeration in the large country. One precondition for this result is perfect international capital mobility, i.e. there are no transaction costs when capital holders invest in other countries.

Thus with regard to the development of specialization patterns, the following factors are the main driving forces: differences with respect to per-capita-income, intermediate and final product demand, exports, factor productivity growth, relative prices and the vertical organization of production, i.e. inter-industry division of labour (for a detailed overview see Schettkat and Yocarini 2006).

According to Fujita et al. (1999), larger countries are more likely to be persistently more specialized in large industries compared to smaller countries. This is due to the fact that first intra-industry linkages gain in importance the larger an industry is and second to the fact that larger countries are more favorable destinations for industries characterized by a great number of intra-industry linkages. In these industries, the effect of decreasing trade costs on demand proximity is outweighed by the effects of intra-industry linkages. Larger countries tend to reduce specialization in smaller industries as economic integration unfolds, since proximity to markets and the concurrent decrease in transportation costs becomes less important, while smaller countries can gain shares in those industries where their initial disadvantages vanish due to a better access to intermediate goods. In general, however, larger countries tend to be less specialized than smaller countries. Especially if home market effects, economies of scale and comparative advantages prevail, a high degree of specialization in small countries but only small degree of specialization in large countries is observable at early stages of integration (Fujita et al. 1999). This is due to the fact that large countries operate in many industries (and there is also a high concentration of overall production in core countries) whereas at lower trade costs larger countries become more specialized as opposed to de-specialization processes in smaller countries. Krugman (1991) and Krugman and Venables (1995) show that core-periphery pattern also depend on industry characteristics as will be discussed in the following section.

## 2.2.4 Industry Characteristics

One factor explaining the opposing concentration is the limited ability of some industries to exploit economies of scale and market size (Helpman and Krugman 1985 or Haaland et al. 1999). In this respect we have to distinguish between intra-industrial externalities (Marshall 1920, Arrow 1962, Romer 1986 and Romer 1990) and inter-industry externalities (Jacobs 1969)[6]. In the former case only

---

6    For studying the impact of economies of scale on concentration processes, internal economies of scale (both pecuniary and technological) are only of minor interest. Even though we should not neglect that larger firms may have competitive advantages com-

firms within the same industry are able to benefit from agglomeration whereas in the latter case knowledge can spill over between firms in different industries. In both cases the local supply of non-tradable and factor inputs by specialized suppliers (including the availability of an adequately skilled local labour pool) makes it more profitable for firms to concentrate production in order to minimize production costs and make full use of spillovers and the use of a common infrastructure. The pooled labour market is beneficial for workers by lowering the probability of unemployment, increasing the incentives for acquiring special skills and raising wages as more employers demand for specialist workers (Matouschek and Robert-Nicoud 2005). Yet whereas intra-industry externalities lead to concentration of industries, inter-industry externalities do not necessarily imply industry concentration but more likely the concentration of overall production within a small number of places, i.e. absolute concentration of overall economic activity.

This also implies that concentration is high in imperfectly competitive industries characterized by a large number of up- and downstream linkages (Krugman and Venables 1995 and Venables 1996) or a high level of non-tradable intermediate inputs in production (Fujita 1988 and Rivera-Batiz 1988): Under these circumstances, the location decisions of producers become interdependent and the incentives to locate where other firms are located increase. If an upstream industry in a location expands the production variety of intermediate goods, the downstream industry benefits both because it has better (or more) access to specialized inputs and because it obtains these inputs at lower transportation costs. In general, firms can then provide non-tradable and specific inputs in greater variety and at lower cost due to intense competition within larger market areas at economic centers than in the periphery. This reinforces concentration forces. The more mature manufacturing industries are however, the more standardized production gets and thus the less important a pooled labour market, specialized inputs, and information and knowledge spillover become (Krugman 1991b). This implies if economies of scale decrease due to technical reasons (as could be the case if human capital becomes more relevant in production processes than physical capital or the production becomes more service-oriented such that the service part in manufacturing rises), the general trend will be deconcentration even if economic integration processes continue. For high tech industries on the other hand the availability of specialized and highly skilled labour is important.

---

pared to smaller firms as the former can purchase intermediate input factors lower prices due to market power and can better cope high fix costs, it is mainly external economies of scale we will deal with in this dissertation.

For industries that are characterized by constant returns that operate under perfect competition with an immobile work force, there is no supplier-proximity effect. Only for industries that produce differentiated products with increasing returns to scale operated by a mobile work force, a change in trade costs can have an effect on the location of this industry (Krugman 1991 a). Thus concentration can arise because of self-reinforcing forward and backward linkages between firms in the same industry as well as across industries. These forces stem from a combination of increasing returns to scale, trade costs, and the fact that firms are linked via their input–output structures (Krugman 1991a, Fujita et al. 1999). Downstream firms use inputs from upstream firms as intermediate inputs. The forward linkage implies that whenever trade incurs positive costs, the larger the number of upstream firms in near distance available, the lower the prices for intermediate inputs. More downstream firms, however, also imply a larger home market for upstream firms increases sales and profits for those firms.

Differentiated products and increasing returns to scale tend to increase productivity more in larger countries than in smaller ones even if they have identical per capita resources and access to the same technology due to higher demand in larger areas. Thus, the importance of big countries is not the size of a country per se or the number of inhabitants but the demand associated with larger areas. The larger a region, the more varieties or intermediates will be produced locally. Compared with smaller regions, fewer goods have to be imported, saving transportation costs.

Production structures of European countries should become more similar also due to the fact that intra-industry trade is rising whereas inter-industry trade is not. Thus, countries do not specialize in different industries but diversify production in the same industries. This is already discussed in Jones and Kiezkowski (1990 and 2001) who describe this phenomenon as the result of increased fragmentation of production, i.e. the value chain of production is split into an increasing number of tasks, which are performed in different countries since as Arndt and Kiezkowski (2000) pointed out, there is no need for spatial proximity for sequential production.

The more standardized the production of goods and services becomes (i.e. the more mature industries are), the lower the necessity to locate production close to consumers and the lower the importance of a pooled labour market, specialized inputs, and information and knowledge spillover (Krugman 1991b). This implies that upon a decrease of economies of scale due to technical reasons, the general trend will be de-concentration and de-specialization since endowment differences can be arbitraged away (Isard 1960) even if economic integration processes continue.

In cases where the gains from a fall in fixed costs outweigh the gains from declining trade costs, de-concentration processes occur, since the importance of forward and backward linkages vanishes (Ekholm and Forslid 2001). Forces of de-concentration can also be set free by decreasing transportation costs, since resources become more easily transferable from one location to another. Production factors then move to countries where they were initially scarce and where factor-rewards are high. By this process, not only the endowments of countries but also their respective production structures ought to become more similar. Economic integration in Europe has for instance increased capital mobility and thus enforced foreign investments in Southern European Countries due to higher rates on return. As a consequence, countries that had comparative advantages in capital-intensive industries before are now faced with new competition from lagging countries, leading to structural convergence (Aiginger et al. 1999).

In this economic environment, proximity to demand (home market effects) loses importance (Fujita et al. 1999), since it becomes cheaper to export final goods and import intermediate goods for production. The better access of peripheries to other producers as well as a larger number of consumers makes them more competitive, since they are then able to export to larger market areas, leading to de-concentration (Rossi-Hansberg 2005). Aiginger und Leitner (2002) show that the deepening of integration reduced the disadvantages of smaller countries since strongly segmented markets lead to strong incentives to locate production where the largest home market is to be found, favouring large countries. Due to the ongoing economic integration, industries with economies of scale will locate where costs of production are lowest giving smaller countries better opportunities to attract such industries.

Industries thus become locally concentrated if intra-industrial economies of scale prevail since the location decisions of producers become interdependent and the incentives to settle where other firms are located increase. If an upstream industry in a country expands the production variety of intermediate goods, the downstream industry benefits both because on the one hand it has better (or more) access to specialized inputs and firms can provide non-tradable and specific inputs in greater variety, and on the other hand because it obtains these inputs at lower transportation costs. Improved access to suppliers and other complementary activities facilitates the exploitation of economies of scale and raises productivity in larger economic areas and in economic centers compared to small countries and peripheries (Krugman and Venables 1995 and Venables 1996). Furthermore, the demand for specific products is higher, yielding opportunities for a better division of labour, specialization and efficiency gains (Fujita et al. 1999 and Braunerhjelm et al. 2000). By this mechanism, production in large countries in the center of custom unions becomes favoured over production in small, periphery countries (Venables 1996 and Fujita et al. 1999) especially in cases where production is dependent on a high level of non-tradable intermediate inputs (Fujita 1988 and Rivera-Batiz 1988). Krugman (1980) and Helpman and Krugman (1985) argue that the competitiveness of economic centers will further rise at the expense of periphery regions due to the better access to larger markets anda higher number of prosperous consumers – even more so if labour is immobile as in the case of European countries (for details on this argument see 2.2.2).

Davis (1998) shows that agglomeration tendencies in increasing return industries stemming from large home markets vanish if the trade costs for all goods are equal. If spillover effects between or within industries are low as it is the case for constant return industries or transportation costs are high, then production (and employment) tend to be located more equally across space. As a country grows, new producers locate close to existing production places, widening the production differences between lagging and leading locations. When wage gaps widen up, industries start to spread to places characterized by low wages. Yet, this does not imply that all countries develop towards the same steady state. Instead, economic development (and specialization as well as concentration processes) takes place in waves. If the real world resembles the theoretical neoclassical models that being behind can be an advantage—since countries that are lagging farther can catch up faster. Yet if the real world is likely to resemble the New Economic Geography model with agglomeration economies, then the farther locations are behind, the tougher it is to catch up: Since economies of scale are more likely to prevail in economic centers as well as in core countries, it is more probable that innovative, dynamic industries concentrate in the core countries, whereas the periphery countries are left with mature industries which face fierce competition from world markets. As a consequence, peripheral countries may grow more slowly in terms of income and employment, and may be more vulnerable to adverse macroeconomic shocks. Empirical studies show an increase in concentration for industries such as Chemicals and Transport Equipment from the mid–1980s onwards, but starting from very low concentration levels. For a detailed analysis of the concentration of industries see Chapter 4.

## 2.2.5 Migration

In Krugman (1991a), the fact that a fraction of the population is immobile builds a centrifugal force into the model: in the presence of trade costs, firms have an incentive to locate close to the immobile population. If employees are mobile, the core-periphery pattern occurs due to forward linkages between firms that make firms in economic centers more competitive as they can produce at lower costs and make workers to migrate from the lower paying periphery to the high-wage centers. Firms moreover benefit from increasing returns to scale as trade costs on imported goods tend to decline and consumers benefit from a greater variety of goods that can be consumed at even lower prices.

International migration can offset inter-regional wage-differentials (Krugman 1991b or Venables 1996). Thus, whenever workers are characterized by differences in their willingness to migrate, concentration rises in sectors where an over proportional weight of mobile workers is employed (Forslid and Ottaviano 2003). In Krugman type models, workers in the manufacturing sector are mobile, whereas farmers in the agricultural sector are not mobile with the effect that workers in the manufacturing sector migrate from the small country in the periphery that pays low wages to the large country in the economic center where wages are higher and the probability to get unemployed is lower. Yet Egger et al. (2007) show that in the case of multinational firms, migration of low-skill workers leads to less concentration than migration of high-skill workers. Additionally, inter-regional migration is considered to have a strong impact on agglomeration, while inter-sectoral migration will not have such an effect.

Moreover, workers are characterized by differences in their willingness to migrate. In economic models such as Forslid and Ottaviano (2003) it is presumed that high-skill workers are more willing to migrate and therefore concentration should rise in sectors where an over proportional weight of high-skill (i.e. mobile) workers is employed. In European reality, however, it is the low-skill and low-wage workers that are (or have to be) more willing to migrate; thus concentration ought to be affected mostly in these industries. Alonso-Villar (2005) moreover demonstrates that the willingness of people to migrate might not be sufficient to lead to concentration – especially when transportation costs of intermediate goods are high.

Additionally, economic activity ought to be spread more unevenly across space as captured by Tabuchi and Thisse (2002) who account for individual preferences to live in the home country (region) even though other regions would pay higher wages. Concentration may however occur even if workers are immobile as unemployment may act as a factor creating divergence; as wage differences between countries are not reduced by migration, the incentives for firms to move to peripheral areas where production costs are lower, rise.

Ottaviano (1999) models migration that is costly and assumes forward-looking agents. He shows that the initial advantages of large and central places can only disappear if migration costs are low enough and/ or transportation costs are low enough. Behrens et al. (2010) elaborate a selection model that also builds on Melitz and Ottaviano (2008) where ex ante identical individuals decide whether or not to move from a common rural hinterland to cities. Their heterogeneity is revealed after this decision has been made and the decision itself is assumed to be irreversible so as to rule out sorting. They show that larger market size increases productivity not only through a .higher degree of labour division driven by pecuniary externalities (easier and higher availability of intermediate goods) but also through a selection process, whereas higher productivity increases market size by providing incentives for rural-urban migration. At low transportation costs combined with limited labour mobility, wage differentials across countries also can lead to a reallocation of production, promoting deconcentration as shown by Puga (1999).

As for Europe and the prevalence of different languages, education systems and so forth, we have to face the fact that migration costs might still be rather high even though the Single Market had been already created in 1992. Thus in European reality there are many institutional factors that still hinder both temporary and permanent migration. European labour markets are thus quite rigid and international labour mobility is low. Bentivogli and Pagano (1999) indicate that less than 1.5 per cent of EU citizens live in another member state. Bentolila and Dolado (1991) estimate that the elasticity of migration to interregional wage differentials in Europe is close to zero which has been confirmed in other studies (Eichengreen 1993, Decressin and Fata 1995, Faini et al. 1997). De la Fuente (1999) reports that one has to take into account the unemployment rate in order to describe the probability of migration correctly. They can show that if the employment rate is much higher in the country of origin than in other parts of the world, then migration is more likely to happen. Therefore models that explain agglomeration forces without a mobile working force seem to be apt to describe Europe's reality. Moreover, it is argued that European labour unions and the wage rigidities caused by them weaken dispersion forces since the downward pressure on wages in peripheral regions is reduced. The relatively low labour mobility in Europe contributes to a lower level of agglomeration and hence less heterogeneity between countries than predicted in models of new economic geography or new trade theory (Tabuchi and Thisse 2002). Labour market rigidities and initial comparative advantages could lock a country in its specialization pattern slowing down the reallocation of production factors and thus increasing heterogeneity between countries (Peri 2002). Hence, in determining the location of specific industries, it is crucial to take into account the combination of transport costs and factor mobility (Norman and Venables 1995).

## 2.2.6 Imitation

Arguments for increasing concentration of industries are to be found in the New Economic Growth literature as well. Whenever investments in new technologies and the accumulation of human capital differ considerably across countries, industries in which production crucially depends on specific skills and new technologies will be concentrated (Romer 1990). Even assuming perfect knowledge spillovers between countries, differences in the production structure could continue to persist, since knowledge spillovers over proportionally reduce production costs in economic centers[7] (Helpman and Grossman 1992) leading at least to inter-regional concentration. Concentration may thus occur even though productivity and/or labour cost convergence prevails (Fujita et al. 1999). As countries harmonize their laws, rules and product standards, it is easier and less costly for foreign firms to set up subsidiaries in other countries, because national regulations do not have to be followed any more. If multinational firms can transmit parts of the knowledge they obtain in plants in one country to their plants in other countries through intra-firm communication channels (internal spillovers), de-concentration can emerge. Thus, diversification processes could set in particularly when transaction costs are low.

Evolutionary models moreover emphasize the cumulative and path-dependent character of technological change as an explanation for persistent economic structures (Fagerberg et al. 1994 and Fagerberg 2000). Whenever small and "random" initial events (also called "historical accidents") have re-enforcing effects, long-term concentration processes are initialized (David 1985, 1986, 1988, 1992, 1993a, 1993b, 1994 and Arthur 1988, 1989, 1994). Due to tacit knowledge accumulated in the past this results in first-mover advantage, leading to both increasing concentration and one-country specialization. In such cases, other countries are not able to catch up over time unless there is a shift to a new technological paradigm and de-lock-in occurs. David (1985), Arthur (1986 and 1994), and Krugman (1991a, 1991b, 1993) have shown that the location of industries characterized by economies of scale can be easily determined by historical accidents, causing their development to occur path-dependently. However, as pointed out by Holmes (1999), the impact of historical factors is much smaller in cases where the level of industrial mobility is high. The evolutionary approach argues that the selection pressure of existing spatial structures is rather weak when new industries emerge. Thus, the windows of location op-

---

7    We have to bear in mind that there is a negative effect of distance on the flow of technology, i.e. for certain kinds of technology spillovers, proximity is crucial. Thus spillovers are strongest within cities or small economic centers and decrease the larger is the market area (Keller 2002).

portunity are open in emerging industries – yet rather closed in traditional industries (Boschma and Frenken 2003).

The potential of foreign direct investment and knowledge-spillovers in the catch-up process of lagging countries, as well as their impact on structural convergence should not be underestimated. As new technologies become available to a group of technologically lagging countries, they can accumulate new factors of production faster and more easily (de la Fuente 1997 or Pigliaru 2003). As shown by Los and Verspagen (2006) in the context of international trade possibilities, technological backwardness entails the possibility of benefiting from technological spillovers. Thus, path dependent concentration processes are not stable over time due to the limited adaptability of first-movers to cope with new competitors (whenever technological advancement in other countries occurs and creative destruction takes place), and due to the fact that often specific and localized input factors turn into universal ones. In all the cases described above, market dominance is split up and firms in other countries gain ground (Witt 2003). Moreover, if local knowledge and productivity advantages spill over to other sectors in the technologically leading country, this ensures the country a technological leadership over other countries in many industries. This will lead to de-specialization patterns in the technologically leading country as more and more industries benefit from increases in productivity from the innovating industry. De-specialization is thus the consequence of technological leadership in one industry that induces pressure to make the production more efficient in other industries too. Puga and Venables (1998) show that de-specialization could be driven by relocation of production in regions where labour is cheaper. Knowledge spillovers can reduce production costs. Suppose firms can transmit some of the knowledge it obtains in plants in one country to its plants in other countries through intra-firm communication channels (internal spillovers). Then de-concentration can emerge even though geographical proximity implies intensive competition between firms: the presence in the agglomeration helps firms to obtain technological knowledge that they can use to increase their profits in locations where they have greater market power. We have to bear in mind, however, that there is a negative effect of distance on the flow of technology, i.e. for certain kinds of technology-spillovers proximity is crucial. Thus spillovers are strongest within cities or small economic centers and decrease the larger the area gets (Keller 2002).

Concerning the relationship between structural change and the types of products/ technologies, it can be argued that more sophisticated products are more difficult to transfer across borders, as production techniques for these products are complex and hence hard to codify (Dosi et al. 1990). Therefore, we would expect high-tech products to be more stable across national borders, when compared to other more low-tech products. This idea is consistent with the so-called product-life-cycle theories (Vernon 1966, Grossman and Helpman 1991 and Hill 2007), in which high-tech products are developed in the home country, while more mature products spread out to be produced abroad (in less sophisticated countries).

If local growth of technology and productivity may spill to other sectors in the region this grant to the region a technological leadership. At some point, the temptation of some workers in the region to use their technological lead to produce more efficiently also in the other sector will generate tendencies towards spin-off in the other industries and towards a reduction of the specialization. The "advanced regions" will tend to de-specialize while the other regions will still remain more specialized.

## 2.2.7  Firm and Worker Heterogeneity

As studied by Ottaviano (2012), firm heterogeneity has a remarkable effect on agglomeration patterns. Whereas in other NEG models, countries and industries move from dispersion to full agglomeration due to declines in trade barriers, Ottaviano (2012) creates a more realistic model in which there is only partial agglomeration taking place as transportation costs fall over time This is a stable outcome and also in this model it is true that the larger markets is more attractive for many firms and consumers as these places exhibit more entrants, more sellers with lower average mark-ups, offer a higher degree of product variety which is produced at lower average costs. The reason why this model does not create full agglomeration is that larger markets provide lower expected profits since firms face a lower success rate of entry.

Behrens et al. (2010) present a model in which agglomeration is driven by technological externalities. They distinguish between ex ante heterogeneity (e.g. skills), known to workers before they decide where to locate, and ex post heterogeneity (e.g. luck) revealed to each agent after they decided where to live. Workers choose their living places based on their skills and occupation possibilities. The more talented people are, the better their chances of finding better jobs in larger locations, are. Thus, larger areas attract higher skilled people and in the model better skilled workers are concentrated in larger markets. This makes these places more productive and offers more productive occupation possibilities.

Forslid and Ottaviano (2003) elaborate the impact of skill heterogeneity of workers on agglomeration. In their model, there is a positive effect of highly-skilled workers on agglomeration since these workers have higher wages and thus higher purchasing power leading to more production in places that can more than proportionally attract high-skilled workers. This forms an incentive for firms to localize in regions with high-skill workers too, aggravating agglomeration tendencies as in other Krugman-type models.

Last but not least, increased international competition between firms as well as the internationalization of home markets increases the potential of exports for firms. At the same time, firms themselves become more globalized, manifested by the rising percentage of multinational firms. Thus inefficient high-cost producers have to exit the market, especially in previously protected industries. Surviving firms will likely benefit from better opportunities to exploit economies of scale (Davies and Lyons 1996). The declining set-up costs of new plants could be a driver for de-concentration since multinational firms also ease the imitation of production processes between countries.

Taken together these arguments, patterns of increasing specialization are likely to be driven by divergence that occur in industries which exhibit economies of scale and are technology- and knowledge-intensive, since these industry characteristics are also likely to interact with path-dependencies causing catch-up potential to be smaller. In the service sector, economic integration might play a minor role, since many services are regionally bound and cannot be shipped like manufacturing goods. Yet with the developments in information and communication technology, spatial proximity has lost importance in many service industries. In service industries like financial intermediation, however, the ICT should lead to massive concentration as cost-competitiveness starts outweighing the advantage of proximity to end customers. On the other hand, regionally bound services like hotels/restaurants are not expected to show high degrees of convergence or divergence.

## 2.3 Empirical Evidence

### 2.3.1 The Impact of Industry Characteristics

Amiti (1998) reports that in general a rise in scale economies of one percent leads to a 0.5 percent increase in concentration. This is supported by the results of Brülhart (1998a) and Haaland et al. (1999). Both studies show that increasing return industries, technology-intensive and science-based industries are more concentrated than other industries, although they also detect a decline of spatial concentration in these sectors. Brülhart and Torstensson (2007) find evidence that the concentration of manufacturing industries is highest for industries that are least characterized by economies of scale such as textiles, clothes, shoes and leather. The impact of an increase in the intensity of intermediate goods in the production on concentration is even stronger since a one percent increase almost leads to a one percent increase in concentration (Amiti 1998).

When we turn to the effects of other specific industry characteristics such as the need for technology and skill in production, theory predicts convergence for low and medium technology industries, due to the fact that technology diffusion across European countries is much easier than in technology-intensive industries (Posner 1961). Posner's technology gap theory postulates that there is a competitive advantage if a country introduces new goods as it enjoys monopoly rents and other countries have to import this good until they learn how to produce this very good. Thus, as long as other countries are not able to compete in this industry, trade is enhanced causing an imitation lag. As empirical findings show, however, the location patterns in traditional industries are not particularly formed by technology diffusion processes but rather by cost-advantages. Thus, the comparative advantages inherent in South European Countries at the beginning of the observation period continued to exist, making economic structures sticky and concentration levels even rise as indicated by a number of studies (Krugman 1991b, Amiti 1998, Amiti 1999, Brülhart 1998a, Brülhart 2001, Gao 1999 and Midelfart-Knarvik et al. 2003). For a detailed analysis see also chapters 4 and 5.

Brülhart et al. (1995) and Brülhart (1998a) show that both labour- and resource-intensive industries are more dispersed across space than the average. Yet, especially, labour-intensive industries are characterized by substantial increases in concentration after the implementation of the European Single Market. The empirical evidence for the Unites States however shows that agglomeration is highest for labour and resource-intensive industries (Krugman 1991a). Amiti (1999) finds no correlation of economic concentration for European countries with labour intensity neither. Haaland et al. (1999) report a weak positive correlation with labour intensity in 1992, but not for 1985, and the reverse for human capital intensity. These results are supported by Midelfart-Knarvik et al. (2003) whose simple correlations suggest a positive effect of skill intensity only in the 1970s and no effect of capital intensity for any period. They find that concentration increased for twelve industries and decreased for the remaining 24 industries. There is considerable variation over time. In the 1970s, eleven industries became increasingly concentrated, while 25 became less so. This pattern was reversed in the 1980s, with increasing concentration the norm (23 industries relative to 13 industries) before reversing again in the 1990s (15 industries increasing relative to 21). With regard to the development of high-tech industries, Krugman moreover highlights the problems associated with the measurement of concentration in this category of industries. According to his empirical work, data is biased insofar as some much localised technologically advanced industries are excluded and high tech products are buried in meaningless aggregates. However he concludes, that *"whatever drives industries to concentrate in one place, it is not sole a matter of technological spillovers"* (Krugman 1991a).

The evidence on the role of demand and cost linkages is mixed: Whereas Brülhart (1998a) finds that economic concentration takes places in high market potential areas, Amiti (1999) concludes that there is a positive correlation for the intermediate input cost variable, while the own input variable of Haaland et al. (1999) is associated with increased absolute - but not relative - concentration. In contrast, Midelfart-Knarvik et al. (2003) find no significant correlation with intra- or inter-industry inputs. Nor do they find any correlation with final demand.

Midelfart-Knarvik et al. report that industrial concentration declined until the 80s but increased from then onwards. The authors show that some industries that were initially concentrated (basically high returns to scale industries like motor vehicles, aircraft, electrical products, chemicals, petroleum and coal) remained concentrated whereas fast growing high-tech and high-skill industries such as office, computing, machinery and radio got more dispersed. Low-tech, low increasing return industries, low-skill and low-wage industries being initially dispersed such as textiles, leather, furniture, transport equipment got more concentrated especially in low wage and low skill abundant countries. Results from regressions indicate that forward and backward linkages are important for localization and that the importance of economies of scale is declining. The authors attribute this to the fact that a very low level of transport costs seems to be reached.

Interesting is also the fact, that even though concentration patterns can be sticky over time, there are good examples that highly concentrated industries can become rather de-concentrated and vice versa over time. Amiti (1998) also reports that the level of geographic concentration increased over time for a majority of industries between 1968 and 1990. Amiti (1998) state that the level of geographic concentration has increased over time for a majority of industries, with the highest coefficient rising from 0.32 in 1968 to 0.41 in 1990. Interestingly, the industries that were the most geographically concentrated in 1968 are not necessarily the same in 1990. For 17 out of 27 industries, concentration increased. Above all, industries characterized by high economies of scale and inter-industry linkages are highly concentrated. A disadvantage of the results however is that the concentration measures are only calculated for the years 1968 and 1990 and therefore the development during this time span is not recorded. Similar to Midelfart-Knarvik et al. (2000 and 2003) they show that those industries that were the most geographically concentrated at the beginning of the observation period are not necessarily the same in 1990. For example, the chemical industry turned from one of the highest concentration levels to the most dispersed industry.

## 2.3.2 European Integration

The fact that European consumers tend to stick to locally manufactured goods, making use of the new consumption possibilities to a lesser extent than expected by economic theory and simulations, ought to reduce the effects of any forces leading to divergence. The impact of European integration as well as globalization is moreover assumed to have a lesser impact on the service sector than on the manufacturing sector, because not all services are as easily tradeable. Therefore we expect to observe differences between locally oriented branches (which still require a high degree of proximity between producers and consumers) and globalized industries. Within the service sector, concentration is expected to have risen especially in the banking and insurance industry. This is because this industry will benefit like no other from economic integration that brought about the free movement of capital after 1992. Whereas Krugman (1991a,b) predicted that the Single Market should boost economic concentration and empirical results show increasing concentration for some but decreasing concentration for other industries, industry specific characteristics seem to dominate the process of (de-)concentration. If one is willing to argue that the European integration process was pushed to a higher level after the completion of the single market and the conclusion of the Treaty of the European Union (Maastricht Treaty) in the early 1990s, one may interpret the Krugman hypothesis as implying that the localization of economic activity across industries and countries should increase at an accelerated pace after the early or mid-1990s. In this case there should have been a structural break in the evolution of localization in Europe: the localization of economic activity in the EU as a whole, the concentration level of individual industries across EU countries, and the specializations of EU countries should have all increased faster after the early 1990s. Cutrini (2010) and Brülhart and Träger (2005) do, in fact, report evidence for such a structural break. Cutrini finds that the decrease of localization of manufacturing between countries came to a halt in the early 1990s, and Brülhart and Träger (2005) report evidence that the tendencies of industries to concentrate (disperse) have tended to be somewhat stronger (weaker) after the early 1990s. Even though this result is not supportive of the Krugman hypothesis proper, it offers some support for the hypothesis that structural inequalities between countries have increased relative to those within countries (Brülhart and Träger 2005). Unfortunately many studies such as Cutrini (2010) focus only on the manufacturing sector, which, as will be shown below, should not be taken as representative for the economy as a whole because its localization patterns and dynamics differ markedly from those of the services sector. Regarding the concentration in the services sector, Jennequin (2008) reports a small increase of concentration after 1986, yet remaining at a moderate level. He shows that business and financial services are the most agglomerated industries. In chapter 4 we explore the evidence on the Krugman hypothesis more consistently and comprehensively.

Non-tariff barriers seem not to be correlated with relative concentration while absolute concentration is associated with high trade barriers (Haaland et al. 1999). According to Forslid et al. (2002), economic integration affects the location of industries in different ways. Distance influences production costs and firms' competitiveness. At high transaction costs both internal and external economies of scale can be exhausted only to a certain degree – thus as trade barriers vanish, the industry characteristics should become more important in order to explain concentration and specialization processes (Helpman and Krugman 1985, Krugman 1991, Fujita et al. 1999). Empirical results however show that competition is far lower than expected and thus it can hardly be spoken of an internal market for services yet. This is especially true for industries that provide non-tradable goods, whereas industries such as telecommunications have become integrated which can be seen by more competition and lower customer prices.

According to Krugman (1991) many of the agglomeration enhancing processes have already taken place both in the US and in Europe, whereas the potential for higher levels of country specialization in Western Europe have not yet been reached in the early 1990s. The reason is that trade costs at the national level decline and thus economic integration should lead to the degree of specialization of European countries becoming more similar to that of United States. The specialization of regions within European countries should however not increase to the same extent since regions within a country have already been highly integrated with each other. Since the European countries are expected to specialize in different industries, the concentration of industries across countries should also increase as economic integration proceeds in Europe. Comparing European nations (France, Germany, Italy and UK) with U.S. regions (North-East, Middle-West, South and West), Krugman (1991) shows that the former are less specialized in manufacturing industries because until the completion of the Single market many non-tariff barriers of trade existed and still language barriers exist and migration flows across countries remained low.

### 2.3.3 Country Size and Location

Krugman (1991) however poses the question whether larger countries in reality are really favourable to smaller countries, i.e. whether it is accurate to presume big countries to consist bigger regions than small countries or whether it would be more accurate to think of big countries consisting of more regions than smaller countries implying that economies of scale do not prevail more easily in big countries and larger home markets are not the case. Krugman (1991b) pointed out that the poorer European countries in general also are more distant from large home markets and thus are disadvantaged in their economic development since the poorer these countries are, the lower are incomes and thus the home demand remains lower than in central, rich countries. Comparing European nations (France, Germany, Italy and UK) with U.S. regions (North-East, Middle-West, South and West), Krugman (1991) shows that the former are less specialized in manufacturing industries because until the completion of the Single market many non-tariff barriers of trade existed and still language barriers exist and migration flows across countries remained low. Brülhart and Torstensson (2007) additionally address the question of where the more concentrated industries are located. They compare industry Gini coefficients with industry centrality indices, which indicate the industry bias towards central EU countries. Using employment data for eleven countries and eighteen industries as well as for nine EU regions and seven industries, they find a positive correlation between industry concentration and centrality indices. These findings confirm the results of Brülhart (1998). Brülhart (2001) states that countries that are both big and in the core (France, Germany, and the UK) tend to be the least specialized when compared to the EU-average[8]. Small countries in the core tend to be slightly more specialized (Austria, Belgium, the Netherlands). Only Cohesion countries (Greece, Ireland and Portugal) tend to be more specialized than the small Scandinavian countries (Sweden, Denmark, Finland). According to Brülhart (2001a) the reasons for the higher levels of specialization in smaller countries are manifold: first, in comparison to larger countries they have fewer natural resources (in fewer branches), moreover whereas in small countries, economies of scale might still prevail, large countries are too large such that economies of scale prevail over the whole country. As Brülhart (2001a) stresses, *'this is not surprising, since large countries are likely to have more heterogeneous economic and natural endowments, and scale economies may be exhausted for a larger number of industries'*.

---

8    Note however that larger countries have more weight when calculating the EU-average. To some extent the lower degree of specialization could thus likely be a mere statistical effect.

Amiti (1998) gives evidence that there was a significant increase in specialization between 1968 and 1990 in Belgium, Denmark, Germany, Greece, Italy, and the Netherlands; no significant change in Portugal; and a significant fall in specialization in France, Spain, and the UK. Even though specialization decreased for some countries when comparing 1968 to 1990, there was a significant increase in specialization for all these countries in between 1980 to 1990. Other studies, such as Hine (1990), and Greenaway and Hine (1991), also provide evidence of increasing specialization in EU countries in the 1980s,[7] using a different measure of specialization. Amiti (1998) also calculated relative Gini indices for the period 1968 to 1990 comprising 27 industries. The results of this study are listed in Table 1 with the countries being ranked from the most to the least specialized.

*Table 1 Specialization Levels in Amiti (1998)*

| Ranking | 1969 | 1980 | 1990 |
|---------|------|------|------|
| 1 | UK and France | UK | UK and France |
| 2 | | France | |
| 3 | Germany | Germany | Germany |
| 4 | Italy | Spain | Italy |
| 5 | Belgium and Spain | Italy | Spain |
| 6 | | Belgium | Belgium |
| 7 | Netherlands | Netherlands | Netherlands |
| 8 | Denmark | Portugal | Denmark |
| 9 | Greece | Denmark | Portugal |
| 10 | Portugal | Greece | Greece |

Source: Own calculations based on Amiti (1998)

The declines in specialization - above all in France and the UK - in Amiti (1998) are due to the high level of industrial aggregation used in the construction of the Gini index. Moreover, it is remarkable that according to Amiti's results large countries like the UK, France, Germany and Spain decreased their specialization levels whereas the small countries like Belgium, the Netherlands and Denmark became more specialized. The exceptions to the rule are Italy that became more specialized over time and Portugal which economic structure became more even. Amiti reports that the data exhibit increasing specialization for all countries between 1980 and 1990 – this is not true, however, looking at Table

1 which is based on Amiti (1998). This is only true when comparing 1980 with 1989. The fact that altering the reference year by only one year from 1990 to 1989 having such an effect on the results can be seen as a first hint on the robustness of empirical results – a topic that we will discuss in more detail in chapter 3. Anyhow, specialization increased for most countries during the 1980s which Amiti attributes to the increasing trade liberalization and its effects on production structures. The results then are in line with what Krugman (1991a) expected for European Countries to occur once economic integration processes become more important. If we compare the specialization levels of 1990s with 1969, however, it becomes clear that there are no major changes in the levels of specialization.

According to Amiti (1999) specialization could fall after the accession to the EU in countries that first face fiercer competition leading to structural adjustments. This would especially be true for countries that before the accession to the EU were characterized by high trade barriers protecting important home industries in which they did have comparative advantages, such as textiles in Portugal. This is somehow contradictory to Barry (1996), who reports that peripheral countries could lose competitiveness in industries characterized by strong increasing returns to scale as trade costs decrease and thus peripheries are condemned to specialize in low-growth industries. After a period of intensified integration, these countries should however be able to absorb R&D and to benefit from learning by doing; more educated people such that these countries start to catch up in technology-leading countries.

Midelfart-Knarvik et al. (2002 and 2003) calculate specialization indices for Western European countries. The results indicate that the majority of countries converged until the mid-1980s, but from then onwards all countries but the Netherlands increased relative specialization. In general, they find a positive effect of becoming a member of the European Union on specialization. Moreover, they report dramatic structural changes for both Finland and Ireland with regard to technological upgrade of their economies. These two late-comers started out with levels far below average and turned out to be leaders in major high-technology industries. This development is in sharp contrast to Greece in Portugal, which started out at low levels of high-tech, fast growing industries and remained to be so over the investigation period. Similar results hold for high-skill industries. The results for country specialization by Midelfart-Knarvik et al. (2002) are listed in Table 2 below, where the countries are ranked from the most to the least specialized one.

*Table 2 Specialization Levels in Midelfart-Knarvik et al. (2002)*

|             | 1970/1973 | 1980/1983 | 1988/1991 | 1994/1997 |
|-------------|-----------|-----------|-----------|-----------|
| Ireland     | 1         | 1         | 2         | 1         |
| Finland     | 2         | 5         | 6         | 3         |
| Denmark     | 3         | 4         | 4         | 4         |
| Portugal    | 4         | 6         | 3         | 5         |
| Greece      | 5         | 2         | 1         | 2         |
| Netherlands | 6         | 3         | 5         | 6         |
| Spain       | 7         | 11        | 11        | 12        |
| Sweden      | 8         | 7         | 7         | 7         |
| Italy       | 9         | 9         | 9         | 9         |
| Belgium     | 10        | 8         | 8         | 8         |
| Germany     | 11        | 10        | 10        | 10        |
| Austria     | 12        | 12        | 12        | 11        |
| UK          | 13        | 13        | 13        | 13        |
| France      | 14        | 14        | 14        | 14        |

Calculation based on results reported in Midelfart-Knarvik et al. (2002)

Aiginger and Leitner (2002) compared the concentration levels of the US States with European EU-NUTS 1 regions in ten manufacturing industries and found a higher level of concentration in the US due lower transportation costs and due to the unrestricted forces of economies of scale since markets are not nationally segmented as in Europe implying that in smaller European countries industries are not able work at a minimum efficient scale. Moreover labour is more flexible in the US since employees are characterized by a higher degree of mobility – therefore it is easier for firms to attract workers with adequate knowledge. Even though economic integration has facilitated concentration processes, industries remain fragmented and spread over Europe.

Amiti (1998) and Midelfart-Knarvik et al. (2001, 2002, 2003) moreover report decreasing specialization patterns for Western European countries until the mid-1980s, but a reversal trend from then onwards. In general, they find a positive effect of becoming a member of the European Union on specialization.

Midelfart-Knarvik et al. (2003) report that overall manufacturing activity measured by the absolute Gini index to be concentrated in the four biggest countries of the EU, using production data from the OECD STAN database. In the mid-1990s, Germany accounted for roughly 30% of total output, followed by France, Italy and the UK - with shares ranging between 14 and 15%. In this regard, it is remarkable that the patterns of overall manufacturing output are rather stable between 1970 and the mid-1990s at the national level. France and the UK are the biggest losers with roughly a two and a three percentage point decline, respectively. Italy wins production shares, increasing from 12.5 per cent to 14.5

per cent. The picture is different at the regional level, however, where overall concentration (as measured by the coefficient of variation) has increased considerably - at least from 1980 onwards. These results are based on data for 36 manufacturing industries calculated for the following year averages: 1970-73, 1980-83, 1990-93, and 1994-97.

Helg et al. (1995) present specialization figures for twelve EU countries based on the OECD Indicators for Industrial Activity for eight 1-digit ISIC industries. Their results suggest that nine countries become more specialized over time, whereas the specialization levels of France, Portugal and Spain declined between 1975 and 1995. Their results are hard to compare with other studies, however, as they are based on the shares of output of each industry in each country. Changes in the composition of output that are common across EU countries (say a move from textiles in to chemicals) will show up as increased specialization. Thus, these numbers capture both the change in individual countries relative to the rest of the EU and the change in the EU relative to the rest of the world. More recent studies have tended to focus on shifts in countries specialization patterns relative to the rest of the EU as the key variable of interest. The drawback of this study however is that the output of only eight industries is considered such that the results might not be very robust and the implications are less clear compareable to other studies that analyze a larger sample (A detailed analysis of the implications using different aggregation levels on the results is to be found in Chapter 3).

The factors described above imply that the advantages and disadvantages of countries could become more evident as globalization and economic integration processes become more and more important, giving firms incentives to relocate production to more favourable destinations. This in turn implies increased specialization on the one hand and leads to changes in the demand patterns of costumers for domestic and foreign goods on the other hand. Given these developments, we aim to shed light on the development of industry structures in Western Europe in chapter 5. More precisely, the question is whether lagging countries were able to change their economic structures such that structural convergence in the sense of catching-up to the technologically leading countries in Western Europe was attained, this would lead to de-concentration processes. Divergence of production structures between countries is of great relevance, as low labour mobility is not able to offset the negative effects of asymmetric shocks (OECD 1999). Countries would therefore be more vulnerable to shocks that create divergence in the labour market, with rising unemployment and falling wages in some countries and labour shortages and inflationary pressures in other countries (Braunerhjelm et al. 2000). The arguments advanced in this chapter are finally summarized in Table 3.

*Table 3: Driving Forces of Convergence and Divergence*

| Convergence | Divergence |
|---|---|
| Supply Side Effects | |
| • Cost-differential in production between core and periphery (i.e. high wages and rents in the center), letting firms spread to the periphery at very low costs of trade<br>• Increases in labour productivity in lagging countries, (i.e. technological catch-up, imitation of new techniques), combined with the slow-down of increase in labour productivity in the leading countries<br>• Outsourcing of agricultural and labour-intensive production in the manufacturing sector from Southern Europe to other countries, i.e. increase in trade with low-wage countries (leading to a decline of labour intensive industries across Europe).<br>• Homogeneity of products leads to fierce price competition at economic centers, thus giving firms incentives to move production to peripheries with lower competition in order to sell at higher prices. | • Technological gap (differences in productivity), implying comparative advantages of advanced countries in high tech industries<br>• Pecuniary Externalities leading to advantages due to shorter or less expensive ways of transportation.<br>• Industry-specific technological externalities lead to concentration by the higher supply of sophisticated and specially trained people.<br>• Input-output-linkages, leading to concentration of production at the center<br>• High spatial concentration of one specific input factor (natural resources, special skills)<br>• Different industrialization and/or tertiarization patterns<br>• Economies of scale: in large countries the market area is larger and firms can exploit economies of scale better than in smaller countries.<br><br>• Hub effect, i.e. lower transport costs for economic centers than for peripheries |
| Demand side effects | |
| • Convergence in demand structures, leading to convergence in production - especially in the service sector<br>• Increasing demand for non-standardized products, customized products leading to less specialization and concentration than under mass production | • Home market effects, i.e. more sales in big markets where demand is large.<br>• Preference of consumers for product variety, which can easier be produced at economic centers. |

| Convergence | Divergence |
|---|---|
| European integration | |
| • Structural funds for lagging countries by the EU fostering firm localization in the periphery.<br>• The more production depends on immobile production factors, the more will production be spread across space. | • Economic integration, leading to lower transaction costs and better possibilities to exploit economies of scale<br>• Inter-industry trade caused by economic integration, fostering specialization and concentration.<br>• European integration should increase both labour and firm mobility in order to make advantage from best employment possibilities, again favouring economic centers. |

# 3 Measurement of Specialization

## 3.1 Introduction

Economic integration during the 1990s was expected to alter specialization and concentration patterns across Europe (Krugman 1991a). Several empirical studies tried to capture this phenomenon but came to contradicting results between the 1970s and the late 1990s. According to Combes and Overman (2004) this could be due to different data bases as well as due to the use of different specialization measures. Due to the increasing interest on the effects of economic integration on the specialization of countries, the necessity to measure heterogeneity across countries as well as its effects on the competitiveness of individual countries has risen. Empirical research on international trade and international specialization patterns uses a wide array of statistical tools, ranging from simple descriptive indicators to complex econometric techniques. Yet there seems to have been no agreement on which index is best to capture specialization, although the empirical results depend heavily on the statistical methods and measures employed.

In the aftermath of the economic depression of the 1930s and also in the wake of the establishment of a common currency in Europe in the 1990s, both the dangers and merits of over-specialization on economic stability and long-term growth have been discussed at length (Conkling 1963 and Krugman 1991a). From the Great Depression until the 1970s there was widespread belief that highly specialized cities and regions (such as Detroit) were suffering more heavily from economic downturns than more diversified economic entities (Hoover 1948, Rodgers 1957, Conklin 1963 and Conroy 1975). In this respect, the interrelations between economic growth and the development of economic structures as well as the specialization patterns of individual countries have been tackled. As countries, that are structurally lagging behind in strongly growing industries and that are specialized mainly in declining (labour-intensive, low-wage) industries, will not only grow more slowly than economically leading countries, but also face higher unemployment and lower income levels. Measuring structural heterogeneity appropriately also hence allows for tracing processes of economic development and catching-up processes. Neglecting the potential of regions in certain sectors just for the sake of diversification could lead to ignoring comparative advantages and hinder economic growth (Smith and Gibson 1998).

The possible negative impacts of over-specialization in today's economic environment should not be underestimated, either: The likelihood of members of the European Monetary Union to be exposed to asymmetric shocks increases as labour mobility has remained low (OECD 1999). Countries are therefore vulnerable to shocks that create divergence in the labour market, with rising unemployment and falling wages in some countries and labour shortages and inflationary pressures in other countries (Braunerhjelm et al. 2000).

According to this strand of literature, the advantages of diversification lie in fewer and weaker exposure to seasonal and cyclical fluctuations and economic diversity is also regarded to have a positive impact on the stable long-term economic performance of countries, thus a positive effect on employment, per capita income and growth. This is due to the easier replacement of declining industries - since problems of maturing clusters are avoided and since it is easier to take advantage of better employment possibilities in new sectors. At the regional level, over-specialization could also pose a problem due to the higher sensitivity of business cycles compared to more diversified regions where unemployment in declining sectors can be compensated more easily by employment possibilities in growing sectors. In this respect, the problem of ageing clusters and the nature of life cycles of industries have been tackled (Klepper 1996 and Porter 1998). It thus became a primary goal of economic policy to take measures to diversify the economy in order to keep the exposure to external shocks low. During the last decades however, there was a change in paradigm, now emphasizing the advantages of specialization and international division of labour – in particular factors that lead to lower costs of production and make better use of economies of scale, the pool of skilled workers, benefit most from knowledge spillover as well as stronger forward and backward linkages (Krugman 1991b and Porter 1998) - in short: factors that lead to the clustering of economic activity. In order to draw meaningful policy conclusions, however, it is important to use appropriate measures of specialization.

In this chapter we aim to compare the most common specialization indices, discussing their properties, strengths and weaknesses. In order to unravel the differences between the indices, we apply them to European employment structures in 2005, spanning up to 51 industries and 24 European Countries. Note that we restrict our analysis to the calculation of specialization indices, leaving out such issues as the development of geographic concentration patterns, the difference between heterogeneity arising from unrelated small plants located closely in a region and heterogeneity arising from one monopoly firm dominating an industry in one region (Ellison and Glaeser 1997, Maurel and Sédillot 1999 and Devereux et al. 2004), or the interdependencies between specialization and concentration processes per se (Aiginger and Davies 2004). Moreover, we focus on the specialization patterns at the country level only and also leave aside regional specialization patterns (Brülhart and Träger 2005 and Ezcurra et al. 2007) as well as the development of trade specialization (Minondo 2011 and Cadot et al. 2007).

One of the first to measure economic concentration was McLaughlin (1930). He measured concentration of value added in the five (twenty) largest manufacturing industries in order to capture the relationship between high economic concentration and the severity of economic fluctuations. The deficiencies of this measure are obvious, and widely recognized. The choice of $N$ is arbitrary, much information is needed; dramatic shifts in industrial structure can occur which the index would not be able to mirror. Think of the case in which the industry structure of the top $N$ industries remains unaffected while the development of all other industries changes. Then, the index would be unaffected, not being able to mirror the underlying structural change.

It is not the aim of this chapter, however, to discuss whether specialization or diversification has a more positive influence on growth and welfare. Instead, we will discuss different measures of specialization, their advantages and disadvantages in applying them in empirical work. Empirical research on international specialization patterns uses a wide array of indices without giving any explanation why the actual index is chosen. As long as the choice which index to use does not influence the results or leads to contradicting results, this is no problem. Otherwise, robustness checks are necessary and it is of relevance which index to choose. According to Amiti (1998), Aiginger (2000) and Combes and Overman (2004), results could differ substantially due to which index and which data is implemented.

In particular, Amiti (1998) shows that even holding the index used constant (in this study the Gini index) and altering the level of data aggregation between 27 and 65 industries, the average increase in specialization is on average around one per cent whereas with the more disaggregated data the average increase is two per cent. Aiginger (2000) points out that the results depend on both the indicator to measure specialization as well as on the underlying time period – in his case altering the beginning of the time span from 1985 to 1988 or even 1990s since the data show de-concentration from 1985 until the early 1990s and increasing concentration afterwards. If you therefore analyze years in the 1990s only, concentration appears to have increased much more than when starting the analysis in the mid 1980s.

## 3.2 Absolute vs. Relative Specialization

We focus on two different groups of indices: The first group (*specialization indices*) describes a country's absolute specialization. Using such an index, a country would be considered specialized if a small number of industries exhibit high shares of the overall employment of the country (Aiginger and Davies 2004). This is the case for instance for Italy, which is specialized in textiles, for Scandinavian countries, which are dedicated to the production of pulp and paper, or for Poland, which is specialized in agriculture and food. The second group of indices (*heterogeneity indices*) focuses on the deviation of a country's industry structure from the average industry structure of the reference group of countries. This kind of relative specialization – measured for example by the Krugman Index- would thus reveal countries' comparative advantages in relation to the reference group. For instance, Finland is relatively more specialized in Communications Technologies than any other Western European country, although the absolute share of this industry on the Finnish industry is low. This means, if a country is specialized in industries which the other countries are also specialized in, the first group of indices will indicate high specialization while the second group will indicate a low degree of specialization.

These distinctions are necessary since these different forms of heterogeneity may, but need not necessarily go hand in hand. Aiginger and Davies (2004) for instance show that the average specialization of EU countries in the manufacturing sector increased since the mid-1980s while the concentration of manufacturing industries across EU countries decreased in the same period. Concentration and specialization moving into opposite directions is often considered counterintuitive as they are evidently two sides of the same coin. In fact, relative localization measures as those used in Cutrini (2010) or in the present paper are measures of both average concentration and average specialization. Thus, for these measures, average relative concentration and specialization cannot diverge from each other by definition. The present chapter solves this puzzle by showing that the increases of average specialization measures of the kind used by Aiginger and Davies are driven predominantly by the *aggregate* structural change from mature to modern industries. We also show that there is no such dominance of aggregate structural change for their average concentration measures as there is actually very little aggregate regional structural change between regions or countries in the data. Thus, the average concentration measure of Aiginger and Davies (2004) is not dominated by shifts of aggregate employment across regions but by changes in the relative concentration patterns of the individual industries (Bickenbach et al. 2010).

The difference between the two groups of indices can be explained also comparing the benchmark they use: For the group of absolute measures, the reference level is the equal distribution of employment shares across all industries, i.e. $1 / I$ as the uniform distribution of employment shares is the reference point, absolute specialization indices give evidence on how the economic structure (the degree of specialization) of one specific country changes over time, regardless of the development of other countries. On the other hand, the average economic structure of countries under study is taken as the benchmark for relative specialization measures. Specialization indices of this kind provide data on the dissimilarity in the sectoral composition of each region compared with the structure of the selected reference level.

The second reference level is the average distribution of employment of a (arbitrarily chosen) reference group. Since this benchmark itself is changing over time due to structural change and altering specialization patterns, the specialization of a specific country with regard to the changing reference level could vary even though the economic structure remains constant (Chisholm 1968). In this case, one should speak of a change of comparative advantages (or competitiveness) rather than of changing specialization patterns. Moreover, larger countries contribute more to the benchmark than smaller ones; therefore the specialization of large countries is underestimated, while the specialization of smaller countries is overestimated. Taking the EU-average without the country under investigation as the reference level ameliorates the results since the bias towards the own country reflected by the standard EU-average reference level is larger for large countries such as Germany than for Austria.

Both benchmarks have been criticized as being arbitrary (Gratton 1979 and Brown and Pheasant 1985): Absolute indices neglect that certain industries naturally are larger than others. Since the industry classification is much finer for modern growing industries such as in the information and communication industries than for traditional industries or the fact that industries are much finer disaggregated within the manufacturing sector than in the service sector, the equiproportion of employment shares is doubtful to be a good reference level. The neglect of these peculiarities of classification systems implies that absolute specialization measures will increase over time in (almost) any empirical application just as a consequence of a general structural change from "old" to "new" industries or from broad to narrow defined industries (Krugman 1991, Bickenbach et al. 2010). Moreover, an increasing number of services have been outsourced from manufacturing industries over the past decades. Thus, the assignment of employment to industries has changed even though the tasks of employment remained the same. This is especially true for the rise of business services or R&D employment. In this context, it is of special interest how indices are affected by the change of employment shares due to a re-classification of employment to individual industries. It is quite likely that changes in the employment distribution towards service industries may change the level of specialization even without "real" changes in employment patterns. Krugman (1991b) discussed this problem for the case of Information and Communication

Technologies that are higher disaggregated than other industries such as textiles, thereby leading to an underestimation of absolute specialization in ICT industries. Additionally the interpretation of results is questionable if neglecting the potential of regions in certain sectors just for the sake of diversification. This could lead to ignoring comparative advantages and hinder economic growth (Smith and Gibson 1988). Moreover, sticking closely to such a reference point assumes that every country possesses identical factor endowments and the same market area, which does not hold true in reality (Conroy 1975b, Combes and Overman 2004). The distribution of employment shares could also become concentrated in fewer industries independent of changes in trade costs more easily. In cases where consumer preferences change or technological change affects one single industry in all countries in a similar way, absolute specialization patterns would report rising specialization (Amiti 1999) which might be attributed to wrong causes and leading to wrong policy conclusions. In this respect, relative specialization patterns are superior since they better control for natural size differences between industries. Yet, a different shortcoming is associated with relative indices: In contrast to the absolute measures of specialization, a country with a much more equilibrated structure than a highly specialized reference country group will thus receive a high level of relative specialization, whereas a country specialized in the same industries as the reference countries will receive low level of relative specialization.

## 3.3 Preferable Characteristics of Indices

In order to evaluate the (dis-)advantages of the indices under investigation, it is necessary to define characteristics which indices should fulfil in order to be appropriate measures of specialization. These characteristics will also help us to understand why empirical results could differ depending on the index applied.

Most indices studying structural heterogeneity are borrowed from the research on income inequality or from the analysis of market concentration. Consequently we also borrow the characteristics which sound indices ought to fulfil from these two strands of research[9]. In the following we shortly describe the relevant characteristics that a good measure ought to fulfil:

---

9   The main difference between income inequality and structural heterogeneity is their interpretation: whereas income inequality can be seen as unjust, e.g. when the income distribution strongly favors a small fraction of people, structural heterogeneity does not have fairness implications, since unequal industry structures do not necessarily imply inequality of productivity and income, but can stem from different specialization patterns all leading to the same level of income.

*Axiom of Anonymity:* If the distribution of employment shares $d_{A'}$ is obtained from a distribution of employment shares $d_A$ through permutation (i.e. through changing the order of industries in calculating the heterogeneity index), then the degree of specialization should be the same for both distributions (Kolm 1969 or Atkinson 1970). In our case this would imply that the re-ordering of employment shares used for the calculation of the specialization indices should have no effect on the resulting level of specialization.

*Axiom of Progressive Transfers (also referred to as the Pigou-Dalton Principle or rank-preserving equalization):* According to this "Transfer principle" (Dalton 1920, Atkinson 1970, Sen 1973 or Hannah and Kay 1977), a country should become less absolutely specialized if one hour of employment is transferred from an industry a country is stronger specialized in towards an industry a country is less specialized in as long as the transfer between the two industries does not completely reverse the raking of these two. On the other hand, if employment is transferred from an industry with low employment share to an industry with higher employment share, absolute specialization is expected to increase. This is equivalent to the concept of a mean preserving spread as introduced by Rothschild and Stiglitz (1970).

*Bounds:* Bounds are important in order to put the obtained specialization values into perspective. Only by having defined bounds, does it become clear whether a country is highly specialized or not. Studying absolute specialization, the upper bound, which signifies complete specialization, is reached if a country is characterized by having employment in one industry only. This bound of relative specialization is attained if a country is completely specialized in one industry, while every other country is specialized in other industries. In that case, the employment share $b$ is 1 in one industry and zero in all other industries. The employment shares in the country group, $i$, on the other hand is of equal size in all industries, such that the $i = 1 / I$. The lower bound signifies total equality, i.e. in the case of absolute measures all industries having equal employment shares, whereas in the case of relative measures the respective country having the same specialization patterns as the reference group. Ideally, the values of the upper and lower bound should be independent from the number of countries and industries (Combes and Overman 2004) in order to make reasonable comparisons across the development of country groups and time (if industries or countries are added). Yet typically, the bounds vary with the number of countries and/or industries. When making international comparisons, one should therefore use the same number of industries for all countries and hold the number of countries constant in order to avoid distortions.

Calculating the lower and upper bound of indices is of major importance since they set the various results of empirical research into respective. Therefore it is necessary to not only report the level of specialization but set it in proportion with the minimum and maximum level, which can vary widely across the different indices. It is also due to this fact that it is not meaningful to compare the levels of specialization based on different indices without a further reference to the bounds of each index.

*Decomposability:* A decomposable inequality measure is defined as a measure which allows inequality to be split into a weighted average of the inequality existing within and between subgroups (Bourguignon 1979). In our case, a good index should thus be decomposable into inter-sectoral and inter-industry heterogeneity on the one hand and inter- and intra-regional heterogeneity on the other hand. The inter-industrial part of specialization ought to be scaled by the average share of the respective sector $k$. The smaller a sector (i.e. the smaller its employment share $\overline{b}_{kE}$ ), the smaller should be the impact of inter-industry heterogeneity on the aggregate index. This means for instance that since the service sector has been growing, inter-industry heterogeneity in the service sector contributes more to overall specialization in 2005 than it did in 1970, even if the actual degree of inter-industry heterogeneity has not changed.

By decomposing a country's specialization into 'between-' and 'within-' components, it is possible to distinguish comparative advantages that are inherent to the whole country in relation to all other countries on the one hand (i.e. the between-country component), and regional competitiveness within this country, i.e. comparative advantages of some regions compared to the national level on the other hand (the within-country component). Thus, when investigating the economic structure of Italy for instance, the between country analyses would attribute Italy competitiveness in Textiles and Leather relative to the economic structures of Germany or the UK. Investigating the economic structures of Italian provinces would however shed light on the fact that not the whole country is more competitive in the production of leather and textiles than other European Countries, but that this over-proportional competitiveness is restricted to some provinces, implying heterogeneity within Italy.

*Classification of industries:*[10] In this context it is interesting how specialization is affected by splitting industries into a larger number of sub-industries or merging industries to one larger industry. Ideally, if we split one industry into

---

10    Combes and Overman (2004) also stress the importance of bias of results due to arbitrary changes in the spatial classification of regions or countries. Since changing borders of countries is a problem for Germany (re-unification) only, we do not deal with this in this paper. One shortcoming has to be kept in mind, however: Employment in the same industry in neighboring countries is treated in exactly the same way as employment that takes place at the opposite end of Europe. Thus the distance between sub- units of the sample is not taken into account.

two sub-industries, the level of absolute specialization should decrease, since each industry now has a smaller employment share. On the other hand, if two small industries are combined to a larger industry, then absolute specialization ought to increase, since the employment share of this industry is now larger than before. This implies that changes in industry classification over time should influence results – causing problems if the classification of industries changes over the investigation period. This is a problem particularly if the level of disaggregation varies systematically with activity types. If the sectoral disaggregation for example is finer for manufacturing than it is for services, then changes in the composition of output towards services may change measures of concentration even if the location patterns of firms remain unchanged. Krugman (1991b) discussed the problem that Information and Communication Technologies are disaggregated much finer than other industries such as textiles, thereby leading to an underestimation of specialization and concentration of ICT industries.

Regarding relative specialization, however, we have to distinguish the following two cases. With regard to the shift of employment on specialization, it has to be taken into account whether the reallocation is from a small towards a larger industry which should increase specialization or from a big industry towards a small industry since this would need to lead to a decrease in absolute specialization. In this respect, the disaggregation of data can play an important role and we will show whether the inclusion of very big and very small industries has the same effects in all indices. This is illustrated by two examples: First, let the country under study be more specialized than the reference group in all branches of an industry $i$, then the employment share in every sub-industry, $b_{ji}$, has to be larger than in the reference group (in our case, the EU-average), i.e. $b_{ij}^A > \bar{b}_{ij}, \forall j$.

*Table 4: Specialization in industry i for Case 1*

|  | Country $A$ | Reference Group | Heterogeneity | Degree of Heterogeneity |
|---|---|---|---|---|
| $b_{i1}$ | 0.3 | 0.2 | $b_{i1}^A > \bar{b}_{i1}$ | 0.1 |
| $b_{i2}$ | 0.2 | 0.1 | $b_{i2}^A > \bar{b}_{i2}$ | 0.1 |
| $b_{i3}$ | 0.4 | 0.3 | $b_{i3}^A > \bar{b}_{i3}$ | 0.1 |
| $b_i$ | 0.9 | 0.6 | $b_i^A > \bar{b}_i$ | 0.3 = 0.1+0.1+0.1 |

In order to quantify the degree of heterogeneity between the economic structures of country $A$ and the reference group, we could either build the sum of heterogeneity obtained in every single sub-industry, $b_{i1}, b_{i2}, b_{i3}$, i.e. $\sum_{j=1}^{J} \left| b_{ij}^{A} - \bar{b}_{ij} \right|$, or we could calculate the heterogeneity after adding all sub-industries to one large industry, i.e. $\left| b_{i}^{A} - \bar{b}_{i} \right|$. If $b_{ij}^{A} > \bar{b}_{ij}, \forall j$, then the degree of heterogeneity obtained by the calculation of sub-industries should be equal to the level of heterogeneity obtained by the proper industry (see last row in Table 4). Merging or splitting up industries therefore must not alter the degree of specialization in cases in which the country is more specialized in all sub-industries.

Case two applies if the country under study is more specialized in industry $i$ even though only in some sub-industries the employment shares are higher than in the reference group (i.e. the reference group is relatively more specialized in some sub-industries) and in others they are lower. This is shown by the example in Table 5: Country A is relatively more specialized than the reference group in sub-industries $I_{i2}$ and $I_{i3}$, while the reference group is more specialized in $I_{i1}$.

Table 5: Specialization in industry i for Case 2

|  | Country A | Reference Group | Heterogeneity | Degree of Heterogeneity |
|---|---|---|---|---|
| $b_{i1}$ | 0.1 | 0.2 | $b_{i1}^{A} < \bar{b}_{i1}$ | 0.1 |
| $b_{i2}$ | 0.2 | 0.1 | $b_{i2}^{A} > \bar{b}_{i2}$ | 0.1 |
| $b_{i3}$ | 0.4 | 0.3 | $b_{i3}^{A} > \bar{b}_{i3}$ | 0.1 |
| $b_{i}$ | 0.7 | 0.6 | $b_{i}^{A} > \bar{b}_{i}$ | $0.1 < 0.1 + 0.1 + 0.1$ |

Merging the employment shares of the sub-industries $b_{11}$, $b_{12}$ and $b_{13}$ to one industry $b_1$ in such a case would then imply that the total heterogeneity caused by adding the heterogeneity in all sub- industries is larger than the heterogeneity obtained by the sum of all sub-industries, i.e. $0.3 > 0.1$, since over- and underspecialization patterns in the sub-industries partially cancel each other out in this second case (see Table 5).

*Number of industries:* The introduction of an industry with an employment share of zero or a very small employment share should have no or only negligible impact on the level of absolute specialization of a country (Hannah and Kay 1977). Thus, the following distributions of economic structures ($d$) $d_c(0,6;0,4)$, $d_{c'}(0,6;0,4;0)$ and $d_{c'}'(0,6;0,3999;0,0001)$ ought to be considered as almost equally specialized. Similarly, the addition of an industry with an employment share of zero both in the country under study and in the average of the reference group should have no impact on the level of relative specialization of a country.

## 3.4 Indices

In the following section, we describe the characteristics of all indices we use for our empirical comparisons. We draw on standard indices which are common tools for measuring income inequality and market concentration, adapting them slightly for our purposes. The notation is the same for all indices: There are $i = 1...I$ industries, $b_i^n$ is the share of industry $i$ of total employment in country $n$, and $\bar{b}_i$ is the average share of industry $i$ of total employment across the entire reference group, i.e. $\bar{b}_i = \sum_{n=1}^{N} b_i^n \big/ N$ (in our case $N = 24$ European countries).

### 3.4.1 Specialization Indices

Helg et al. (1995) present absolute specialization figures computed with Gini indices for the EU 12 countries based on the OECD Indicators for Industrial Activity for eight 1-digit ISIC industries. Their results suggest that all countries, except France, Portugal and Spain become more specialized between 1975 and 1985. The periphery countries – Greece, Italy, Portugal and Spain – were the least specialized countries throughout the investigation period. The least specialized country appeared to be Luxembourg. The results differ somewhat from Brülhart (2001a) who conducts a similar exercise using employment data for 12 of the EU 15 countries. Brülhart's results are hard to interpret, however. First, he excludes Belgium, Ireland and Luxembourg due to limited data availability. Second, he presents the change of specialization between 1972 and 1996 only. It is thus difficult to know whether his findings are driven by structural differences, or just differences in the business cycle across countries.

#### 3.4.1.1 Hirschman-Herfindahl-Index

The Hirschman-Herfindahl index (Herfindahl 1950 and Hirschman 1964) is widely used in industrial economics (Scherer 1990) to measure market concentration and to investigate the existence of an oligopoly or cartels in particular (Hannah and Kay 1977[11], Waterson 1984 or Tirole 1988). The Hirschman-

---

11    A variation of the HHI as being proposed by Hannah and Kay (1977) is

$$\frac{1}{I}\sum_{iI}^{I} b_i^2 - \frac{1}{I^2}\left(\sum_{i=1}^{I} b_i\right)^2$$
.

Herfindahl (*HHI*) index has also been used as a measure of economic diversity (Tauer 1992) and for macroeconomic specialization analyses (Sapir 1996, Davis 1998, Storper et al. 2002, Aiginger and Pfaffermayr 2004 and Beine and Coulombe 2007). It has the following form:

$$HHI = \sum_{i=1}^{I} b_i^{\alpha}$$

In industrial economics, $\alpha = 2$ has a theoretical meaning[12], whereas in the field of specialization this value is arbitrary. For this reason, the value of $\alpha$ has to be chosen carefully. In general, the higher $\alpha$, the more weight is given to the largest industries in the distribution and the lower is the impact of small industries. When applying and interpreting the *HHI*, one therefore has to be aware of the fact that choosing an appropriate value for α can be crucial. In order to counter the effect of giving much weight to large industries, we could also implement a variation of the *HHI* introduced by Keeble and Hauser (1971) and used by Chisholm and Oeppen (1973): They used the square root of the *HHI*, such that:

$$HHI_{KH} = \sqrt{\sum_{i=1}^{I} b_i^2}$$

If a value of $\alpha$ closer to 1, the index is more similar to the Shannon Entropy Index that is described below. Note that when $\alpha < 1$, then *HHI* is an inverse measure of specialization. For $\alpha = 1$, the *HHI* is 1 no matter how strong or weak a country is specialized. Similar to this, for $\alpha = 0$ the *HHI* is always equal to *I*.

The *HHI* implicitly takes the equi-proportion as a reference, since this is the lower bound of the index. This implies that the lowest degree of specialization is reached if each industry has the same employment share; the highest degree of specialization is reached if the country is specialized in one industry only – irrespective of the specialization of other countries. For $\alpha = 2$, the lower bound thus is $1/I$ and the upper bound 1.[13] In general, the relative sizes of industries are more important for the absolute value of the *HHI* than is the absolute number of industries, since the index weights each industry by the relative employment share (Hall and Tideman 1967). Whereas the *HHI* tends to decrease with the number of industries, it increases with the dispersion in size between the industries.

The Axiom of Anonymity holds, as the level of specialization is independent of the sequential ordering of industries. Transferring employment shares from a small to a large industry increases specialization, whereas transferring employ-

---

12   The Hirschman-Herfindahl Index determines if a monopoly exists. Thus it also makes sense that the calculation gives higher weight to larger firms.

13   As α→0, the upper bound is 1, but the lower bound also tends to be close to 1, whereas for α→∞, the upper bound remains 1 and the lower bound converges towards zero.

ment from an industry which a country is specialized in an industry a country was not specialized into before, decreases specialization – even more than when using other indices. The *HHI* itself is not decomposable, but if we calculate the *HHI* as a measure of diversity (where specialization = 1 – diversification), then total *HHI* diversification can be split up into intersectoral *HHI* diversification and inter-industry *HHI* diversification (Acar and Sankaran 1999).

The *HHI* also possesses two favourable criteria connected with the size and the number of industries: Splitting an industry into two smaller industries decreases specialization over proportionally since larger industries are given relatively more weight. Merging industries has the opposite effect in line with the Axiom. Adding a new industry with employment share zero holds the degree of specialization constant. Concerning the level of the index, the relative size of industries is more important than the absolute number of industries, since the index weights each industry by the relative employment share (Hall and Tideman 1967). Whereas the *HHI* tends to decrease with the number of industries, it increases with the dispersion in size between the industries.

Some studies also implement the concentration ratio as an index (Aiginger 2000). Since this indicator uses information on the largest $i$ industries only, it uses less information compared to the HHI, has identical (dis-)advantages and will therefore not be implemented in this study. Moreover, economic theory does not provide suggestions as to how many industries should be included in calculating the concentration ratio.

### 3.4.1.2 Shannon Entropy Index

The Shannon Entropy Index (*SEI*) belongs to the group of entropy indices[14] that is widely used in the research of income distribution (Cowell 1995 and Cowell 2000) but only rarely applied in the context of specialization (Attaran and Zwick 1987, Smith and Gibson 1988, Aiginger and Davies 2004 and Aiginger and Pfaffermayr 2004).

$$SEI = -\sum_{i=1}^{I} b_i \ln(b_i)$$

The *SEI* is defined as the negative sum of employment shares multiplied by the natural logarithm of employment shares of each single industry $i$. Due to the ln-form, the influence of large industries is reduced compared to the *HHI*. This

---

14 In information theory, entropy generally refers to the uncertainty associated with a random variable. The Shannon entropy quantifies the expected value of the information contained in a message. Therefore, the Shannon entropy is a measure of the average information content missing if the value of the random variable is unknown (Shannon 1948).

means that countries which specialize in large industries instead of small industries are marked as more specialized by the *HHI* than by the *SEI*. Note that due to the natural logarithm the *SEI* is an inverse measure of specialization, i.e. it increases with decreasing specialization so that the lower bound (lying at zero) gives absolute specialization and the upper bound (at ln *I*) complete diversification, with each industry having the same employment share.

The value of the Shannon Entropy Index is independent of the ordering of industries and can be decomposed. Additionally, this index satisfies the Axiom of Progressive Transfers. The *SEI* does not completely fulfill one criterion of a good specialization index, however: As the ln(0) is not defined, it is not possible to calculate the *SEI* for any employment distribution containing industries with employment shares equal to zero. When adding an infinitely small industry, however, the *SEI* does not change significantly, implying that very small industries only have a negligible effect on the level of specialization. Merging subindustries to one larger industry decreases the value of the *SEI*, signifying increasing specialization in line with the Axiom of the Classification of Industries.

### 3.4.1.3 Ogive Index

First employed by Tress (1938) to study diversity in the field of economics, the Ogive Index has been implemented in the context of country specialization by Bahl et al. (1971), Hackbart and Anderson (1975), Wasylenko and Erickson (1978) and Attaran and Zwick (1987).

$$O = \sum_{i=1}^{I} I \left( b_i - \frac{1}{I} \right)^2$$

Specialization is analyzed using the equal distribution of employment across all sectors as an explicit benchmark for maximum dispersion. The index is a linear transformation of the *HHI*[15]. Therefore, the country ranks of both indices are perfectly correlated if $\alpha = 2$. The lower bound of the Ogive Index is zero; the upper bound is $(I - 1) / I$ The Ogive Index puts relatively more weight on industries which deviate much from $1 / I$ (i.e. both on industries that are heavily over- and under-represented in the country's economic structure) due to the fact that

---

15 We can show that the Ogive Index is a linear transformation of the traditional Hirschman-Herfindahl Index (i.e. in case that $\alpha = 2$) by the following operation:

$$O = \sum_{i=1}^{I} \frac{\left( b_i - \frac{1}{I} \right)^2}{\frac{1}{I}} = \sum_{i=1}^{I} \left( \frac{b_i^2 - 2b_i \frac{1}{I} + \frac{1}{I^2}}{\frac{1}{I}} \right) = I \sum_{i=1}^{I} b_i^2 - 2 \sum_{i=1}^{I} b_i + \sum_{i=1}^{I} \frac{1}{I} ; HHI = \sum_{i=1}^{I} b_i^2 \Rightarrow$$

$$O = I * HHI - 2 + 1 = I * HHI - 1.$$

the numerator is squared. Therefore the Ogive measure can easily overestimate the degree of diversity between countries. To overcome this problem, one could use the modified Ogive Index of Jackson (1984), which employs absolute deviations instead of squared values. Using simple deviations only (instead of absolute values) as Florence (1948) or Siegel et al. (1995) is problematic, however, since over- and under-specialization could cancel out one another, leading to an underestimation of specialization.

The Ogive Index fulfills the Axiom of Anonymity and the Axiom of Progressive Transfers. Moreover, the classification of industries (splitting them up or merging them) alters the level of specialization remarkably. The Ogive Index does not fulfill two characteristics of a good specialization measure, however, and can therefore be considered to be inferior compared to the (related) Hirschman-Herfindahl Index, which fulfills all criteria. First, the Ogive Index is not decomposable. Second, adding an industry with employment share zero alters the results significantly, since the size of the reference level $1 / I$ is affected. The same problem arises if industries with small employment shares are introduced, leading to a large rise in the degree of specialization since under-represented industries are weighted heavily.

### 3.4.1.4 Diversification Index

Rodgers (1957) introduced the Diversification Index *(DIV)*. For its construction, the employment shares of each industry of country $n$ are calculated and then sorted in ascending order according to their size. Summarizing the progressive totals gives the *crude diversification index (CDI)*. Let $b'_j$ be the sorted index of the ranked industry shares, so that $b'_j < b'_{j+1}$ for all $j$. Then the sum of the progressive totals can be written as

$$CDI = b_1 + \sum_{j=2}^{n}\left(\sum_{k=1}^{j-1} b_k\right), \text{ with } b'_j, j = 2,....,I; k = 1,...I.$$

After calculating this Crude Diversification Index, we have to determine the average index for all countries, *aCDI*, and as the upper bound the (hypothetical) Index of Least Diversity which, *ICDI = I*, since overall employment is then concentrated in one single industry and thus the progressive totals sum up to $I$. The Refined Diversification Index, *RDI*, is then defined as follows:

$$RDI = \frac{CDI - aCDI}{ICDI - aCDI}.$$

Note that the index - although taking into account a reference group - does not compare the shares of each industry by pairs, but only compares the degree of specialization. That means that even if the industry structure of the country under analysis deviates widely from the average, the index may be low as long as the degree of specialization is similar to the reference group.

The *RDI* turns negative whenever the economic structure of the reference country group deviates from the equi-distribution of industries while the country under study at the same time is more specialized than the reference country group, i.e. $CDI > aCDI > lCDI$. For the case where the reference group has equal employment shares in all industries while the specific country is specialized in one single industry, the index is not defined, since then $lCDI = aCDI$, which would imply that the denominator turns zero. The *RDI* hence only turns positive when the economic structure of the reference country group deviates from the equi-distribution of industries and the country under study is less specialized than the reference country group, i.e. $aCDI > CDI \geq lCDI$. This implies that the *RDI* is an inverse measure of specialization with the lower bound at 1. It is reached if the country under study is characterized by an equi-proportional industry structure, i.e. $CDI = lCDI$. This is true irrespective of the degree of specialization of the reference group – as long as $aCDI \neq lCDI$. The upper bound is not defined since in such a case *CDI* is maximized, whereas $aCDI = lCDI$, turning the numerator of the *RDI* zero. In addition to this deficiency, the Diversification Index is not decomposable. Moreover, adding an industry with an employment share of zero (or even a very small industry) may lead to a considerable change in results, since the level of *lCDI* is not affected as much as the levels of *CDI* and *aCDI*. It may therefore yield results that indicate a high level of specialization even though this is not the case in reality. The Diversification Index fulfills the three other criteria of a good specialization measure– the Axiom of Anonymity, the Axiom of Progressive Transfers and the Classification of industries.

### 3.4.1.5  Absolute Gini-Index

The Gini Index (Gini 1912 and Gini 1921) is a common measure of income equality and heterogeneity of economic structures. Yet it is widely applied as a relative measure only. To our knowledge, the Gini Index has not yet been applied as an absolute measure in the field of specialization. We introduce it in order to give a full account of indices and to compare the different outcomes of the Absolute and the Relative Gini Indices.

In order to calculate the Absolute Gini Index of Specialization (*Abs. GINI*), the relative employment shares of the country are ranked in ascending order for the construction of the Lorenz curve. Since the reference level is $1 / I$, the ordering of the employment shares is the following: $b_i / I \geq b_{i-1} / I$. The Lorenz curve is generated by ordering the progressive totals of the employment shares $b_i$ on the y-axis and the progressive totals of $1/I$ on the x-axis and then connecting the points. Next, the 45° line is introduced, which is equal to the progressive totals of $1/I$. In order to finally determine the Gini coefficient, we define $A_L$ to be the area under the Lorenz curve. The Gini coefficient $G$ then is $(1 - 2A_L)/I^2$. The Gini coefficient thus represents the difference between a country's actual distribution of employment and the equal distribution of employment over all industries. The lower bound of the absolute Gini Index is zero. It is reached when all industries are of equal size, i.e. $1/I$ and hence the Lorenz curve represents the 45° line. The upper bound of the Absolute Gini Index is $(I-1)/I$ but it converges towards one for a very large number of industries.

The Absolute Gini Index is characterized by several shortcomings: First, they are not decomposable. Second, total heterogeneity cannot simply be split up into intersectoral and inter-industry (or similarly inter- and intraregional) heterogeneity, but includes a third term, called *transvariation* (Dagum 1997), which does not have a clear interpretation in the context of specialization. Third, the Index does not satisfy the Axiom of Progressive Transfers, since values in the middle part of the distribution are weighted more heavily than values at the tails of the distribution (Cowell 1995 or Amiti 1999). Therefore e.g. a country $A$ characterized by the economic structure $d_B : (b_1 = 0.1; b_2 = 0.25; b_3 = 0.25; b_4 = 0.4)$ should have a lower absolute specialization level than country $B$ with the following economic structure $d_{B'} : (b_1 = 0.1; b_2 = 0.1; b_3 = 0.4; b_4 = 0.4)$; this is not the case if the level of specialization is calculated with the help of a Gini index. Moreover, the index is sensitive to the splitting and merging of industries, as well as to adding industries with an employment of zero: Merging sub-industries to one larger industry decreases the level of specialization measured by the Gini index, which contradicts the intuition that absolute specialization should increase when industries are merged. The employment distribution $d_C : (b_1 = 1; b_2 = 0)$, for instance, would result in a lower Gini index value than $d_D$: ($b_1 = 0.5$; $b_2 = 0.5$; $b_3 = 0$; $b_4 = 0$), even though intuitively a country ought to be considered more specialized if the economic structure is represented by distribution $d_C$ rather than distribution $d_D$. Introducing new industries with an employment share of zero – which should not alter a good specialization index strongly - leads to a significant increase in the level of specialization due to changes in the reference level $1/I$. Therefore, the Absolute Gini Index only fulfills the Axiom of Anonymity.

Last, a specific value of the Gini coefficient can thus correspond to different distribution. It is therefore quite difficult to interpret the absolute value derived (Aiginger 2000).

### 3.4.1.6 Absolute Theil-Index

Similar to the Gini Index, also the Theil Index (Theil 1967) is mostly applied as a relative measure. The absolute Theil Index (Abs. T) has only been applied by Aiginger and Davies (2004). It builds on information theory, borrowing from Shannon (1948) and can thus be regarded as a variation of the Shannon Entropy Index as it is a transformation of this index. It is generated by dividing the employment shares of a country, $b_i$, through the number of industries, $1 / I$. Therefore the results obtained are perfectly negatively correlated. For this reason, in the empirical part of the paper results are not reported for the *SEI*.

$$Abs.T = \frac{1}{I}\sum_{i=1}^{I} b_i I \ln b_i I$$

The Absolute Gini Index does not satisfy the Axiom of Progressive Transfers, since values in the middle part of the distribution are weighted more heavily than values at the tails of the distribution (Cowell 1995 or Amiti 1999).

In summary, for the analysis regarding the absolute level of specialization, the Hirschman-Herfindahl Index is not only an easily computable index but also fulfils more criteria than all other indices presented (see Table 6). It can thus be regarded as superior to other measures, especially if $\alpha$ is chosen closer to 1 in order to counterweight the influence of large industries. Likewise, one could use the Shannon Entropy index, but it has to be kept in mind that the index is problematic if industries with employment shares of zero are contained in the sample. Both the Diversification Index and the Absolute Gini Index are not only more time-consuming to calculate but also fail to satisfy important criteria of good specialization measures.

*Table 6: Criteria of Absolute Specialization Measures*

|  | Anonymity | Progressive Transfers | Decomposability | Splitting/ Merging | Industries with $b_i = 0$ | Bounds |
|---|---|---|---|---|---|---|
| *HHI* | ✓ | ✓ | ✓ | ✓ | ✓ | ✓ |
| *SEI* | ✓ | ✓ | ✓ | ✓ | x | ✓ |
| *Ogive* | ✓ | ✓ | x | ✓ | x | ✓ |
| *DIV* | ✓ | ✓ | x | ✓ | x | x |
| *Abs. GINI* | ✓ | x | x | x | x | ✓ |
| *Abs. Theil* | ✓ | ✓ | ✓ | ✓ | x | ✓ |

There are large differences between the absolute specialization indices. This first of all stems from the fact that the Hirschman Herfindahl Index is a specialization (and concentration) index whereas the Gini and the Theil Index are disparity measures. Thus these indices are taken from different strands of research: whereas the HHI has its roots in measuring the concentration of firms within an industry, the latter two stem from income inequality research and therefore measure two different things.

When deciding which index to implement for empirical studies, one has to be aware of the following caveats: The relative size of industries drives the value of the Hirschman-Herfindahl Index more than the number of industries since the *HHI* is shaped by the employment shares of the industries under study. As a consequence, large industries drive the *HHI* index much more than it is the case for any other index. This is a problem if there is one single industry only, as it would be the case when including the agriculture sector opposed to manufacturing industries. For empirical research it is thus important to check for robustness in results and check for the presence of one big industry in the data set.

The specialization levels of the Gini and the Theil Index on the other hand are more driven by the number of industries since the reference point is (1 / I). This is of special importance if the number of industries in the sample is low. Then even adding a small industry can alter the results significantly by shifting the point of reference.

## 3.4.2 Heterogeneity Indices

### 3.4.2.1 Krugman Specialization Index

The Krugman Specialization Index $(K)$ is the standard index among the specialization measures. Basically, it is the standard error of industry shares, i.e. it calculates the share of employment which would have to be relocated to achieve an industry structure equivalent to the average structure of the reference group. The reference value $\bar{b}_i$ can be either one other country, as originally in Krugman (1991a), or it can refer to the mean of all other countries, as in Midelfart-Knarvik et al. (2000), Longhi et al. (2004) and Palan and Schmiedeberg (2010).

$$K = \sum_{i=1}^{I} | b_i - \bar{b}_i |$$

Before this index received widespread acceptance, it was known as the coefficient of regional specialization and implemented by Hoover (1948), Leser (1949a and 1949b) as well as by Isard (1960). The Krugman Specialization Index can take values in between zero and $2(I-1)/I$. If relative specialization is zero, the economic structure of a single country resembles the economic structure of the reference level (i.e. the EU-average in our case). The higher the index, the more the economic structure of a country deviates from the reference group and the more a country is considered to be specialized. In contrast to the absolute measures of specialization presented above, a country with a much more equilibrated structure (and thus a lower *HHI*) than a highly specialized reference country group will thus receive a high K-value, whereas a country specialized in the same industries as the reference countries will receive a low K-value (irrespective of the high *HHI* of both the country and the reference group). A favourable property of the Krugman Specialization Index is that splitting one industry into sub-industries will not alter the degree of specialization if the country is relatively more specialized than the reference group in *all* sub-industries. On the other hand, if the country under study is relatively more specialized in some sub-industries, while being relatively less specialized in some other sub-industries compared to the reference group, then merging industries would decrease the level of specialization since patterns of over- and under-specialization cancel each other out. Adding industries with zero or very low employment shares does not alter the level of specialization. Hence, the Krugman Specialization Index fulfills all criteria but decomposability. Using the standard deviation has some drawbacks as it highly weights both positive and negative outliers. One advantage stems from the fact that absolute differences are used and small industries are weighted correctly (Aiginger 2000).

### 3.4.2.2 Index of Inequality in Productive Structure

The Index of Inequality in Productive Structure (*IP*) was introduced by Cuadrado-Roura et al. (1999), but variations thereof have also been employed by Haaland et al. (1999), Landesmann (2000) and Percoco et al. (2005)

$$IP = \sum_{i=1}^{I} \left( b_i - \bar{b}_i \right)^2$$

The *IP* is simply the variance of employment shares. It is similar to the Krugman Specialization Index, but by adding up the squared deviations of employment shares, it gives more weight to large deviations as shown in Table 7. Even if the economic structure of country *A* does not change, the specialization level of country *A* falls compared with the second reference group since the deviations in every single industry are smaller compared with the first distribution. Thus, even if the sum of the single distributions is the same, in the first case the larger deviation in industry 1 outweighs smaller differences in the other industries (see Table 7). This implies that a country with a larger deviation in one single industry will be regarded as more specialized than a country with smaller deviations in more industries. Larger industries per se do not a lead to a bias, as long as all countries have large employment shares in these industries. It is large absolute deviations – which, however, are more likely to occur in larger industries – that are weighted more by this index than e.g. by the Krugman Specialization index. Moreover, large differences in few industries are given more weight than small differences in many industries.

*Table 7: Heterogeneity of Employment Shares*

| | Country A | Reference Group Case 1 | Heterogeneity Case 1 | Reference Group Case 2 | Heterogeneity Case 2 |
|---|---|---|---|---|---|
| $b_1$ | 0.4 | 0.1 | 0.3 | 0.2 | 0.2 |
| $b_2$ | 0.3 | 0.4 | 0.1 | 0.2 | 0.1 |
| $b_3$ | 0.2 | 0.3 | 0.1 | 0.3 | 0.1 |
| $b_4$ | 0.1 | 0.2 | 0.1 | 0.3 | 0.2 |
| $\sum_{i=1}^{I} b_i - \bar{b}_i$ | | | 0.6 | | 0.6 |
| IP | | | 0.12 | | 0.1 |

The *IP* can take values between zero and $(I-1)/I$. Adding industries with very low employment shares does not alter the level of specialization if the employment share is low in all countries. Moreover, the Axiom of Anonymity and the Axiom of Progressive Transfers are fulfilled. It yields problematic results if industries are split or merged, however: Splitting an industry which the country is relatively specialized in sub-industries leads to a decline in specialization also if the country under study is relatively more specialized in all sub-industries than the reference group. This is due to the fact that the employment share deviations are squared and thus adding up all deviations before squaring gives higher values than squaring each deviation individually and then summing up the individual deviations. If the country has lower employment shares in some sub-industries and higher employment shares in other sub-industries than the reference group, then merging these industries leads to a decline of specialization in line with the Axiom of the Classification of Industries. One further deficit of the *IP* is that it is not decomposable.

### 3.4.2.3 Relative Gini Index

The Relative Gini Index (*Rel. GINI*) is a common index in many fields of economics, with many applications also in the context of industry structure and specialization. The first to use this index in the field of specialization measurement was Hoover (1936), who studied industrial localization. In recent years, it has been employed by Conkling (1963), Kim (1995), Amiti (1998 and Amiti 1999), Haaland et al. (1999), Brülhart (2001a), Aiginger and Leitner (2002), Midelfart-Knarvik et al. (2000), Beine and Coulombe (2007), Südekum (2006), Brülhart and Torstensson (2007), and Ezcurra and Pascual (2007) in the empirical analysis of both specialization and concentration.

In order to calculate the Gini Index for a single country, the Balassa Index has to be calculated similar to the Absolute Gini index. The only difference is that the employment shares of every industry in the country under study are set in relation to the employment share in the reference group instead of using the reference level 1/I. The lower bound of the Relative Gini Index is zero, since whenever the economic structure of the country under study completely mirrors the economic structure of the reference group, the Lorenz curve coincides with the 45° line. Its upper bound is $1 - (1 / I^2)$, which converges to 1 for large numbers of industries.

The Relative Gini Index is only decomposable if the range of the values taken by the variable of interest does not overlap across subgroups of individual observations (Cowell 1980 or Dagum 1997), so that the transvariation is zero. This is evidently not to be suspected the case in our context: different countries may well have similar degrees of specialization in a particular industry. A further drawback of the Relative Gini Index is that not all deviations from the economic structure of the reference group are treated equally. This can be illustrated by the following example: Let the economic structure of the reference group be $d_r$: ($b_1 = 0.1$; $b_2 = 0.2$; $b_3 = 0.3$; $b_4 = 0.4$). If country $A$ is characterized by the economic structure $d_A$: ($b_1 = 0.1$; $b_2 = 0.1$; $b_3 = 0.4$; $b_4 = 0.4$), it is considered to be less specialized than if it had the economic structure $d_{A'}$: ($b_1 = 0.15$; $b_2 = 0.2$; $b_3 = 0.3$; $b_4 = 0.3$) or $d_{A'}$: ($b_1 = 0.15$; $b_2 = 0.25$; $b_3 = 0.25$; $b_4 = 0.35$). Thus the more closely the smallest and largest employment shares are distributed, the more specialized a country appears to be, even though $\sum_{i=1}^{I} b_i - \bar{b}_i$ is the same in all three cases. Hence, the Axiom of Progressive Transfers is not satisfied. Adding industries with an employment share of zero both at the country and at the reference group level results in impossibility to calculate the Gini Index, since 0 / 0 is not defined. Adding industries with negligibly small employment shares strongly increases the level of specialization (even more than in case of the Absolute Gini Index), giving rise to misleading conclusions. Moreover, we obtain misleading results when merging industries. Since the area between the Lorenz curve and the 45° line automatically gets smaller, the level of specialization decreases if industries are merged – irrespective of whether if the country is over- or under-specialized in the respective sub-industries.

### 3.4.2.4 Relative Theil Index

It has been implemented for the analyses of specialization and concentration by Maasoumi (1993), Duro Moreno (2001), Brülhart and Träger (2005) and Ezcurra and Pascual (2007).

The Theil Index ($T$) is a variation of the Shannon Entropy Index, which sets all employment shares of a country, $b_i$, in relation to the employment shares of the reference group, $i$:

$$T = \frac{1}{I} \sum_{i=1}^{I} \frac{b_i}{\bar{b}_i} \ln \frac{b_i}{\bar{b}_i}$$

Due to its decomposition qualities, the Theil Index has been used widely in the research of income inequality (Shorrocks 1980 and Shorrocks 1984). This is doubtless the greatest advantage of the Theil Index, since it is the only decomposable relative specialization measure. Yet the Theil Index is not superior to other heterogeneity indices in all aspects: Adding an industry with an employment share of zero would lead to an undefined index. A problem arises for the definition of the upper bound: Perfect relative specialization implies that the country is completely specialized in one industry while $\bar{b}_i = \frac{1}{I}, \forall i$, but in that case, the Theil Index is equal to negative infinity; yet it converges towards $I \ln I$ if we allow for the existence of negligible small industries. If the economic structures of the country and the reference group are identical, then the Theil Index is zero. This, however, is not the lower bound of this index: If the country is under-specialized in more industries than it is over-specialized in relation to the reference group, then the Theil Index turns negative.

The largest difficulty with respect to the Theil Index is that it may yield distorted results, since not all deviations of a country's economic structure from the reference level are weighted equally. This can lead to an erroneous perception of specialization levels and consequently to misleading conclusions. To illustrate the problem, take the following example: Country $A$ has the employment distribution $d_A$: ($b_1 = 0.5$; $b_2 = 0.1$; $b_3 = 0.2$; $b_4 = 0.2$) and the employment distribution of the reference group is $d_R$: ($b_1 = 0.5$; $b_2 = 0.25$; $b_3 = 0.2$; $b_4 = 0.05$). Note that the employment shares in industry 1 and 3 are identical; there are only deviations in industries 2 and 4. The Theil Index gives a value of 1.29 in this case. If the distribution of country $A$ changes to $d'_A$: ($b_1 = 0.1$; $b_2 = 0.3$; $b_3 = 0.4$; $b_4 = 0.2$) and the economic structure of the norm changes such that $d'_R$: ($b_1 = 0.1$; $b_2 = 0.15$; $b_3 = 0.4$; $b_4 = 0.35$), then again industries 1 and 3 are characterized by identical employment shares in country $A$ and in the reference country group. The deviations in industries 2 and 4 are identical as in the other case – each is 0.15. But for the latter distributions the Theil Index is only 0.39. So, even though the deviations from the economic structures are identical, the index values obtained vary. In addition, the Theil Index leads to irrational results if industries are split into sub-industries because specialization rises under all circumstances whereas a merger of industries leads to de-specialization (irrespective whether the country under study is more specialized in all or only some sub-industries).

To summarize, the Index of Inequality in Productive Structure should not be used as a measure of specialization, since it only has disadvantages compared to the closely related Krugman Specialization Index. The Relative Gini Index is widely used in the empirical analysis of specialization patterns, yet both the Krugman Specialization Index and the Theil Index seem superior. Whether the Krugman Specialization Index or the Theil Index is more suitable for analysis depends on the research question and the aims of empirical analysis. If the focus is on differences between interregional and international specialization patterns, then the Theil Index is better suited since this index is the only one that possesses the decomposability property. This could be of special interest if studying the economic development of countries with large interregional differences such as Italy or Spain, where large interregional disparities within the respective countries are found. In cases where the analysis focuses on the development of economic structures over time, in which the appropriate estimation of specialization levels is important, the Krugman Specialization Index must be recommended since it is the only measure that possesses the criterion of the classification of industries.

One problem of the relative Gini and the relative Theil index is that large deviations in small industries drive the results more than for other indices. This is why developments in small industries (if deviations from the reference country are large) can lead the Gini and the Theil index to change significantly whereas these developments to not alter other indices much.

*Table 8: Criteria of Relative Specialization Measures*

|  | Anonymity | Progressive Transfers | Decompos-ability | Splitting/ Merging | Industries with $b_i = 0$ | Bounds |
|---|---|---|---|---|---|---|
| *K* | ✓ | ✓ | x | ✓ | ✓ | ✓ |
| *IP* | ✓ | ✓ | x | x | ✓ | ✓ |
| *Rel. GINI* | ✓ | x | x | x | x | ✓ |
| *Rel. Theil* | ✓ | ✓ | ✓ | x | x | x |

# 3.5 Sensitivity Analysis: Specialization of European Countries

## 3.5.1 Data and Variables

In the following section we present a specialization ranking of 24 European countries in the year 2005 in order to illustrate that the indices described above produce quite different results, according to their characteristics. We use employment data from the KLEMS data base (see Timmer et al. 2007), which provides data collected from the national accounts of the EU countries. We include 51 industries, covering the agricultural, manufacturing and service sectors. The variable we use is annual employment in full-time equivalents, a common measure for industry structure. Similarly, we could focus on e.g. value added - a variable which is less prone to productivity biases, but might be susceptible to measurement errors and exchange rate biases. But as our focus is the measurement methods rather than the specialization itself, the choice of variables is of minor importance. However, it should be born in mind that also this choice will influence the results.

Due to the different domains of definition of the indices, the index values cannot be compared directly, but only the rankings obtained by calculating the indices for all countries. In Table 9 and Table 10 we present the rankings of the absolute and relative specialization measures, respectively, with the least specialized countries on the top. For the comparison we apply Spearman correlation coefficients in order to learn about (dis-)similarities of the indices.

*Table 9: Country Rankings for Absolute Specialization Indices in 2004*

| Rank | Absolute Specialization | | | | | | Absolute Gini Index |
|---|---|---|---|---|---|---|---|
| | Hirschman-Herfindahl Index[*] | | Shannon Entropy Index | | Diversification Index | | |
| 1 | CZ | .044 | EST | 2.583 | CZ | -.065 | CZ .471 |
| 2 | EST | .045 | CZ | 2.559 | SVN | -.023 | EST .500 |
| 3 | IT | .046 | SVN | 2.534 | SVK | -.016 | IT .500 |
| 4 | MLT | .047 | MLT | 2.527 | DE | -.006 | DE .502 |
| 5 | SVK | .047 | SVK | 2.526 | IT | .006 | HUN .513 |
| 6 | SVN | .048 | HUN | 2.487 | EST | .010 | SWE .524 |
| 7 | DE | .049 | IT | 2.485 | HUN | .013 | FIN .538 |
| 8 | HUN | .049 | SWE | 2.462 | MLT | .017 | AUT .540 |
| 9 | AUT | .051 | DE | 2.459 | SWE | .059 | IRL .545 |
| 10 | FIN | .055 | LVA | 2.453 | AUT | .068 | ESP .548 |
| 11 | LVA | .055 | FIN | 2.420 | FIN | .076 | LVA .548 |
| 12 | FRA | .057 | IRL | 2.411 | IRL | .096 | FRA .550 |
| 13 | IRL | .057 | CYP | 2.390 | FRA | .105 | DK .553 |
| 14 | SWE | .057 | LTU | 2.378 | UK | .119 | NLD .555 |
| 15 | UK | .058 | PRT | 2.372 | ESP | .124 | UK .555 |
| 16 | ESP | .058 | BEL | 2.368 | NLD | .129 | BEL .559 |
| 17 | GRC | .060 | DK | 2.361 | DK | .130 | SVN .569 |
| 18 | CYP | .061 | UK | 2.356 | BEL | .136 | SVK .571 |
| 19 | NLD | .061 | AUT | 2.356 | LVA | .139 | PRT .581 |
| 20 | DK | .062 | POL | 2.354 | POL | .153 | GRC .584 |
| 21 | PRT | .062 | ESP | 2.352 | GRC | .176 | MLT .585 |
| 22 | BEL | .062 | GRC | 2.344 | PRT | .194 | LTU .593 |
| 23 | LTU | .064 | NLD | 2.337 | LTU | .218 | CYP .594 |
| 24 | POL | .081 | FRA | 2.330 | CYP | .232 | POL .640 |

[*] The ranking is identical for the *HHI* and the Ogive Index but with different index values. We therefore do not list the Ogive Index separately. Source: EU KLEMS database, March 2008.

*Table 10: Country Rankings for Relative Specialization Indices in 2004*

| Rank | Krugman Specialization Index | | Index of Inequality in Productive Structure | | Theil Index | | Relative Gini Index | |
|------|------|------|------|------|------|------|------|------|
| 1 | AUT | .148 | AUT | .001 | ESP | -.049 | CZ | .169 |
| 2 | FRA | .170 | FRA | .002 | FRA | -.007 | DE | .181 |
| 3 | DE | .212 | DE | .003 | AUT | -.002 | HUN | .207 |
| 4 | UK | .256 | CZ | .004 | BEL | .027 | SVK | .212 |
| 5 | ESP | .257 | IT | .004 | UK | .044 | IT | .224 |
| 6 | NLD | .260 | UK | .005 | NLD | .103 | SVN | .242 |
| 7 | IT | .262 | NLD | .005 | DE | .104 | FRA | .246 |
| 8 | FIN | .299 | HUN | .005 | POL | .207 | AUT | .271 |
| 9 | CZ | .299 | SVK | .005 | PRT | .236 | SWE | .278 |
| 10 | HUN | .301 | FIN | .005 | IT | .238 | NLD | .281 |
| 11 | DK | .316 | MLT | .006 | DK | .259 | ESP | .282 |
| 12 | IRL | .324 | ESP | .006 | LVA | .276 | UK | .283 |
| 13 | SVK | .329 | IRL | .006 | SVN | .288 | MLT | .290 |
| 14 | SVN | .343 | SVN | .007 | HUN | .299 | IRL | .305 |
| 15 | BEL | .345 | GRC | .008 | FIN | .300 | FIN | .306 |
| 16 | GRC | .345 | BEL | .008 | SWE | .305 | BEL | .320 |
| 17 | SWE | .376 | DK | .009 | GRC | .310 | EST | .325 |
| 18 | MLT | .389 | SWE | .010 | CZ | .315 | POL | .333 |
| 19 | PRT | .438 | PRT | .011 | SVK | .354 | DK | .344 |
| 20 | LVA | .465 | LVA | .011 | LTU | .418 | GRC | .356 |
| 21 | EST | .469 | EST | .012 | IRL | .525 | LVA | .426 |
| 22 | POL | .473 | LTU | .018 | EST | .729 | PRT | .441 |
| 23 | LTU | .516 | CYP | .018 | MLT | .729 | LTU | .468 |
| 24 | CYP | .553 | POL | .034 | CYP | .794 | CYP | .514 |

Source: EU KLEMS database, March 2008

In a next step we present the specialization patterns of ten to fourteen European countries for 35 to 51 industries between 1970 and 2005 using the indices described above. In order to investigate whether the results depend on the choice of indices as well as on the aggregation of data, we apply the seven indices to different samples of countries and industries. We use employment data from the

KLEMS data base (see Timmer et al. 2007), which provides data collected from the national accounts of the EU countries. The industries cover the agricultural, the manufacturing and the service sector. The variable we use is annual employment in total hours worked, which is a common measure for industry structure in the literature. Similarly, we could focus on value added - a variable which is less prone to productivity biases, but might be susceptible to measurement errors in service industries, the fact that the value added of multinational firms is assigned to headquarters, which in the case of Ireland has a strong bias on the results (Barry 2001). As our focus is the measurement methods rather than the specialization itself, the choice of variables is of minor importance.

We proceed as follows: The absolute and relative specialization patterns are calculated for every year for the whole range of available data. Then, the correlation of the indices over the investigation period is calculated for every single country separately in order to then compute the average correlation for the whole country sample between two indices in a last step. Indices were calculated using a range of 35, 46 49 and 51 industries. The reasons are the following: For all fourteen countries in the sample, data was available for 35 industries only. For ten countries (excluding Germany, Italy, the Netherlands and Portugal) the data were available for up to 51 industries. In order to study the impact of large and small industries on the results, indices were constructed for 46 and 49 industries, respectively, as well. According to economic theory, the more detailed data available, the higher the reported degree of specialization should be. This holds true in Amiti (1998) who studied specialization patterns using 27 and 65 industries respectively.

With regard to absolute specialization, Aiginger and Davies (2004) used the Absolute Theil Index to study 99 industries and 14 countries over the period 1985 to 1999. Except for the years 1990 and 1991 specialization was reported to increase. In contrast, Sapir (1996) found constant levels for most countries between 1977 and 1992 and increase for France only using the Herfindahl Index. With regard to relative specialization, Amiti (1998 and Amiti 1999) found a steady increase of specialization for several countries during the 1970s with Relative Gini Indices, whereas Midelfart-Knarvik et al. (2002) using Krugman Indices report a decrease in specialization over this period. Since the studies use one measure of specialization only and use different data base, it is the aim of this paper to show to which degree the choice of indices has an impact on results. At first sight it thus seems to make no difference which index is applied and which level of disaggregation is chosen since the results are robust. This is no longer true, however, if we compare the results for indices computed with 35 industries with the results obtained with 51 industries as shown in Table 11:

*Table 11: Correlation between Absolute Measures with different industry levels I*

|  | $HHI^{51}$ | $T^{51}$ | $G^{51}$ |
|---|---|---|---|
| $HHI^{35}$ | .116 | .081 | .049 |
| $T^{35}$ | .245 | .210 | .178 |
| $G^{35}$ | .377 | .342 | .309 |

Source: EU KLEMS database, March 2009.

It is remarkable that correlation levels vary widely across countries. Whereas for Austria and France low and even some negative correlations exist, all correlations turned out to be negative for Finland, Greece, Ireland and Sweden whereas the correlation for Belgium, Denmark and the UK remained around .900 and even above. The level of disaggregation thus seems to have diverse effects on indices depending on the individual characteristics of countries and industries. In the following, we try to capture reasons for the diverging results. In order to evaluate the differences as well as the (dis-)advantages of the indices under investigation, we can check to which degree fulfil some criteria as proposed by Combes and Overman (2004).

*Table 12 Country Ranking for Absolute Specialization in 2005*

| Country | HHI 51 | Theil=-SEI 51 | GINI 51 | HHI 35 | Theil 35 | GINI 35 |
|---|---|---|---|---|---|---|
| AUT | 10 (.054) | 10 (.412) | 9 (.495) | 8 (.071) | 8 (.611) | 8 (.591) |
| BEL | 12 (.050) | 11 (.379) | 11 (.470) | 5 (.080) | 5 (.663) | 5 (.610) |
| DK | 5 (.058) | 4 (.465) | 4 (.526) | 1 (.088) | 2 (.721) | 3 (.629) |
| FIN | 8 (.056) | 7 (.429) | 7 (.503) | 14 (.058) | 14 (.453) | 14 (.517) |
| FRA | 11 (.053) | 12 (.370) | 12 (.470) | 7 (.077) | 7 (.621) | 7 (.593) |
| GER | 14 (.047) | 14 (.314) | 13 (.436) | 12 (.066) | 12 (.533) | 12 (.557) |
| GRC | 2 (.067) | 2 (.564) | 2 (.570) | 6 (.079) | 3 (.704) | 2 (.632) |
| IRL | 3 (.064) | 3 (.497) | 3 (.534) | 10 (.069) | 10 (.587) | 10 (.582) |
| ITA | 7 (.057) | 9 (.416) | 10 (.488) | 13 (.061) | 13 (.508) | 13 (.548) |

| Country | HHI 51 | Theil=-SEI 51 | GINI 51 | HHI 35 | Theil 35 | GINI 35 |
|---------|--------|---------------|---------|--------|----------|---------|
| NL | 9 (.056) | 6 (.436) | 6 (.510) | 2 (.087) | 1 (.726) | 1 (.633) |
| PRT | 1 (.068) | 1 (.572) | 1 (.573) | 9 (.070) | 9 (.606) | 6 (.593) |
| ESP | 4 (.061) | 5 (.465) | 5 (.517) | 11 (.068) | 11 (.565) | 11 (.572) |
| SWE | 6 (.057) | 8 (.426) | 8 (.496) | 3 (.081) | 6 (.530) | 9 (.588) |
| UK | 13 (.048) | 13 (.323) | 14 (.431) | 4 (.081) | 4 (.583) | 4 (.612) |

Source: EU KLEMS database, March 2009.

## 3.5.2 Specialization Indices

Within the group of absolute specialization measures we did not identify notable differences in the results for our sample. When calculating correlations for results based on 51 industries, the values decrease slightly but remain high between .871 and .970.

*Table 13: Correlation between Absolute Measures with same industry level*

|  | $HHI^{35}$ | $T^{35}$ | $G^{35}$ |  | $HHI^{51}$ | $T^{51}$ | $G^{51}$ |
|--------------|-------|-------|-------|--------------|------|------|---|
| $HHI^{35}$ | 1.000 |       |       | $HHI^{51}$ | 1    |      |   |
| $T^{35}$ | .975 | 1.000 |       | $T^{51}$ | .956 | 1 |   |
| $G^{35}$ | .966 | .993 | 1.000 | $G^{51}$ | .871 | .970 | 1 |

Source: EU KLEMS database, March 2009.

It thus seems to make no difference, which index to apply and which level of disaggregation we use as results are robust. This is no longer true, however, if we compare the results of 35 and 51 industries with one another as shown in Table 14.

*Table 14: Correlation between Absolute Measures with different industry levels I*

|            | $HHI^{51}$ | $T^{51}$ | $G^{51}$ |
|------------|------------|----------|----------|
| $HHI^{35}$ | .116       | .081     | .049     |
| $T^{35}$   | .245       | .210     | .178     |
| $G^{35}$   | .377       | .342     | .309     |

Source: EU KLEMS database, March 2009.

It is remarkable that correlation levels vary widely across countries. Whereas for Austria and France low and even some negative correlations exist, all correlations turned out to be negative for Finland, Greece, Ireland and Sweden whereas the correlation for Belgium, Denmark and the UK remained around .900 and even above. The level of disaggregation thus seems to have diverse effects on indices depending on the individual characteristics of countries and industries. In the following, we try to capture reasons for the diverging results. In order to evaluate the differences as well as the (dis-)advantages of the indices under investigation, we can check to which degree fulfil some criteria as proposed by Combes and Overman (2004).

With regard to the number of industries, we have to distinguish two cases: If the number of industries increases, is this due to a higher level of disaggregation or due to the inclusion of more industries in the sample or both. Switching from 35 to 51 industries, there are both new industries (agriculture, mining, electricity and construction) added and also the number of manufacturing and service industries is more disaggregated – this is especially true for the transport industries. With regard to the inclusion of new industries, the impact on the level of specialization is likely to depend on the size of the new industry. The biggest change in this respect is the inclusion of agriculture and mining; the impact of this industry varies widely across countries, however (see Table 15) and thus the impact on the indices should also be quite different. Moreover, agriculture loses in importance over the course of time; therefore the indices should become more homogenous for the end of the investigation period compared to 1970. Both hypotheses are also supported by the figures in the Appendix.

*Table 15: Employment Shares in Agriculture*

| Country | Employment share agriculture 1970 | Employment share agriculture 2005 |
|---------|-----------------------------------|-----------------------------------|
| Austria | .182 | .063 |
| Belgium | .044 | .018 |
| Denmark | .100 | .033 |
| Finland | .269 | .071 |
| France | .192 | .054 |
| Greece | .378 | .117 |
| Ireland | .276 | .067 |
| Spain | .271 | .059 |
| Sweden | .095 | .032 |
| UK | .039 | .019 |

Source: EU KLEMS database, March 2009.

In order to extract the impact of the agriculture sector on the specialization indices, we again calculated the indices including 49 manufacturing and service industries only. The results are as follows:

*Table 16: Correlation between Absolute Measures with different industry levels II*

|          | $HHI^{35}$ | $T^{35}$ | $G^{35}$ |
|----------|------------|----------|----------|
| $HHI^{49}$ | .884 | .896 | .885 |
| $T^{49}$   | .921 | .944 | .936 |
| $G^{49}$   | .929 | .954 | .950 |

Source: EU KLEMS database, March 2009.

Comparing Table 16 with Table 17, it becomes evident that the HHI reacts stronger to the inclusion of a large industry than any other index. Therefore, the smaller the agricultural sector gets, the more similar results get to the specialization levels of the Gini and the Theil indices. The introduction of an industry with a very small employment share must not have no or only negligible impact on the level of absolute specialization of a country (Hannah and Kay 1977). For this reason, we checked for the impact of the transport industries. For 49 industries, the transport industries contain four industries – as a robustness check, we aggregated them to one larger industry and calculated specialization indices for 46 industries as a comparison. The results are as follows:

Table 17: Impact of Small Industries

|  | $HHI^{49}$ | $T^{49}$ | $G^{49}$ |
|---|---|---|---|
| $HHI^{46}$ | .999 | .986 | .971 |
| $T^{46}$ | .979 | .999 | .995 |
| $G^{46}$ | .944 | .953 | .950 |

Source: EU KLEMS database, March 2009.

### 3.5.3 Relative Specialization

Regarding the group of relative specialization measures, the most similar results are given by the Krugman Index and the Index of Inequality in Productive Structure (see Table 18). This is not unexpected as these two indices are similarly constructed. Differences stem from the fact that the *IP* puts more weight on large deviations than on smaller ones whereas the Krugman Index puts the same weight on all deviations, no matter how large they are.

Table 18: Correlation between Relative Measures

|  | K | IP | T | Rel. G |
|---|---|---|---|---|
| K | 1.000 | | | |
| IP | .726 | 1.000 | | |
| T | .153 | -.032 | 1.000 | |
| Rel. G | .234 | .039 | -.500 | 1.000 |

A favorable property of the Krugman Specialization Index is that splitting one industry into sub-industries will not alter the degree of specialization if the country is relatively more or less specialized than the reference group in *all* sub-industries. On the other hand, if the country under study is relatively more specialized in some sub-industries, while being relatively less specialized in some other sub-industries compared to the reference group, then merging industries would decrease the level of specialization since patterns of over- and under-specialization cancel each other out. Adding industries with very low employment shares does not alter the level of specialization. A shortcoming of the

Krugman Index is its insensitivity against shifts within under or overspecialized industries as pointed out by Krieger-Boden and Traistaru-Siedschlag (2008).

The relative Theil Index puts more weight on highly under-proportional industries than any other index. Therefore changes in small industries can have tremendous impact on the overall index. The relative Theil Index is thus higher for those countries that are characterized by few but large deviations from the reference economic structure than for countries with many but smaller deviations (corr = .850). The results of the relative Theil Index are, however, not highly correlated with the sum of the absolute deviations from a country's economic structure from the reference level. This becomes clear by the following examples: Country $A$ has the employment distribution $d_A$: ($b_1 = 0.5$; $b_2 = 0.1$; $b_3 = 0.2$; $b_4 = 0.2$) and the employment distribution of the reference group is $d_R$: ($b_1 = 0.5$; $b_2 = 0.25$; $b_3 = 0.2$; $b_4 = 0.05$). Note that the employment shares in industry 1 and 3 are identical; there are only deviations in industries 2 and 4. The Theil Index gives a value of 1.29 in this case. If the distribution of country $A$ changes to $d'_A$: ($b_1 = 0.1$; $b_2 = 0.3$; $b_3 = 0.4$; $b_4 = 0.2$) and the economic structure of the norm changes such that $d'_R$: ($b_1 = 0.1$; $b_2 = 0.15$; $b_3 = 0.4$; $b_4 = 0.35$), then again industries 1 and 3 are characterized by identical employment shares in country $A$ and in the reference country group. The deviations in industries 2 and 4 are identical as in the other case – each is 0.15. But for the latter distributions the Theil Index is only 0.39. So, even though the deviations from the economic structures are identical, the index values obtained vary. In addition, the Theil Index leads to unreasonable results if industries are split into sub-industries because specialization rises under all circumstances whereas a merger of industries leads to de-specialization (irrespective whether the country under study is more specialized in all or only some sub-industries).

The Theil Index and the *IP* are negatively correlated due to the fact that the Theil Index gives much weight on large deviations in little industries whereas the *IP* almost neglects such heterogeneity. As has already been pointed out in a previous section, a problem with using the Gini Index is that it puts more relative value on changes in the middle parts of the industry distribution. Therefore, a transfer from a big to a small industry has a much greater effect on the level of specialization, if the industries are close to the middle rather than at either end of the distribution (see Cowell 1995 and Amiti 1999). This means that movements between industries that are the closest to the European average will get the largest weights in the country Gini coefficient. As these industries may vary from year to year, the weighting of industries could also vary significantly over time. Midelfart-Knarvik et al. (2003) report another shortcoming of the Relative Gini Index: Comparisons across industries or time can be problematic since the Lorenz curves cross for more than fifty percent of the changes over time in their empirical study. This flip happens whenever employment shares in an industry decline both in countries where this industry is over- and underrepresented. In order to clarify differences between the indices characterized above, we give the following examples:

The first example deals with the relevance of small industries (country A vs. Country B) as well as the relevance of industry classification (country C vs. Country D):

*Table 19: Number of industries and industry size influences results*

|  | Reference country with $b_i = 1/I$ | | | |
|---|---|---|---|---|
|  | country A | country B | country C | country D |
| industry 1 | 0.10 | 0.09 | 0.10 | 0.05 |
| industry 2 | 0.25 | 0.25 | ---- | 0.05 |
| industry 3 | 0.25 | 0.25 | 0.90 | 0.45 |
| industry 4 | 0.40 | 0.40 | ---- | 0.45 |
| industry 5 | ----- | 0.01 | ---- | ---- |
| **HHI** | **0.30** | **0.29** | **0.82** | **0.41** |
| **Theil** | **0.10** | **0.29** | **0.37** | **0.37** |
| **Gini** | **0.23** | **0.38** | **0.04** | **0.04** |
| **K** | **0.30** | **0.60** | **0.80** | **0.80** |
| **IP** | **0.05** | **0.09** | **0.32** | **0.16** |

With respect to the *HHI*, adding a small industry does not alter the results substantially whereas both the Gini and the Theil Index are characterized by significant changes in their results. This is due to the fact that the reference point alters for the latter whereas it is kept constant for the *HHI*. Regarding the Theil Index one has to mention that small industries can increase the specialization level much, in the example even by almost three times. It is thus questionable whether building on the Theil Index only gives a good and adequate inside into the structure of a country's economy under these circumstances. In the example the results for the *IP* and the Krugman Index vary widely too, i.e. specialization doubles due to the introduction of a small new industry. Turning to the impact of industry classification on the results it is remarkable that only the HHI and the *IP* react whereas the values of the other indices remain the same. These two problems are most severe if the sample under study is characterized by a small number of industries which size varies widely. With regard to the Krugman Index and the *IP* it has to be noted that the results remain unchanged if the new industry is small in both the reference country as well as in the country under study, whereas the relative Gini and the relative Theil Index react to these changes.

Regarding relative specialization indices, there are more problems to be aware about. The largest problem arises from the fact that the differences in employment shares between the country under study and the reference country are weighted quite differently as example 2 shows:

The starting point is that economies consist of four industries. The reference country is characterized by lower employment shares than country E in industries 1, 2 and 3. Country E* has a higher employment share than the reference country in industries 2 and 3 but a lower employment share in industries 1 and 4. Comparing the results obtained by the various indices, it shows that the Krugman Specialization Index is the same for both countries, whereas the *IP* and the Relative Gini Index are smaller for country E* than for country E, whereas the Theil Index reports a higher level of specialization for country E* than for country E.

Inconsistent results are also produced when the distribution of employment shares changes such that the distance between the country under study and the reference country rises (as it is the case for country F compared to country E or E*) or declines (as it is the case for country G compared to country E or E*). A rise in the distance between the countries should lead to a higher level of specialization, which in our example is not the case for the Gini Index. A decline in the distance between the countries should lead to a lower level of specialization, which in our example is not the case for the Theil Index. The problematic results of the Gini and the Theil Index respectively, stem from the fact that the level of specialization is very much driven by the distribution of employment shares and that industries with highly under- or over proportional employment shares receive more weight – even if these industries are very small.

*Table 20: The distribution of employment drives results*

|  | Reference country | country E | country E* | country F | country G |
|---|---|---|---|---|---|
| industry 1 | 0.200 | 0.350 | 0.300 | 0.300 | 0.200 |
| industry 2 | 0.100 | 0.150 | 0.200 | 0.300 | 0.300 |
| industry 3 | 0.300 | 0.350 | 0.350 | 0.200 | 0.200 |
| industry 4 | 0.400 | 0.150 | 0.150 | 0.200 | 0.300 |
| **K** | | **0.500** | **0.500** | **0.600** | **0.400** |
| **IP** | | **0.090** | **0.085** | **0.100** | **0.060** |
| **Theil** | | **0.350** | **0.452** | **0.822** | **0.702** |
| **Gini** | | **0.401** | **0.370** | **0.292** | **0.323** |

In the last example we analyze the importance of the reference country with respect to the results obtained:

*Table 21: The reference country drives results*

|  | Reference country | country E | Reference country | country G |
|---|---|---|---|---|
| industry 1 | 0.100 | 0.100 | 0.100 | 0.100 |
| industry 2 | 0.200 | 0.100 | 0.100 | 0.200 |
| industry 3 | 0.300 | 0.400 | 0.400 | 0.300 |
| industry 4 | 0.400 | 0.400 | 0.400 | 0.400 |
| **K** | | **0.200** | | **0.200** |
| **IP** | | **0.020** | | **0.020** |
| **Theil** | | **0.293** | | **0.090** |
| **Gini** | | **0.263** | | **0.425** |

For the specialization values of both the Krugman Index and the *IP* it is not relevant which country the reference country is since the basis for the indices are the deviations of employment shares. For the Gini and the Theil Index it matters which country is the reference country since employment shares are divided by the reference values.

# 3.6 Conclusion

To summarize, we find that results differ widely according to which measure is used. As expected, results from measures of absolute specialization cannot be compared to indices of relative specialization, since they follow two distinct concepts of specialization. But even within both groups the indices differ from each other due to different construction and weighting schemes. As a result, the rankings do not consistently match. While the Krugman Specialization Index and the Index of Inequality in Productive Structure, which are constructed similarly, are concordant in a large number of cases, all other comparisons show only occasional congruence. Hence, the pictures these rankings draw are somewhat arbitrary.

A general problem of specialization indices is that they are only able to give a very aggregate picture and thus convey only a limited understanding of the development of the economic structure of a country, since they give no information about the underlying developments, i.e. in which industries countries are specializing. None of the presented aggregate indices is able to indicate which industries drive specialization patterns in a country. Moreover, all indices presented above focus on the distribution of employment across industries only and do not to account for inter-industry linkages. Due to the quite limited availability of consistent input-output data over a long time horizon, the application of more sophisticated measures of specialization is hard to accomplish in empirical studies.

To summarize, the Index of Inequality in Productive Structure should not be used as a measure of specialization, since it has disadvantages compared to the closely related Krugman Specialization Index. The Relative Gini Index is widely used in the empirical analysis of specialization patterns, yet both the Krugman Specialization Index and the Theil Index seem superior. Whether the Krugman Specialization Index or the Theil Index is more suitable depends on the research question and the aims of empirical analysis. If the focus is on differences between interregional and international specialization patterns, then the Theil Index is more appropriate since this index is the only one that possesses the decomposability property. This could be of special interest if studying the economic development of countries with large interregional differences such as Italy or Spain. In cases where the analysis focuses on the development of economic structures over time, in which the appropriate estimation of specialization levels is important, the Krugman Specialization Index must be recommended since it is the only measure that satisfies the criterion of the classification of industries.

A general problem of specialization indices is that they are only able to give a very aggregate picture and thus convey only a limited understanding of the development of the economic structure of a country, since they give no information about the underlying developments, i.e. in which industries countries are specializing. None of the presented aggregate indices is able to indicate which industries drive specialization patterns in a country.

Moreover, all indices presented above focus on the distribution of employment across industries only and do not to account for inter-industry linkages. Due to the quite limited availability of consistent input-output data over a long time horizon, the application of more sophisticated measures of specialization is hard to accomplish in empirical studies. The decomposition property is of great importance for studies at the inter-regional level in order to account for differences in the competitiveness of regions within and across countries. This property implies that an index should allow the overall amount of specialization to be split into a weighted average of the specialization resulting from within and between subgroups (Bourguignon 1979 and Cowell and Jenkins 1995). At the country level, an index should be decomposable into inter-sectoral and inter-industry heterogeneity as well as within and between clubs of countries. This criterion is equivalent to the first criterion in Combes and Overman (2004) since they want indices to be comparable across activities. It has to be noted that with regard to absolute specialization, only the Gini index fails to fulfil this criterion whereas with regard to relative specialization indices, the Theil index is the only decomposable index available.

# 4 The Location of Industries in Western Europe[16]

## 4.1 Introduction

At the beginning of our observation period in 1970, the European Economic Community (EEC) only comprised the six founding members, i.e. Belgium, France, Germany, Italy, Luxembourg and the Netherlands. These countries created a customs union that already comprised a large number of industries and also set up common agricultural and trade policies (Molle 2006).[17] Although intra-European quotas and tariffs were abolished, many non-tariff barriers remained to exist due to differences in national regulations (e.g. with regard to product standards, licensing procedures, indirect taxation) hindering the creation of trade and specialization. Moreover, at that time the mobility of labour was restricted since different school and university degrees were not easily recognized in all other member states. In the first half of the 1980s the European Commission aimed to complete the integration of product (for both goods and services) and factor (both capital and labour) markets, thereby setting an end to the fragmentation of Western European economies; the object was to complete the internal market by 1992, as laid out in the Single European Act of 1986. As stated in Article 159 EC, the objectives are the following: higher competiveness by speeding up structural change and altering the specialization profile of countries towards high-wage and high-growth industries and facilitating the exploitation of both economies of scale and scope (also by fostering co-operations among firms). With regard to the free movement of goods and capital, full market integration has been realized, whereas the free movement of services and workers has not yet been realized even though a free internal labour market has been achieved by the harmonization of social security, residence permits, diploma recognition, work conditions, health and safety conditions (Commission of European Communities 1997). Thus the level of both permanent and temporary migration has remained at three percent of the European labour force since the

---

16  This chapter is mainly an extension of joint work with Claudia Schmiedeberg and the paper "Structural Convergence of European Countries", published in Structural Change and Economic Dynamics, 2010, vol. 21, 85-100.

17  At the same time the European Free Trade Association (EFTA) was established as an alternative to the EEC and included some later EEC member countries such as Denmark, United Kingdom (both left the EFTA to join the EEC in 1973), Portugal (which became a member of the EEC in 1986) as well as Austria, Finland and Sweden (which are members of the EEC since 1995).

1970s and remained behind expectations (Molle 2006). This low level of mobility[18] implies that workers have not yet taken full advantage of the benefits of free movement – i.e. better opportunities to capitalize special qualifications via higher wages – nor have employers been able to optimize the factor input mix since nationally segmented labour markets still support a mis-match between the skills required by expanding industries and the skills obtained by employees in declining industries. Thus structural change is slower than expected and the degree to which specialization patterns of countries have changed has remained low. The adoption of a common currency in 1999 as well as the enlargement of the European Union into Central and Eastern Countries in 2004 has led to a further removal of institutional and non-tariff barriers within Europe and unified former segmented national markets (for a more comprehensive historical overview, see Watts 2008). The wage differentials between Western and Eastern European countries have put many labour-intensive industries under pressure. In some industries shifts of production sites were remarkable.

## 4.2 The Index of Structural Heterogeneity

In order to detect structural convergence (or divergence, respectively) we implement the classical approaches of σ- and β-convergence that were initially introduced by Barro and Sala-i-Martin (1992 and 1995) in the context of income convergence. In this context, we speak of σ- convergence whenever the dispersion of income per capita across country groups diminishes. If economies with lower income per capita grow faster than more advanced economies, then there is a negative correlation between income growth and the initial level of income. This concept is referred to as β-convergence. As Barro and Sala-i-Martin (1992)

---

18  In the early 1970s, only three percent of the labour force within Europe migrated to one of the neighbor Western European countries. On the one hand, this is due to the non-coordinated labour policy (recognition of diplomas), but on the other hand is caused by the economic downturn in the aftermath of the oil crisis. As a consequence governments applied more restrictive measures to prevent increasing pressure of migrants from non-European countries on home labour markets and even fostered programs aimed at return migration to home countries (Böhning 1979 or Hammar 1985). Back then, it was above all Irish citizens migrating to the UK and Italians moving to Germany and other more favorable countries. Intra-EU migration as a share of the total work force even fell between three and two percent from the 1980s onwards. This could be due to the fact that the push- and pull-factors lost importance for this country group, i.e. differences in wages, job opportunities, education systems, capital accumulation. The share of extra-EU 15 migrants remained constant over time and even rose slightly in the aftermath of the single market program can be traced to the increasing activities of multinational firms in foreign countries (Molle 2001).

showed, β-convergence is a necessary but no sufficient condition for σ- convergence and therefore it is fruitful to investigate both concepts in our context of the development of economic structures. We are aware of the limitations of this kind of analysis and the potential threat of misspecification problems (Quah 1993 and Bernard and Durlauf 1995) and therefore adopt a time-series approach. Thereby we can study the structural gap between countries over time and analyze whether disparities are persistent over time. As opposed to mere cross-sectional studies, time-series tests for convergence in general tend to not reject the no-convergence hypothesis for all countries.

For empirical tests of structural convergence, a measure of heterogeneity is required, since increasing (decreasing) heterogeneity is interpreted as divergence (convergence). A number of indices developed for this purpose can be found in the literature (see Chapter 2). Since we want to investigate relative concentration patterns in Western European Countries, we implement an index of structural heterogeneity, the *SHE*, which is constructed analogously to the Krugman Specialization Index (Krugman 1991a)[19], but is specified in two types to capture inter-sectoral heterogeneity ($sSHE^N$) and inter-industry heterogeneity ($iSHE^N$) separately.[20]

With regard to inter-sectoral heterogeneity (i.e. the $S=3$ aggregate sectors agriculture, manufacturing, and services) we use the $sSHE^N$ index calculated as the sum of the $N$ countries' absolute deviations from the average employment share of each sector $s$ of total employment (marked with the subscript $E$). Moreover, we decided to employ the Krugman Specialization Index:

$$sSHE^N = \frac{1}{N}\frac{1}{S}\sum_{n=1}^{N}\sum_{s=1}^{S}\left|b_{s,E}^n - \bar{b}_{s,E}\right|$$

The employment share $b_{s,E}^n$ of sector $s$ in country $n$ is calculated by dividing employment $l$ in sector $s$ by total employment in country $n$, i.e. $b_{s,E}^n = l_s^n \Big/ \sum_{s=1}^{S} l_s^n$ ;

---

19   For more detailed information on the Krugman Specialization Index and its characteristics, see section 3.4.2.1.

20   With this index we do not overcome the fundamental shortcomings of aggregate national-level indices which do not account for localization, i.e. the role of firm clustering and concentration effects on country specialization. In addition, these indices do not enable us to see which countries (de-)specialize in which industries. For these aspects, a more detailed analysis based on regional or firm-level data would be required (see Duranton and Overman, 2005), which is beyond the scope of this chapter. However, in contrast to the existing indices the SHEN permits the decomposition into inter-sectoral and inter-industry parts, conforming to the emphasis of the present analysis. We use absolute deviation instead of variance in the calculation of the index in order to maintain the intuitive interpretation of the index as the employment share which would have to be relocated to achieve the European average.

similarly, the average employment share is the ratio of employment in sector $s$ in all $N$ countries and total employment in the $N$ countries: $\bar{b}_{s,E} = \sum_{n=1}^{N} l_s^n \Big/ \sum_{n=1}^{N} \sum_{s=1}^{S} l_s^n$. The $sSHE^N$ is used only for the calculation of inter-sectoral heterogeneity shown in Figure 1.

For the analysis of inter-industry convergence/divergence, we focus on only one of these sectors $s$, consisting of $I_s$ industries (i.e. 19 industries in the case of manufacturing and 10 in the case of the service sector), measuring individual manufacturing industries' shares of total manufacturing. We thus implement the $iSHE^N$, which is similar to the $sSHE^N$, but focuses on a different aggregation level: The employment shares $b$ are calculated relative to the total employment of the aggregate sector (marked by the subscript $s$).

$$iSHE^N = \frac{1}{N} \frac{1}{I_s} \sum_{n=1}^{N} \sum_{i=1}^{I_s} \left| b_{i,s}^n - \bar{b}_{i,s} \right|$$

The $SHE^N$ can be interpreted as the share of employment throughout Europe (in total or only in the analyzed sector) which would have to be rearranged between countries to achieve perfect homogeneity. Both types of the $SHE^N$ have their lower boundary at 0, which would indicate perfect homogeneity, i.e. all $N$ countries having the same industry structure and thus implying that $b_{s,E}^n - \bar{b}_{s,E} = 0 \forall s$ .

Perfect heterogeneity on the other hand means that each country is specialized in exactly one industry and does not have any employment shares $> 0$ in all other industries. Obviously, perfect heterogeneity cannot be the case if the number of industries ($I$) exceeds the number of countries ($N$) because then some countries would have to be specialized in more than one industry. Hence we discuss the following three relevant cases:

*Case 1: N=I*

In this case it is possible to observe both complete specialization and complete concentration and the EU average employment share of each industry $\bar{b}$ can be written as $1/N$. From this we can calculate for each industry the (absolute) deviation from the average, regarding the specialized country as $1 - \frac{1}{N} = \frac{N-1}{N}$ and regarding all other countries as $(N-1)\frac{1}{N}$. So, for each industry the sum of deviations can be written as $2\frac{N-1}{N}$. Summing up over all industries gives us the upper bound of the $SHE$, i.e. $\frac{1}{N} \frac{1}{I} I \left( 2\frac{N-1}{N} \right) = 2\frac{N-1}{N^2} = 2\frac{I-1}{I^2}$.

*Case 2: N>I*

In this case, we can observe complete specialization but not complete concentration. There are between 1 and $I$-$N$ industries, in which more than one country specializes. We have to assume an equilibrated industry structure for the

EU average because otherwise we would have to take the size of industries into account. So we assume that each industry has the same average employment share $\frac{1}{I}$. Then we can calculate - for each country separately - the absolute deviation from the average for the industry in which the country is specialized. This is $1 - \frac{1}{I} = \frac{I-1}{I}$, while it is $(I-1)\frac{1}{I}$ for all other industries. This gives us the sum of deviations for each country: $2(I-1)/I$. Regarding this for all $N$ countries yields the *SHE* as $1/N * 1/I * N * (2 * (I-1)/I) = 2 * (I-1)/I^2$.

*Case 3: N<I*

For the case $N < I$ the reasoning of case 2 holds, but the resulting upper boundary implies perfect concentration (instead of perfect specialization). This means that each industry is perfectly concentrated in one country, but countries can specialize in more than one industry. The upper bound then is $2(N-1)/N^2$.

## 4.2.1 σ-convergence

σ-convergence measures the development of heterogeneity between countries in terms of employment or production levels. Furthermore, we can distinguish the concepts of conditional and unconditional convergence. The latter concept would imply global convergence across the sample, whereas conditional – also called club – convergence only implies convergence of countries with similar starting conditions. Therefore it would be possible that countries develop towards different steady states and hence are characterized by long-term differences with regard to their specialization patterns (Baumol 1986, Barro and Sala-i-Martin 1992 and Galor 1996). Using time series econometric methods in order to investigate within and across country convergence is quite a common concept (Bernard and Durauf 1996, Evans 1996, Evans and Karras 1996 and Qi and Pappell 1999), but has not yet been applied to study convergence of employment levels. Since we are interested in the development of 14 countries using 35 industries, we follow the approach taken in many studies to operate with a reference point towards which countries and industries ought to converge. In this study, the reference point is the employment share of the EU-15.

In order to test for σ-convergence we calculate $iSHE^N$ (for both manufacturing and services) and the s$SHE^N$ for each year in the observation period 1970-2005 (1970-2004 for manufacturing industries) and analyze the development of the index over time using the time series methods described below. A growing $SHE^N$ (either $iSHE^N$ or $sSHE^N$) is interpreted as a sign of divergence, while a decreasing $SHE^N$ points towards convergence. We model the development of heterogeneity as an autoregressive integrated moving average process (ARIMA (p,d,q)) with d = 1, using the following (general) equation:

$$\Delta \ln SHE_t^N = \varphi + \mu_1 \Delta \ln SHE_{t-1}^N + ... + \mu_p \Delta \ln SHE_{t-p}^N + \varepsilon_t - \theta_1 \varepsilon_{t-1} - ... - \theta_q \varepsilon_{t-q} \quad 21$$

The estimation result we are most interested in is the constant $\varphi$ which in the case of d = 1 indicates the (deterministic) time trend of the time series. A value of $\varphi$ significantly greater than zero is interpreted as a sign that heterogeneity increases over time, implying divergence, whereas a significant and negative $\varphi$ indicates a decrease of $SHE^N$ and thus convergence.

In contrast to the existing literature, we distinguish between general divergence (convergence) in an industry and one-country specialization (catch up). One-country-specialization can be regarded as a special case of convergence clubs, i.e. groups of countries that converge - but each group at a different level. Accordingly, one could similarly test for "two-country-specialization" and so on. As the typical case in our data is the specialization of one country instead of pronounced convergence clubs, we limit our analysis to this special case. Though the distinction between general divergence/convergence and one-country-specialization/catch-up is relevant for economic policy, it has not yet been accounted for in the literature. The difference between one-country-specialization and a general dispersion trend would be particularly notable in the case of divergence: Whenever economic integration causes all countries to drift apart gradually, this is likely due to the ability of some countries to enhance their competitive advantage at the cost of other countries. This might be the case if larger countries gain from economic integration at the cost of smaller countries, as larger countries can then better exploit input-output linkages and their access to skilled workers. On the other hand, one-country-specialization presumably takes place in emerging industries and highly path-dependent industries, in which case only one (or very few) country gains leadership and can perpetuate and even increase its competitiveness over time.

As the lines between one-country-specialization and general divergence can be blurry, an exact differentiation between general dispersion and one-country-specialization is difficult. As an approximate solution we calculate three measures: $SHE^N$, $SHE^{N-1}$ for the country group without the country deviating the

---

21   To achieve stationarity of variances and co-variances we use the logarithm of the values. First differences have been taken in all cases, since the hypothesis of (trend-) stationarity can be rejected for all time series. Using the Augmented Dickey-Fuller test we cannot reject the hypothesis of a unit root for all time series, but we find stationarity of the first differences for nearly all sectors/industries; the results of the ADF are available from the authors upon request. Lag orders were specified for each time series separately in order to achieve a good fit of the model. However, we are not interested in the values of the AR- and MA-characteristics of the series. Therefore we report the complete results of the ARIMA regressions only in the Appendix C. We moreover are aware of the limited power of the ADF test in the case of short time series.

most, and the employment shares of the country which deviate the most in relation to the European average. The development of these three variables over time can be used to identify the different convergence/divergence types: One-country-specialization is present instead of general divergence in either of the following two cases: First, if the time trend of the maximum deviation is significant and positive, and second if the time trend of $SHE^N$ is insignificant or positive and the time trend of $SHE^{N-1}$ of the remaining countries is significant and negative, insignificant, or significantly smaller than $SHE^N$. As to convergence, a similar distinction is possible for the case that the most specialized country gives up its position. We should expect a negative and significant time trend of the maximum deviation, together with an insignificant time trend of $SHE^{N-1}$. To validate the result in case of one-country-specialization, we must rule out the possibility that the role of the most deviating country devolves from one country to the other from one year to the next. For general divergence, a change in the most deviating country is irrelevant. In our data, we find changes regarding the role of the most deviating country only for general convergence or divergence – or to be more precise, in cases where no country is highly specialized.

*Table 22: Identification of Convergence/Divergence Types*

|  | $SHE^N$ | $SHE^{N-1}$ | max. deviation |
|---|---|---|---|
| General divergence | >0 | >0 | $\geq 0$ |
| One-country-specialization | $\geq 0$ | <SHEN | >0 |
| General convergence | <0 | <0 | $\leq 0$ |
| One-country-de-specialization | $\leq 0$ | >SHEN | <0 |

## 4.2.2 β-convergence

The second approach to measure convergence/divergence is the β-convergence test. We test for unconditional convergence, which implies that all countries ought to converge until all countries have the same employment shares in all respective industries. Therefore, countries whose industrial structure deviates the most from the average structure have to undergo the largest transition and adaptation process. β-convergence thus implies that both the absolute level of heterogeneity as well as the growth rate between countries converges over time. This can only be true if there exists a negative correlation between the initial level of heterogeneity and its subsequent growth rate.

Although this approach has been criticized in the literature due to the fact that a negtive β does not necessarily imply a reduction in dispersion (Quah 1993 and Friedman 1994), $\beta$-convergence is still a commonly used concept. It is based on the appealingly simple idea that countries are considered to converge if the initial value of a variable (in the case of structural convergence this is the industries' employment share) has a significant and negative impact on the growth of the variable over the investigation period 0 - $T$:

$$\Delta e_T^{n,i} = \alpha^i + \beta^i e_0^{n,i} + \varepsilon^{n,i},$$

where $\Delta e_T^{n,i} = e_T^{n,i} - e_0^{n,i}$, and $e_t^{i,s}$ is the deviation of country $n$'s employment share in industry $i$ relative to the average European employment share of this industry at time $t$. We use the deviation from the average instead of simple employment shares to control for structural change which affects all countries similarly, thereby causing a bias in the convergence estimation. The reader will notice that we do not regress growth rates but absolute changes; this is reasonable in the context of deviations from the mean because growth rates (i.e. $\frac{\Delta e_T^{n,i}}{e_0^{n,i}}$) would understate the changes of strongly deviating countries relative to countries near the average. Hence, while growth rates are preferable in case of e.g. productivity convergence, in the case of structural convergence absolute changes are more suited.

In order to fully exploit our cross-sectional time series data, we depart from the aforementioned basic model and estimate the following equation:

$$\Delta e_t^{n,i} = \alpha^i + \beta^i e_{t-1}^{n,i} + \varepsilon_t^{n,i}.$$

Here, $\Delta e_t^{n,i}$ is the annual change of country $n$'s deviation of the employment share in industry $i$ at time $t$ from the European average, i.e. we test the hypothesis that there is a negative (or in the case of divergence, positive) link between the deviation from the European average in the previous year and the growth of the employment share in relation to the European average. For the analysis of $\beta$-convergence, we use a linear[22] random effects estimator, since we don't want to attribute the changes in employment shares to specific (fixed) country effects.[23] Each industry has been analyzed separately in order to distinguish between diverging and converging branches instead of making generalizations across industries.

---

22    One could argue that a linear model does not take into account that our dependent variable, the deviations from employment shares, is limited between -1 and 1 by definition. Since we do not expect any observations near the boundaries however, the OLS model is a reasonable choice, mainly due to its robustness to heteroscedasticity and non-normality.

23    The adequacy of the random effects model is supported by Hausman tests.

# 4.3 Data

Our empirical analysis is based on macro data of 14 EU member states (EU 15 without Luxembourg), covering the observation period of 1970-2004/2005[24]. The data is drawn from the KLEMS database (see Timmer et al. 2007), which provides data collected from the EU countries' national accounts, and additionally from the public Eurostat database.

Above we presented a method of detecting convergence and divergence, respectively. For the implementation of these concepts, we use a classification of three aggregate sectors (agriculture, manufacturing, and services), 19 manufacturing industries and ten service branches, according to the NACE classification.[25] The agricultural sector is not further differentiated, since we do not expect substantial inter-industry structural change within this sector as it contains only three industries. Some industries are not included in the analysis: Data for utilities (Electricity, Gas and Water Supply), Public Administration and Community Services - like Public Waste Disposal or Cultural Activities - are partly missing or available only at a highly aggregated level. Furthermore, we exclude the construction sector, because of its high sensitivity to public spending. As Brülhart and Trionfetti (2004) showed, industries for which public procurement is important, countries tend to specialize into and thus relative concentration should to a large extent be due to differences in public spending rather than due to comparative advantage.

We classify manufacturing industries according to technology intensity, based on the OECD industry ranking on sector average R&D expenditures between 1991 and 1999 (see OECD 2003), which we adapt to our aggregation level of manufacturing branches. Similarly, we build two groups of service industries according to their knowledge intensity (see Laafia 1999), although the classification is somewhat coarse due to the high aggregation level of the branches. For the technology classification of manufacturing industries and the knowledge intensity classification of the service industries, respectively, see the Appendix.

The main variable used is employment, captured in total yearly hours worked by employed persons (i.e. contractual plus unpaid hours). This is the most comprehensive and – at least for our purposes – the robust measure of sec-

---

24    When this analysis was carried out, manufacturing data was available until 2004, whereas service data was available until 2005. We decided to make best use of the available data and therefore the end dates for the industries of the two sectors vary.

25    A description of the industry classification can be found in the Appendix Appendix .

tor (industry) shares available for the time horizon of 1970 to 2005.[26] Although employment data is less problematic than value added, some drawbacks of the long observation period remain: At the beginning of our observation period, the European Community was made up of the six founding member states only. Since then, it has been continuously enlarged and from 1995 on comprises all countries investigated over the observation period. We therefore analyze member and (still) non-member states together, without accounting for potential differences due to membership. A second question is how to treat Germany before and after reunification in 1990: On the one hand, comparability is affected if we switch between Western and unified Germany; on the other hand, excluding Eastern Germany after the Unification and thus including only Western Germany in the analysis for the whole period would result in a biased picture of the German industry structure. Therefore, we follow Timmer et al. (2007) and use the estimated values for Germany at its present size for 1970-1990, which are included in the KLEMS database. By doing so, the influence of Germany on European industry structure in this period is slightly overstated, as the industry structure of West Germany is expanded to the dimensions of unified Germany.

A drawback of our data is that we are not able to take into account the interdependencies between the manufacturing and the service sector. A country specialized in certain manufacturing industries might be specialized also in services associated with these manufacturing industries, e.g. textile industry and fashion design. Our aggregated data do not allow us to distinguish between different types of business services, like fashion design or automotive interior design, so these intra-industry specialization patterns will not be detected. What is more, we cannot preclude measuring errors in the classification of manufacturing and services; e.g. tax and marketing staff is classified as part of the manufacturing sector if directly employed at a manufacturing firm, but if the same services are done by specialized providers like tax advisors, the employees are counted as part of the service sector. This means on the one hand that simple outsourcing processes will appear as tertiarization in our data; yet on the other hand the tertiarization process might be understated as long as the increase of administration

---

26    Total annual hours worked are preferable to the number of employees, which can be biased by national and inter-temporal differences in working hours and the share of part-time workers. A drawback of employment data is a productivity bias: Countries with particularly low productivities in an industry appear more specialized in this industry when focusing on employment data rather than on output data. This could lead to a systematic underestimation of specialization if high productivity and specialization are correlated. To overcome this problem, output-oriented indicators such as value added or exports could be used, but availability of reliable data on these variables over the entire observation period of 1970 to 2005 is limited.

staff in manufacturing – a kind of within-firm tertiarization – is not reflected in the employment data.

Moreover, using value added could more adequately capture the overall importance of an industry and thus the study and its results would be more closely related to the competitiveness of a country. With regard to service sector, it is however far more difficult to use robust figures of output measures due to the lack of market prices for some production as well as the measurement problems associated with productivity growth and choosing an adequate deflator for service output (Grilliches 1992 and Cave and Giovanni 2007). According to Schettkat and Yocarini (2006) however, we have to distinguish between more homogenous industries such as communications opposed to heterogenous industries such as banking or business such that measurement problems are not equally severe for all service industries alike. They draw the conclusion that due to this fact, it is not clear whether the measurement problems are higher than in the manufacturing sector after all. Service industries moreover can be distinguished on the basis of the degree of technological progress. Most studies use the classification of services in this respect first developed by Katouzian (1970) and then altered by Singelmann (1978). According to them, services are assigned to one of the following groups: distributive, producer, social or personal services. Empirical studies of the 1980s using the latter classification show that the rise of employment in service industries is mainly driven by the low productivity growth in these industries, but that also the shift in final demand accounts to some thirty per cent to these changes whereas shifts in intermediate demand are less relevant (Elfring 1989). Differences among countries can be also explained by the degree of openness of an economy, since major part of exports stem from the manufacturing sector and thus reduce the share of service industries employment in the home country(Gregory et al. 2006).

One more issue is associated with measurement problems in the service sector. Often this sector has been defined as the "residual sector", encompassing all industries that are neither part of the agricultural nor to the manufacturing sector. Therefore it comes as no surprise that the service sector in itself is quite heterogeneous compared to the other two broad sectors. The problem of this definition was already clear from the mid of the 20th century. In line with Fuchs (1968) for instance, only labour-intensive industries with little use of capital are considered part of the service sector. As a consequence, transport, communication as well as public utilities would not be part of the service sector.

Different developments of traditional and standardized service industries have not been investigated sufficiently. This distinction is crucial however, as employment and output shares in the service sector have been rising over the past decades and as services have become more easily tradable and since the possibilities of agglomeration in service industries have been on the rise as well. Many services do not depend on the local proximity of buyer and seller any more. Therefore, not only the processes of tertiarization per se are interesting to study, but to highlight the relevance of advanced services that are characterized by trade ability, substantial increases in labour productivity and no necessity of production and consumption at the same point in time (uno-actu principle no longer valid for all services, but still relevant for medical care, education, domestic services). Due to the major advances in information and communication technologies, preconditions for abolishing the uno-actu principle are in effect. Today, many services in financial intermediation or consulting can be transferred from one country to another easily and without incurring high costs. Services thus have become increasingly part of international trade over the last decade (Barth 2001).

## 4.4 Results for Inter-Sectoral Heterogeneity

In the following we provide results both for the development of heterogeneity on the aggregate level (i.e. agriculture, manufacturing and services). We find clear evidence of inter-sectoral convergence between Western European countries, which itself is not a surprising result. It is remarkable; however, that inter-sectoral convergence has not slowed down over time. Tertiarization and catch-up effects of countries that were characterized by a relatively large agricultural sector in the 1970s still persist at the end of the observation period: Inter-sectoral heterogeneity (given by the $sSHE^N$) decreased steadily and in 2004 is only half the level of 1970 (from 0.08 to 0.035) as can be seen from Figure 1.

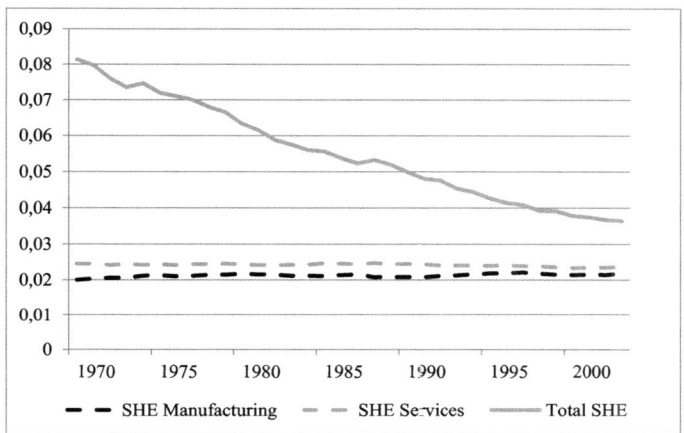

*Figure 1: Structural Convergence over Time*
Source: EU KLEMS Database, March 2007

On the inter-industry level, on the other hand, we find only slight divergence. Note that this result becomes visible only if heterogeneity is analyzed on the inter-industry level, since otherwise all manufacturing and services industries would seem to be converging due to the influence of inter-sectoral convergence. Since we do not use the employment shares of single industries on total employment as in the traditional Krugman Specialization Index, but rather use the shares with regard to sector employment, we focus on convergence/divergence of industries within the same sector, irrespective of the development of the sector itself. The lack of clear convergence or divergence in manufacturing and service industries might be caused by opposing trends in different industries: If some industries diverge and others converge, these (simultaneous) shifts cancel each other out in the aggregate view. An analysis on the industry level is therefore necessary to detect the convergence and divergence tendencies within the manufacturing and service sectors, respectively.

It has to be kept in mind, however, that the size of the Krugman Specialization Index is influenced by the weight we give to the relative size of countries, sectors and industries. Thus the results are - to some extent - sensitive to the exact calculation method of the heterogeneity index chosen. Therefore we do not only present an un-weighted index of structural heterogeneity (which we will use throughout the paper) but also country and sector weighted versions −In general we see that the heterogeneity index weighting with country-size only gives the lowest levels of heterogeneity for both manufacturing and service industries and therefore also for the economy as a whole. The weighted indices are calculated as follows:

1. The country-weighted heterogeneity index (*cwSHE*) gives larger weight to heterogeneity induced by larger countries (such as Germany) than from smaller countries.

$$cwSHE = \frac{1}{S}\sum_{n=1}^{N} w^n \sum_{s=1}^{S}\left|b_s^n - \bar{b}_s\right|; \quad w^n = \frac{total\ employment\ (country\ n)}{total\ employment\ (EU)};$$

2. The sector-weighted heterogeneity index (*swSHE*) addresses the fact that heterogeneity in different sectors is of different importance for economic policy. As such, heterogeneity in larger sectors should be taken more seriously than deviations in small sectors.

$$swSHE = \frac{1}{N}\sum_{n=1}^{N}\sum_{s=1}^{S} w^s \left|b_s^n - \bar{b}_s\right|; \quad w^s = \bar{b}_s;$$

3. The country- & sector-weighted heterogeneity index (*cswSHE*) is a combination of the weighting schemes described above:

$$cswSHE = \sum_{n=1}^{N} w^n \sum_{s=1}^{S} w^s \left|b_s^n - \bar{b}_s\right|;$$

This is likely to be due to the fact that smaller countries deviate more from the EU-average than larger countries. Two reasons underpin this: First, according to both economic theory and the empirical literature (see Chapter 2) smaller countries in general tend to be more specialized than larger countries. Second, the EU average is a weighted average of the employment shares of all 14 Western European countries. Therefore the employment shares of countries such as France, Germany, Spain or the UK obtain more weight than the employment shares of countries such as Austria, Belgium or the Netherlands.

The highest values of heterogeneity are obtained by applying appropriate no weights or sector-weighted indices. This is especially true for the service sector. Thus, the larger the sector (or industry), the more countries seem to deviate from one another. It follows that giving more weight to large countries weakens the divergence trend, whereas favouring large sectors more than smaller ones leads to slight convergence. This shows that it is mainly large sectors and small countries which drive convergence, while small sectors and large countries apparently tend to diverge. This is crucial since the heterogeneity in larger industries should be of more importance for economic policy than deviations in smaller sectors or industries.

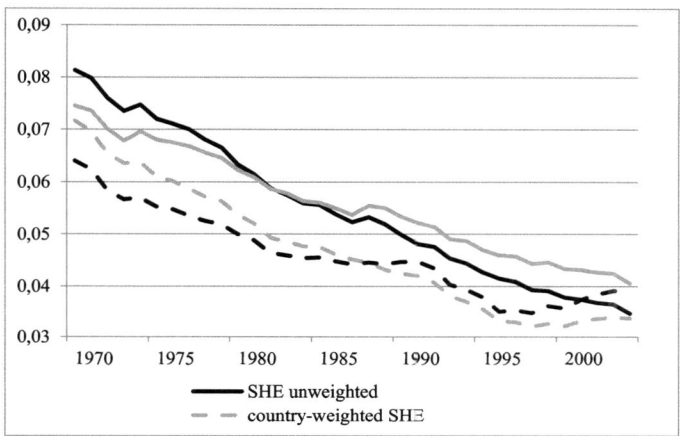

*Figure 2: Weighted Heterogeneity Indices*
Source: EU KLEMS Database, March 2007

It can be noted, that it is likely that mainly large industries that drive the process since the SHE is higher if it is sector weighted than if the index is calculated without weighting the importance of industries in the economic system. With regard to the weights of countries, we can note that using country weights lowers the heterogeneity across countries. This comes as no surprise since large countries such as Germany and France become more important in the calculation of the index meanwhile we have discussed in Chapter 3, that larger countries generally deviate less from the reference group since these countries are weighted more in the calculation of the reference group than smaller countries. From this figure we can also see that applying both country- and sector-specific weights, the results for the level of heterogeneity are lowest, yet close to the country-weighted levels of heterogeneity. The reason is that since country and sector weights work in opposing directions. For reasons of simplicity, we could thus stick to simple calculations of the unweighted *SHE*.

# 4.5 Results for Inter-Industry Heterogeneity

In a next step we turn to the analysis of industry-specific data. In order to analyze concentration processes of individual industries proper, we first provide descriptive data on manufacturing and service industries, respectively. We can either focus on exogenous – thus location dependent - factor such as comparative cost advantages stemming from differences in factor endowments with regard to labour and capital or on endogenous factors, where advantages arise from a firm operating close to other businesses within a region.

## 4.5.1 Descriptive Analysis of Manufacturing Industries

Since the 1970s the overall manufacturing sector showed decreasing employment shares since the proportion of declining industries outweighed the proportion of growing industries as being shown in Table 23. It is mainly industries that failed to innovate or attract human capital that lost employment shares as predicted by economic theory (Pasinetti 1981 and Pasinetti 1993) while innovating industries grew. The figures hint at the degree of structural change: While traditional and labour-intensive industries such as textiles, leather and basic metals substantially lost employment shares, all medium-high tech and high tech industries grew. Differences with regard to the degree of structural change among European countries will be discussed at length in chapter 5.

*Table 23: Employment Shares in Manufacturing Industries*

| Industry | Average employment shares | | Average growth rate |
|---|---|---|---|
| | 1970 | 2004 | |
| Food, Drink & Tobacco (FDT) | .109 | .132 | .005 |
| Textile | .160 | .084 | -.018 |
| Leather | .024 | .016 | -.011 |
| Wood | .031 | .034 | .003 |
| Paper | .026 | .024 | -.002 |
| Printing & Publishing | .042 | .059 | .009 |
| Coke & Fuel | .007 | .005 | -.009 |
| Chemicals | .052 | .053 | .001 |
| Rubber & Plastic | .029 | .047 | .014 |
| Non-metal Mineral Products | .051 | .048 | -.002 |
| Basic Metals | .049 | .031 | -.013 |
| Fabricated Metals | .095 | .111 | .004 |
| Machinery | .102 | .104 | .001 |
| Accounting & Computing Machines | .005 | .005 | .000 |
| Electrical Engineering | .041 | .044 | .002 |
| Communications Equipment | .024 | .024 | .000 |
| Precision Instruments | .027 | .030 | .003 |

| Industry | Average employment shares | | Average growth rate |
|---|---|---|---|
| Transport Equipment | .080 | .089 | .003 |
| Recycling | .047 | .061 | .007 |

Source: EU KLEMS Database, March 2007

Molle (2006) points out that the drop in employment shares in traditional industries was due to the fact that competition in these industries (such as textiles) from Third World Countries started at an early pace. The textile industry is characterized by globalization and easy relocation of production to low-cost countries (in particular China). The textile industry is considered as labour-intensive, low-skill and low-tech, with production taking place mostly in small and medium-sized enterprises.

In high-tech industries on the other hand, the employment shares increased over the course of time. Be aware of the fact, that important developments on the intra-industry level are hidden by the figures. Increasing productivity in the manufacturing and agricultural sector plus low income elasticities as well as outsourcing effects to be the main reasons for the rising share of services (Molle 2006).

This means that in the case of the leather and textile industries, instead of specialization we observe a delayed restructuring process in Southern European countries towards the EU-average due to the liberalization of trade via world-wide agreements and the establishment of the WTO. It is remarkable however, that the five largest industries (textiles, food, machinery, fabricated metals, and transport equipment) in the 1970s are the same as the five largest industries in 2004, implying that low and medium-low tech industries still make up for the bulk of employment in Western European countries. With regard to the relative change of employment shares, we can conclude that structural change mainly-takes place in advanced industries - there, convergence might occur as a consequence of productivity adjustments in lagging countries, but on the other hand in emerging service industries - such as modern telecommunication or financial intermediation - single countries might take the lead, which would cause divergence. Regarding the employment shares, the strong growth of the business services industry is striking. This should be caused by outsourcing e.g. of HR management and accounting services, by which employment is shifted from manufacturing to the service sector. Besides it is remarkable that employment has decreased in advanced service industries such as trade, transport/storage and post/telecommunication. This should not be seen as a sign for the shrinking importance of these industries, as it might be caused rather by standardization and rationalization processes leading to productivity growth. In contrast to that, in traditional services like domestic services or education, which do not exhibit similar rationalization potentials, employment shares have increased.

With regard to the relevance of up- and downward linkages in industries, the degree of intermediate inputs in production is a good proxy. As we see from Table 24, the relevance of intermediate inputs rose over the investigation period – implying that firms more and more rely on the inputs of other firms.

*Table 24: Intermediate Input Shares in Manufacturing Industries*

| Industry | Intermediate input | | Average growth rate |
|---|---|---|---|
| | **1970** | **2004** | |
| Food, Beverages & Tobacco (FBT) | .773 | .742 | -.11 |
| Textile and Leather | .641 | .691 | .21 |
| Wood | .645 | .688 | .18 |
| Paper, Printing & Publishing | .586 | .631 | .20 |
| Coke & Fuel | .893 | .886 | -.02 |
| Chemicals | .635 | .699 | .27 |
| Rubber & Plastic | .568 | .663 | .43 |
| Non-metal Mineral Products | .546 | .636 | .42 |
| Basic and Fabricated Metals | .641 | .677 | .15 |
| Machinery | .580 | .648 | .31 |
| Electrical and Optical Equipment | .557 | .657 | .46 |
| Transport Equipment | .653 | .770 | .46 |
| Recycling | .595 | .670 | .33 |
| **Average** | **.639** | **.697** | **.24** |

Source: EU KLEMS Database, March 2007

The highest shares of intermediate inputs are reported – both in 1970 and 2004 – for the coke & fuel industry followed by Food, Beverage and Tobacco, which are the only two industries where the share of intermediate inputs has fallen over the investigation period. The importance of intermediate products has above all risen in the electrical, transport and rubber & plastic industries, starting from well-below average figures.

As has been stated in 4.3, employment levels are in our study the most robust measure. However, it is also important to take into account productivity levels in order to interpret specialization patterns in a more coherent way. In Table 25 we therefore report the values for gross value added per hour worked for all manufacturing industries under study.

*Table 25: Gross Value Added in Manufacturing Industries*

| Industry | Gross Value Added per Hour Worked | | Average growth rate |
|---|---|---|---|
| | 1970 | 2004 | |
| Food, Drink & Tobacco (FDT) | 52.3 | 107.2 | 2.14 |
| Textile | 42.2 | 118.7 | 3.09 |
| Leather | 44.9 | 96.0 | 2.26 |
| Wood | 45.4 | 132.0 | 3.19 |
| Paper | 43.8 | 133.4 | 3.33 |
| Printing & Publishing | 55.9 | 114.8 | 2.14 |
| Coke & Fuel | 53.8 | 87.9 | 1.45 |
| Chemicals | 21.9 | 133.9 | 5.47 |
| Rubber & Plastic | 37.1 | 130.5 | 3.77 |
| Non-metal Mineral Products | 37.9 | 125.0 | 3.57 |
| Basic Metals | 27.7 | 113.9 | 4.25 |
| Fabricated Metals | 76.8 | 116.0 | 1.22 |
| Machinery | 48.6 | 115.2 | 2.57 |
| Accounting & Computing Machines | 14.3 | 232.3 | 8.55 |
| Electrical Engineering | 42.8 | 128.9 | 3.30 |
| Communications Equipment | 17.8 | 278.1 | 8.42 |
| Precision Instruments | 25.6 | 142.5 | 5.18 |
| Transport Equipment | 44.5 | 131.1 | 3.23 |
| Recycling | 62.5 | 109.3 | 1.53 |
| Average | 42 | 134.0 | 3.47 |

Source: EU KLEMS Database, March 2007

As shown in Table 25, value added per hour increased by almost 3.5 percent annually. There are large differences between the individual industries, however. Communications Equipment started as the industry with the lowest level of value added per hour worked and became the most productive industry in 2004. The development of the Accounting and Computing Machines industry is similar – in both industries, the annual rise in productivity is well about 8.5 percent.

There are, however, industries with slow economic advancements as the Coke and Fuel or the Fabricated Industry.

A first image of the qualitative dimension of structural change in the European countries is sketched in Table 26, where their shares of low, medium, and high tech industries are shown. From the figures, the general shift from low to high technology industries over time as well as the considerable differences between the countries are evident; e.g. the Netherlands had three times as much high technology industry employment as Greece in 1970 (18.7 per cent vs. 5.7 per cent). Regarding convergence tendencies, the rapid development of Finland and Ireland is notable, whereas the share of high technology industries in Portugal has not only remained low, but even decreased between 1970 and 2004. So, although a structural shift towards higher technology intensities occurs in all countries, differences between countries do not diminish; the more developed countries tend to specialize in high technology industries while the lagging countries stick to medium-low and medium-high technology industries. From the top-three countries with the highest shares of high-tech industries in 1970, only Germany was able to substantially increase employment whereas the Netherlands and the UK were rather characterized by a shift towards medium-high-technology industries.

Discussing the results in detail, we observe that Austria, France, Greece, Spain and Sweden exhibited a less than proportional share of high-tech employment, but were able to converge towards EU-average shares until 2004. Countries like Finland, Germany and the Netherlands had above EU average employment shares in high-tech industries but could not gain more advantage and thus converged towards EU-average levels. Countries like Belgium, Denmark and Ireland already exhibited above EU average employment shares in 1970, but were able to even widen the gap separating them from the other Western European countries. The competitiveness of Portugal in high-tech industries has worsened further as evidenced by the low and declining employment share in these industries. Whereas Belgium has a lead in high-tech industries, its employment share in medium-high tech industries is less than proportional and has even diverged from the EU average since 1970. The same is true for Finland. Overall structural change was most dramatic in Finland and Ireland.

*Table 26: Summary Statistics on Industry Shares (Manufacturing)*

| Country | High technology industries | | Medium-high technology indus- tries | | Medium-low technology indus- tries | | Low technology industries | |
|---|---|---|---|---|---|---|---|---|
| | 1970 | 2004 | 1970 | 2004 | 1970 | 2004 | 1970 | 2004 |
| Austria | .116 | .147 | .224 | .315 | .222 | .212 | .441 | .326 |
| Belgium | .158 | .199 | .204 | .264 | .254 | .221 | .384 | .315 |
| Denmark | .119 | .191 | .273 | .312 | .155 | .161 | .454 | .336 |
| Finland | .073 | .193 | .248 | .274 | .119 | .177 | .560 | .355 |
| France | .124 | .150 | .289 | .307 | .193 | .201 | .394 | .343 |
| Germany | .183 | .196 | .284 | .358 | .186 | .178 | .348 | .268 |
| Greece | .057 | .066 | .209 | .208 | .138 | .157 | .596 | .569 |
| Ireland | .135 | .320 | .194 | .194 | .151 | .133 | .519 | .352 |
| Italy | .130 | .135 | .221 | .265 | .202 | .214 | .444 | .385 |
| Netherlands | .187 | .171 | .259 | .351 | .155 | .166 | .399 | .313 |
| Portugal | .073 | .068 | .158 | .191 | .150 | .162 | .619 | .579 |
| Spain | .107 | .116 | .215 | .283 | .212 | .218 | .465 | .383 |
| Sweden | .127 | .173 | .291 | .373 | .196 | .181 | .386 | .273 |
| UK | .167 | .168 | .297 | .328 | .216 | .171 | .320 | .334 |
| EU-Average | .149 | .156 | .264 | .305 | .195 | .191 | .392 | .349 |

Source: EU KLEMS Database, March 2007; for industry classification see the Appendix.

With regard to low-tech industries, countries such as Austria and Denmark had above average shares in the 1970s but could upgrade its employment structure such that until 2004 the share was below the EU-average. The highest shares for low-tech employment were to be found in Finland and Portugal in 1970. Whereas Finland was able to upgrade its economic structure and thus could fill the gap with other European countries, Greece, Portugal and Spain are the countries dominated by low-tech employment shares. In many medium-low and medium-high tech industries, Greece and Portugal are characterized by structural backwardness without being able to close the gap with other European countries.

In a next step we calculate the inter-industry heterogeneity indices $iSHE^N$. Table 27 shows that both the degree of heterogeneity and the rate and direction of its development vary widely across industries: In some cases, like for example in the wood and paper branches, countries are more similar in 2004 than in they were 1970, while in others, such as in the textile and leather industries, heterogeneity in 2004 is higher than in 1970.

*Table 27: Heterogeneity in Manufacturing Industries*

| Industry | $iSHE^N$ | | $iSHE^N$ | $iSHE^N$/branch size | |
|---|---|---|---|---|---|
| | 1970 | 2004 | growth rate in % | 1970 | 2004 |
| Food, Drink & Tobacco (FDT) | .041 | .028 | -1.04 | .052 | .030 |
| Textile | .046 | .064 | 0.98 | .040 | .107 |
| Leather | .009 | .014 | 1.31 | .054 | .123 |
| Wood | .019 | .014 | -0.96 | .086 | .057 |
| Paper | .013 | .011 | -0.63 | .070 | .061 |
| Printing & Publishing | .013 | .015 | 0.40 | .044 | .036 |
| Coke & Fuel | .003 | .003 | -0.22 | .031 | .035 |
| Chemicals | .013 | .019 | 1.17 | .069 | .055 |
| Rubber & Plastic | .005 | .010 | 1.92 | .027 | .017 |
| Non-metal Mineral Products | .011 | .012 | 0.19 | .069 | .085 |
| Basic Metals | .024 | .012 | -2.00 | .026 | .031 |
| Fabricated Metals | .018 | .013 | -0.91 | .042 | .044 |
| Machinery | .030 | .033 | 0.22 | .041 | .053 |
| Accounting & Computing Machines | .003 | .006 | 1.96 | .041 | .041 |
| Electrical Engineering | .013 | .012 | -0.43 | .034 | .050 |
| Communications Equipment | .010 | .012 | 0.43 | .091 | .164 |
| Precision Instruments | .012 | .014 | 0.30 | .046 | .037 |
| Transport Equipment | .023 | .033 | 1.02 | .061 | .071 |
| Recycling | .014 | .018 | 0.82 | .065 | .065 |
| Average | .017 | .018 | 0.01 | .052 | .061 |

Source: EU KLEMS Database, March 2007

Analyzing the individual industries, we can distinguish them according to their level of concentration as well as to their rising or declining heterogeneity levels. Note that comparing the $iSHE^N$ of different industries is difficult, because heterogeneity generally tends to be higher in large industries, since we measure absolute deviations from the average employment share. For example, when considering the $iSHE^N$, e.g. in 2004, the most heterogeneous branch seems to be Textiles with an $iSHE^N$ of 0.893, but if taking into account the size of the branches the (smaller) Accounting and Computing Machines industry is obviously more heterogeneous than the (larger) textile branch, with 0.164 versus 0.107, respectively. In case of an unchanged level of heterogeneity, the $iSHE^N$ should thus grow with the employment share of an industry. More interesting are industries which, without changing their average employment share, exhibit relocation between countries, as indicated by the changes in the $iSHE^N$. This for example is the case in the accounting and computing machines industry.

To obtain a full picture of the development of individual industries over the whole investigation period, we present figures for the developments in each single industry and show which countries lead the development in the individual industries. These figures also help to identify industries in which general convergence or divergence trends occurred as opposed to industries in which one-country or club convergence (divergence) processes took place. In what follows, we will not interpret the developments of each single industry in detail but pay attention to the most significant and interesting results (see Table 28).[27]

*Table 28: Highest and Lowest Concentration Values in the Manufacturing Sector*

| Industry | Lowest SHE 1970 | Highest SHE 1970 | Lowest SHE 2004 | Highest SHE 2004 |
|---|---|---|---|---|
| Food, Drink & Tobacco (FDT) | ITA (-.030) | IRL (.144) | SWE (-.050) | GRC (.076) |
| Textile | SWE (-.076) | PRT (.164) | SWE (-.067) | PRT (.212) |
| Leather | NLD (-.015) | PRT (.025) | SWE (-.014) | PRT (.048) |
| Wood | NLD (-.017) | FIN (.070) | NLD (-.015) | FIN (.036) |
| Paper | ITA (-.012) | FIN (.077) | PRT (-0.12) | FIN (.057) |
| Printing & Publishing | PRT (-.012) | DK (.050) | PRT (-.024) | UK (.040) |
| Coke & Fuel | DK (-.005) | GRC (.009) | PRT (-.004) | GRC (.010) |
| Chemicals | FIN (-.026) | NLD (.019) | PRT (-.031) | BEL (.068) |
| Rubber & Plastic | PRT (-.009) | UK (.012) | PRT (-.022) | UK (.015) |
| Non-metal Mineral Products | NLD (-.028) | ESP (.027) | SWE (-.024) | PRT (.021) |
| Basic Metals | DK (-.034) | BEL (.061) | FRA (-.020) | BEL (.027) |
| Fabricated Metals | FIN (-.047) | ITA (.018) | IRL (-.044( | FRA (.022) |
| Machinery | PRT (-.062) | GER (.036) | PRT (-.061) | DK (.048) |
| Accounting & Computing Machines | PRT(-.005) | IRL (.014) | GRC (-.005) | IRL (.054) |
| Electrical Engineering | GRC (-.029) | GER (.016) | GRC (-.035) | GER (.021) |

[27] For readers who are interested in the deviation of every single country in each industry, the respective figures are listed in the Appendix.

| Industry | Lowest SHE 1970 | Highest SHE 1970 | Lowest SHE 2004 | Highest SHE 2004 |
|---|---|---|---|---|
| Communications Equipment | GRC (-.020) | NLD (.024) | GRC (-.020) | FIN (.060) |
| Precision Instruments | ESP (-.021) | NLD (.022) | PRT (-.023) | IRL (.058) |
| Transport Equipment | AUT (-.044) | UK (.036) | DK (-.051) | SWE (.051) |
| Recycling | UK (-.015) | NLD (.046) | GER (-.025) | NLD (.090) |

Source: EU KLEMS Database, March 2007

From Table 28 it becomes obvious, that both Portugal and Greece have structural deficits in medium to high tech industries not only in the 1970s but that these deficits remain until 2004. On the other hand, Portugal seems to have specialized into low-tech industries over the investigation period. Moreover, to some degree concentration seem to persistent over time since in ten out of 19 manufacturing industries the country with the highest employment share in the 1970s remained the leading country also in 2004. Turning to the industries in detail the following can be concluded:

The Food, Beverages and Tobacco industry was characterized by one-county specialization of Ireland for over two decades. Over this period of time, Ireland de-specialized immensely due to the fact that the catch-up in productivity led to reductions in employment in this industry. On the other hand, Greece was the second most specialized country in 1970 and did not show any sign of convergence with the other countries, which is why it now exhibits the widest gap from the EU average. Thus, while both Greece and Ireland were structurally lagging countries at the beginning of the investigation period, Ireland succeeded in de-specializing out of this low-tech and low-wage industry while Greece did not. In the textile industries, Portugal and Greece were characterized by a relatively high degree of specialization compared to the other countries, which is due to labour cost advantages. At the end of the investigation period, the gap of the two technological late-comers had become even wider – by almost one third in both cases. A similar picture obtains in the leather and footwear industry, where we observe patterns of increasing one-country specialization of Portugal. Especially from the early 1980s until the mid-1990s the gap towards the other Western European countries increased dramatically – by an average of seven per cent annually. Since then, de-specialization has set in, marking a turning point in for Portugal's economic structure. It is also notable that Italy has kept up its comparative advantage in some sub-branches of this industry (hand-made, high-tech and labour-intensive). This shows that specialization in a so-called low-tech, low-wage industry does not exclude the specialization in high-tech and high-wage branches. Apart from specialization due to cost advantages and the availability of specific skills, the abundance of natural resources is a driving force as becomes evident in the wood and the paper industries:

For Accounting & Computing, our results contradict the results of Midel-fart-Knarvik et al. (2000). They claim that strong de-concentration occurred between 1991 and 1997 due to the break-up of the German dominance in this field. Yet our data show that relative concentration mainly occurred and continued to do so until the late 2000 in Ireland. During the 1990s we even observe the highest increases in relative concentration due to one-country specialization. A similar development occurs in Communications Equipment, where Finland is able to take the lead from the 1990s onwards, resulting in enormous one-country specialization effects.

## 4.5.2 Concentration and Industry Characteristics

Industries differ not only regarding the degree of heterogeneity, but also with regard to the rate and direction of the development of heterogeneity. Following Midelfart-Knarvik et al. (2000), we assign the individual industries to one of the following clubs: industries that were concentrated in 1970 and remained so, industries that were dispersed in 1970 and continued to be so and industries that changed from concentrated to de-concentrated and vice versa. The results are reported in Table 29.

It is remarkable, that halve of the investigated industries were dispersed in 1970 and continued to be so for the whole investigation period. The second largest group consists of industries that were concentrated for the last 35 years. There are altogether only four industries that are characterized by a switch between concentration and dispersion or vice versa. Remarkably, three out of the four are to be found in the low-tech industries and only chemicals being a high-tech industry switched from below to above average concentration levels.

*Table 29: Concentration over time, measured by non-weighted SHE*

|  | Concentrated in 2004 | Dispersed in 2004 |
|---|---|---|
| **Concentrated in 1970** | Leather<br>Mineral Products<br>Communications<br>Transport<br>Recycling<br>Machinery | Wood<br>Paper |
| **Dispersed in 1970** | Textile<br>Chemicals | Food, Beverages and Tobacco<br>Printing and Publishing<br>Coke and Fuel<br>Rubber and Plastics<br>Basic Metals<br>Fabricated Metals<br>Machinery<br>Electrical Engineering<br>Accounting and Computer Machines<br>Precision Instruments |

Source: EU KLEMS Database, March 2007

The results in large parts contradict Midelfart-Knarvik et al. (2000). This can be due to the following reasons: We use a different data set (EU KLEMS vs. OECD Stan), we use employment rather than production data and we used the Krugman Specialization Index rather than the Gini Index. Moreover, the impact of using branch size adjusted indices is remarkable as shown in Table 30, where the assignment of industries is closer to the results obtained by Midelfart-Knarvik et al. (2000) who do not use this adjustment in their calculations, however. Empirical results thus do not seem to be as robust as we should have hoped for. The results from Table 30 are interesting with respect to the fact that there is not a single industry that turned from a dispersed to a concentrated industry.

*Table 30: Concentration according to SHE/branch size*

|  | Concentrated in 2004 | Dispersed in 2004 |
|---|---|---|
| **Concentrated in 1970** | Food, Beverages & Tobacco<br>Textile<br>Transport | Wood<br>Chemicals<br>Basic Metals<br>Fabricated Metals |
| **Dispersed in 1970** |  | Leather<br>Paper<br>Printing and Publishing<br>Coke and Fuels<br>Rubber and Plastics<br>Mineral Products<br>Electrical Engineering<br>Accounting and Computer Machines<br>Communications Equipment<br>Precision Instruments<br>Recylcing |

Source: EU KLEMS Database, March 2007

As pointed out in Chapter 2, Brülhart and Torstensson (2008) report that the rank correlation between the ranking of 18 industries based on their level of economies of scale and their ranking according to the Gini Index of Concentration was 0.69, with the results being significant at the one per cent level. Comparing these results with our findings for the non-industry size adjusted values of concentration; we obtain different results as Figure 3 shows. Again, we use the *SHE* values instead of branch adjusted values as did other authors including Brülhart and Torstensson (2008).

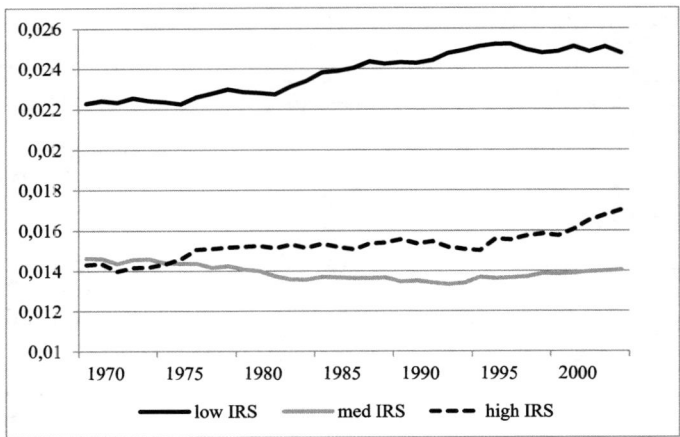

*Figure 3: SHE depending on degree of returns to scale (not industry-weighted)*
Source: EU KLEMS Database, March 2007

Also from the industry heterogeneity indices of Table 27 it becomes obvious that concentration is not positively correlated to the level of increasing returns to scale. On the contrary, on average the concentration of industries characterized by low increasing returns to scale is higher than in industries with medium or even high increasing returns to scale. What is even more striking is that over the period 1970 to 2005 concentration increased above all in low increasing returns industries – from 0.022 to 0.025 - whereas the level of concentration has remained fairly stable for medium IRS industries, falling from 0.015 in 1970 to 0.014 in 2004. For high IRS industries, there is a rise from 0.014 to 0.017 and this rise above all happens above all from the late 1990s onwards, where the effect of both European integration and globalization could be important. This could be even more so since the industry Transport Equipment is –apart from Chemicals – the driving industry. It is contradicting with economic theory, that the concentration of high IRS industries was the lowest at the beginning of the observation period, however.

It is notable that concentration has above all increased in textiles and leather, where international economic pressure ought to have lead to increasing concentration of employment in few Western European Countries, and in wood, where the development is characterized by a shift of specialization of Finland from low-tech and low-wage industries towards more rewarding industries. Thus, other forces than IRS seem to dominate the development[28].

Our data indicate that industries characterized by low increasing returns tend to be industries with highest concentration levels over major parts of the investigation period. This is above due to the divergence effect in Textiles, which was the single most concentrated in 1970 and remained so until 2004.For medium levels of increasing returns to scale, the process is driven by convergence in industries such as Basic Metals. Divergence since the 1990s is driven by Accounting and Computing Machines and Communications Equipment and to a smaller degree by Machinery. In high IRS the development is driven by the development in Transport Equipment as well as in the Chemical industry. If we compare the values with 2004, only two industries turned from below average concentration to highly concentrated industries: chemicals and recycling; and only three industries de-concentrated by a certain degree: wood, basic and fabricated metals. For a more detailed picture see Table 31:

*Table 31: Concentration depending on IRS*

|  | 1970<br>Low IRS | 1970<br>Medium IRS | 1970<br>High IRS |
|---|---|---|---|
| **Below average concentration** | Leather<br>Rubber and Plastics<br>Recycling | Paper<br>Printing & Publishing<br>Mineral Products<br>Accounting<br>Electrical Engineering<br>Communications<br>Equipment<br>Precision Instruments | Coke & Fuels<br>Chemicals |
| **Above average concentration** | Food, Drink and Tobacco<br>Textile<br>Paper | Basic Metals<br>Machinery | Fabricated Metals<br>Transport Equipment |

Source: EU KLEMS Database, March 2007

As a robustness check we also report figures for industry-weighted IRS in Figure 4. From this figure we learn that in all three categories, concentration is rising, above all after economic integration has accelerated since the early 1990s onwards. Moreover, high IRS industries are even getting the least concentrated group – contradicting what theoretical models tell us to expect. Again, low IRS industries are the most concentrated industries, with the process even accelerating over time instead of a decline in the not-weighted industry case.

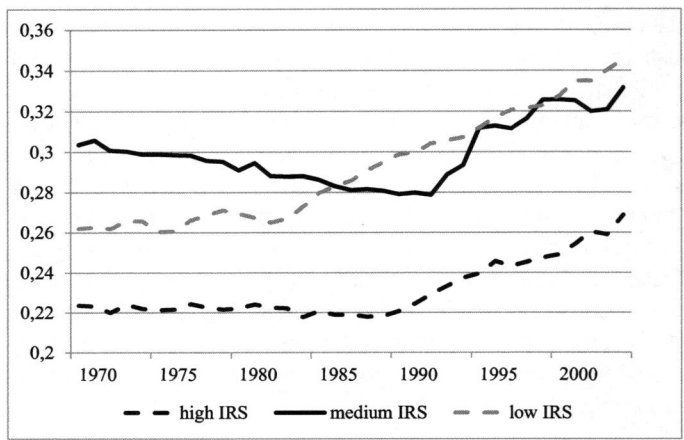

*Figure 4: SHE depending on degree of returns to scale (industry-weighted)*
Source: EU KLEMS Database, March 2007

In a next step we examine whether the degree of inter-industry relations has an impact on concentration. Even though theory would predict concentration to be positively correlated with inter-industry relations, our data do not show this effect. On the contrary, the most-concentrated industry is the textile industry even though it is characterized by low inter-industry relations. Looking at the industries in detail, we can draw the following conclusions from Table 32:

*Table 32 Concentration depending on Inter-industry Relations*

|  | 1970<br>Low inter-industry | 1970<br>Medium inter-industry | 1970<br>High inter-industry |
|---|---|---|---|
| **Above average concentration** | Textile | Wood<br>Fabricated Metals<br>Machinery<br>Transport Equipment | FBT |
| **Below average concentration** | Leather<br>Paper<br>Printing & Publishing<br>Chemicals<br>Communications Equipment | Mineral Products<br>Basic Metals<br>Communications Equipment<br>Precision Instruments<br>Recycling | Coke & Fuel<br>Rubber & Plastic<br>Accounting |

Source: EU KLEMS Database, March 2007

We find that speed and significance of branch specific convergence processes vary considerably. Classifying branches according to their factor intensity, we find that skill- and technology-intense industries tend to converge more strongly than capita-intensive ones. In general, one can observe that in some branches all European countries lose shares (such as textiles) and therefore converge towards a lower level of sector output. At the same time, emerging high-technology industries (such as biotech) are growing in all countries, leading to "high level" convergence. Looking at the industries individually, the following picture prevails:

Again, we can aggregate industries according to their degree of inter-industry relations and get the following picture: Industries that are characterized by low inter-industry relations tend to strongly concentrate economic activity over the course of time whereas the level of concentration remains low for industries with high inter-industry relations and fall for industries with intermediate inter-industry relations until the 1990s and rise sharply from the end of the 1990s onwards. Yet, for both medium and high inter-industry dependent industries, the levels of concentration in 2004 are below the levels of 1970 as shown in Figure 5:

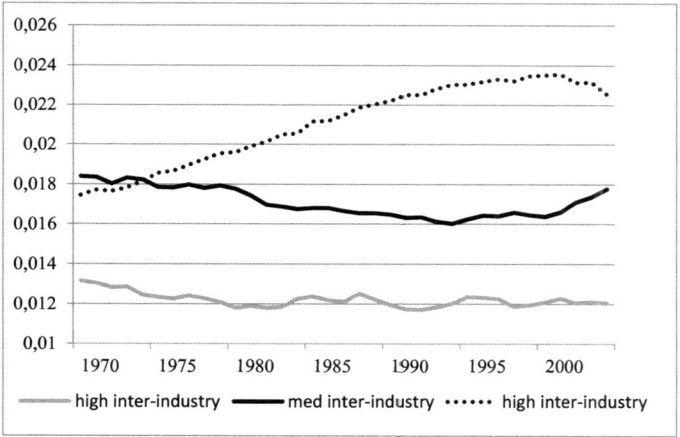

*Figure 5: SHE depending on inter-industry relations (not weighted)*
Source: EU KLEMS Database, March 2007

As a robustness check we also report figures for industry-weighted developments in Figure 6. It becomes evident that industries characterized by high inter-industry relations seem to be much more concentrated if we account for industry-size and that above all there is a huge increase in agglomeration starting in the late 1980s. Also industries with low inter-industry connection become more and more concentrated over time. In the case of low inter-industry relations this is a steady process whereas this is not the case for high inter-industry related industries. It is also noteworthy, that concentration for medium levels of inter-industry relations was low in the 1970s and even declined thereafter. To sum up, the development between industry-weighted and non-weighted figures is again quite diverse.

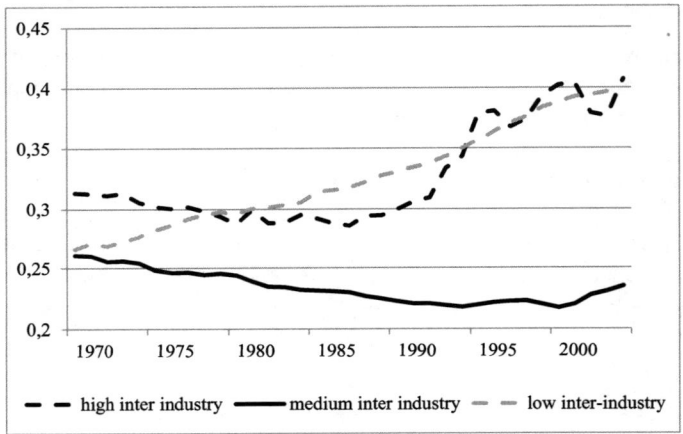

*Figure 6: SHE depending on inter-industry relations (industry-weighted)*
Source: EU KLEMS Database, March 2007

If we turn to the influence of intra-industry linkages on concentration, then on average there is a positive correlation between the importance of intra-industry linkages and the level of concentration, i.e. for industries with low intra-industry linkages the concentration is lowest and increased only moderately over time, whereas concentration is highest for industries with strong intra-industry linkages, and concentration even increased the most in these industries. For intermediate levels of intra-industry linkages, de-concentration processes occurred (see Figure 7).

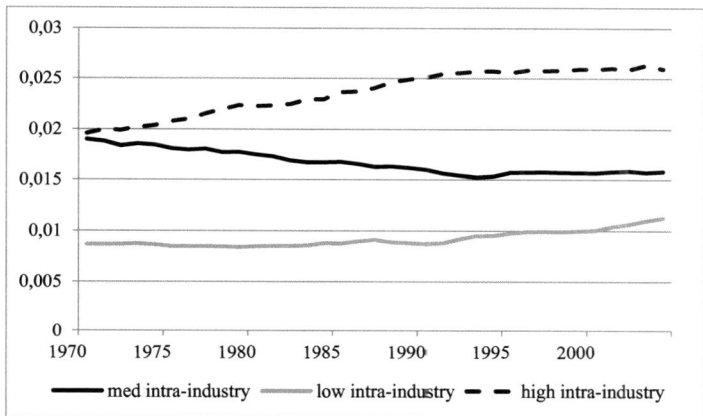

*Figure 7: SHE depending on intra-industry relations (not weighted)*
Source: EU KLEMS Database, March 2007

For a robustness check, we also show the industry-weighted results for the effect of intra-industry linkages on concentration. Here, the results are more robust and show the almost same path of development as in the case of non-weighted industries. The main difference is the increase in concentration after 1990, above all for the low and medium levels of intra-industry linkages (see Figure 8).

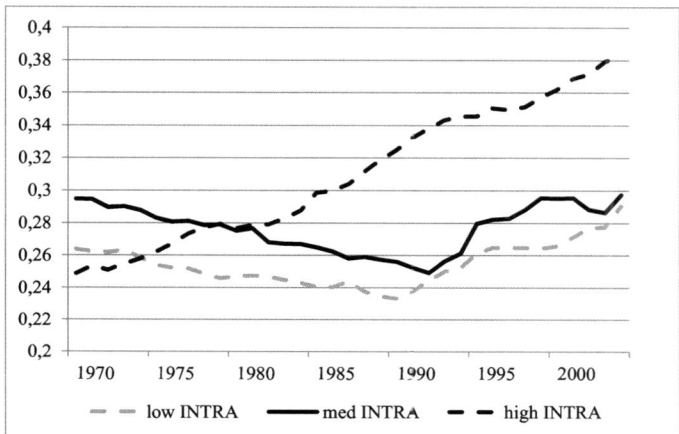

*Figure 8: SHE depending on intra-industry relations (industry-weighted)*
Source: EU KLEMS Database, March 2007

For a more detailed analysis look also at Table 33:

*Table 33: Concentration depending on Intra-industry Relations*

|  | 1970<br>Low intra-<br>industry | 1970<br>Medium intra-industry | 1970<br>High intra-<br>industry |
|---|---|---|---|
| Above average concentration | Coke & Fuel<br>Precision Instruments | FBT<br>Wood<br>Basic Metals<br>Accounting and Computing Machines<br>Communication Equipment | Leather<br>Paper |
| Below average concentration | Rubber & Plastic<br>Recycling | Mineral Products<br>Fabricated Metals<br>Machinery<br>Electrical Engineering | Textiles<br>Printing & Publishing<br>Chemicals<br>Transport Equipment |

Source: EU KLEMS Database, March 2007

Altogether we can conclude that the majority of industries have agglomerated over time. The reasons for rising concentration may however vary between low-tech, low IRS industries opposed to high-tech, high-IRS, high wage industries. Whereas in the former, international cost-competition might drive countries into de-specialization, in the latter it might be due to differences with regard to the ability of countries to be competitive in striving fields.

It can also be argued that the industry level at which we are carrying out our analysis is too broad to find robust results in that subject matter. Either way, it becomes obvious that there are many factors that influence the (de-)concentration processes of single industries and that the development of individual industries cannot be attributed to one single factor.

## 4.5.3  One Country- vs. General Heterogeneity Trends

To obtain a full picture of the development of individual industries over the whole investigation period, we present figures for the developments in each single industry and show which countries lead the development in the individual industries. These figures also help to identify industries in which general convergence or divergence trends occurred as opposed to industries in which one-country or club convergence (divergence) processes took place. In what follows, we will not interpret the developments of each single industry in detail but pay attention to the most significant and interesting results.

In the textile industries, Portugal and Greece were characterized by a relatively high degree of specialization compared to the other countries, which is due to labour cost advantages. At the end of the investigation period, the gap of the two technological late-comers had become even wider – by almost one third in both cases. In other European Countries, such as Austria and France, de-specialization towards the EU average level set in, which is even more a sign that cost-factors play a major role in the location of the textile industry in recent years.

A similar picture obtains in the leather and footwear industry, where we observe patterns of increasing one-country specialization of Portugal. Especially from the early 1980s until the mid-1990s the gap towards the other Western European countries increased dramatically – by an average of seven per cent annually. Since then, de-specialization has set in, marking a turning point in for Portugal's economic structure. It is also notable that Italy has kept up its comparative advantage in some sub-branches of this industry (hand-made, high-tech, labour-intensive). This shows that specialization in a so-called low-tech, low-wage industry does not exclude the specialization in high-tech and high-wage branches. Apart from specialization due to cost advantages and the availability of specific skills, the abundance of natural resources is a driving force as becomes evident in the wood and the paper industries:

In the wood industry as well as in the paper industry, Finland was the most deviating country both at the beginning and at the end of the investigation period. Due to a technological upgrade of the economy's structure, Finland de-specialized in both industries over the investigation period. Similar patterns of development can be found in the case of Sweden. In the paper industry, the initial deviation of Finland and Sweden can also be explained by the better availability of natural resources (similar to the wood industry). It can be noticed that these two countries de-specialize over the whole observation period as employment is shifted to other – more profitable – industries. As a result, two thirds of the gap towards the other countries was closed by 2004. All other countries exhibited only a low degree of heterogeneity, so we are able to identify club convergence (or two-country de-specialization).

We observe one-country-specialization both in Chemicals and in Basic Metals. Whereas in the former industry, Belgium is able to expand its lead, with the only single country able to catch up being Ireland, in the latter industry Belgium lost competitive advantage and moved closer to the EU-average. Thus, in Chemicals we observe one-country specialization and thus increasing concentration, whereas in Basic Metals we observe one-country de-specialization and de-concentration.

In both Electrical Engineering and in Coke & Fuel we find stable, continuous one-country specialization. The reasons might be quite diverse, however. Whereas in Electrical Engineering it is likely that we observe "real" specialization due to specific skills of German employees, in the Coke & Fuel case it is more likely that the relative specialization of Greece is due to under-proportional labour productivity. The over-proportional employment shares are thus not a sign of real specialization but more so of low competitiveness in this industry. In Transport Equipment, Belgium, Germany and Sweden increased their relative concentration immensely over. This process cannot only be attributed to high increasing returns to scale but has to do with consumer preferences for goods in sub-branches, i.e. while the demand for French and Italian cars declined, consumers' desired more Swedish and German cars.

Our data point towards one-country-divergence in the Chemical, Machinery, Office and Computing Machines and Recycling industries, whereas classical divergence obtains regarding printing and publishing, transport equipment, rubber and plastics, textile and leather. It is notable that one-country-divergence is found mainly in high technology industries which are assumed to be both dynamically developing and highly path-dependent. Contrastingly, more mature and less technology intensive branches exhibit rather classical divergence. We interpret this as a hint that path-dependency and the stadium of the industry lifecycle of an industry influence its development, while bearing in mind that the distinction between the two divergence types is vague.

## 4.5.4 Descriptive Analysis of Service Industries

Overall, the service sector expanded at the cost of both agriculture and manufacturing over the last 35 years. Of course, the growth was not distributed equally among the service industries. There are even industries where employment shares declined – mostly due to rationalization and mechanization processes. A detailed overview is given in Table 34:

*Table 34: Employment Shares in Service Industries*

| Industry | Average employment shares | | Average Growth |
|---|---|---|---|
| | 1970 | 2005 | *rate* |
| Domestic Services | .025 | .032 | .007 |
| Hotels & Restaurants | .084 | .089 | .002 |
| Wholesale & Retail Trade | .371 | .261 | -.010 |
| Transport & Storage | .122 | .084 | -.010 |
| Real Estate | .039 | .024 | -.013 |
| Post & Telecommunication | .051 | .049 | -.001 |
| Business Services | .093 | .205 | .022 |
| Health & Social Work | .115 | .148 | .007 |
| Education | .088 | .092 | .001 |

Source: EU KLEMS Database, March 2007

Regarding employment shares, the strong growth of the business services industry is striking. This could be caused by outsourcing of e.g. HR management and accounting services, by which employment shifted from the manufacturing to the service sector. Besides, it is remarkable that employment decreased in advanced service industries such as trade, transport/storage, and post/telecommunication. This should not be seen as a sign for the shrinking importance of these industries, as it might be caused rather by standardization and rationalization processes leading to productivity growth. In contrast to that, employment shares increased in traditional services like domestic services or education, which do not exhibit similar rationalization potentials. Employment in traditional industries declined. On the other hand, intermediary services that provide both services to production as well as private consumers are on the rise like R&D, and ICT. The quick growth of the health and social work industry on the other hand has been linked to the massive build-up of the welfare state, the growth of community services and the overall increased involvement of the public sector in market society (Rose 1985, Saunders and Klau 1985). The fastest growing industry was business services. Since many services in this industry are connected with the production of manufacturing goods it is very likely that the figures overestimate the job creation effects. In earlier days business services tended to be provided in-house by manufacturing firms, whereas nowadays these services are outsourced to specialized firms.

Table 35: Intermediate Input Shares in Service Industries

| Industry | Intermediate Inputs | | Average Growth Rate |
|---|---|---|---|
| | 1970 | 2005 | |
| Domestic Services | .000 | .000 | 0 |
| Hotels & Restaurants | .546 | .490 | -.30 |
| Wholesale & Retail Trade | 1.000 | 1.000 | 0 |
| Transport & Storage | .499 | .571 | .38 |
| Real Estate and Business Activities | .303 | .346 | .37 |
| Post & Telecommunication | .245 | .471 | 1.83 |
| Health & Social Work | .344 | .343 | -.01 |
| Education | .223 | .215 | -.11 |

Source: EU KLEMS Database, March 2007

Table 36: Gross Value Added in Service Industries

| Industry | Gross Value Added per Hour Worked | | Average Growth Rate |
|---|---|---|---|
| | 1970 | 2005 | |
| Domestic Services | 102.9 | 93.0 | -0.29 |
| Hotels & Restaurants | 103.5 | 97.7 | -0.17 |
| Wholesale & Retail Trade | 58.7 | 118.8 | 2.04 |
| Transport & Storage | 46.2 | 120.0 | 2.76 |
| Real Estate | 75.2 | 96.8 | 0.73 |
| Post & Telecommunication | 33,9 | 213.1 | 5.40 |
| Business Services | 77.7 | 91.0 | 0.45 |
| Health & Social Work | 84.2 | 108.3 | 0.53 |
| Education | 78.1 | 93.9 | 0.72 |
| Average | 73.4 | 114.7 | 1.29 |

Source: EU KLEMS Database, March 2007

Table 37: Summary Statistics on Industry Shares (Services)

| Country | Knowledge intensive industries | | Not knowledge intensive industries | |
|---|---|---|---|---|
| | 1970 | 2005 | 1970 | 2005 |
| Austria | .356 | .506 | .644 | .494 |
| Belgium | .407 | .609 | .593 | .391 |

| Country | Knowledge intensive industries | | Not knowledge intensive industries | |
|---|---|---|---|---|
| | 1970 | 2005 | 1970 | 2005 |
| Denmark | .422 | .592 | .578 | .408 |
| Finland | .383 | .561 | .617 | .439 |
| France | .451 | .584 | .549 | .416 |
| Germany | .388 | .549 | .612 | .451 |
| Greece | .335 | .401 | .665 | .599 |
| Ireland | .386 | .545 | .6_4 | .455 |
| Italy | .305 | .421 | .695 | .579 |
| Netherlands | .413 | .569 | .587 | .431 |
| Portugal | .232 | .337 | .768 | .663 |
| Spain | .247 | .399 | .753 | .601 |
| Sweden | .481 | .633 | .519 | .367 |
| UK | .447 | .575 | .553 | .425 |
| EU-Average | .386 | .518 | .614 | .482 |

Source: EU KLEMS Database, March 2007; for industry classification see Appendix A.

There are also large differences between more developed and lagging countries in the service sector (e.g. 48.1% knowledge intensive industry employment in Sweden vs. 23.2% in Portugal in 1970) as well as a pronounced shift towards knowledge intensive service branches for all countries. Note that the gap between leading and lagging countries even widened over time, so that Sweden as the leading country with 63.3% was well ahead of Portugal with 33.7%. This implies that knowledge intensive industries have grown mainly in countries which have been strong in them from the beginning, while the lagging countries even de-specialized in knowledge intensive service industries. Between these extremes, however, there are a number of countries – e.g. Finland and the Netherlands – showing dynamic structural change by catching up with the top countries.

*Table 38: Heterogeneity in Service Industries*

| Industry | $iSHE^N$ | | $iSHE^N$/branch size | |
|---|---|---|---|---|
| | 1970 | 2005 | 1970 | 2005 |
| Domestic Services | .020 | .022 | 0.113 | 0.094 |
| Hotels & Restaurants | .030 | .034 | 0.050 | 0.053 |
| Wholesale & Retail Trade | .028 | .032 | 0.010 | 0.017 |
| Transport & Storage | .019 | .01 | 0.021 | 0.016 |
| Post & Telecommunication | .008 | .006 | 0.065 | 0.051 |
| Financial Intermediation | .011 | .011 | 0.028 | 0.034 |
| Real Estate | .006 | .006 | 0.029 | 0.032 |
| Business Services | .032 | .041 | 0.048 | 0.028 |
| Education | .014 | .013 | 0.041 | 0.041 |
| Health & Social Work | .034 | .044 | 0.022 | 0.020 |

Source: EU KLEMS Database, March 2007

Regarding the service sector, we do not find many references indicating which developments to expect since empirical studies so far have been restricted to the analysis of manufacturing industries. In this respect, the current analysis is of special relevance as it provides new insights into the development of major parts of European economies. Economic theory predicts for traditional services with low productivity growth and for which the proximity of the producer is of high value for the customer, that one should not expect economic integration to set free forces leading to concentration. The developments of industry-weighted heterogeneity indices of traditional service industries such as Domestic Services, Education or Health & Social Work are in line with this argument[29]. However, in more standardized industries, such as Transport & Storage and Post & Tele-communication, where productivity increases in recent years have been high, convergence occurred too. This could be due to catch-up and productivity adjustments in lagging countries. It is mostly hybrid industries (containing both traditional and standardized parts of services) that seem to concentrate, e.g. Hotels & Restaurants, Wholesale & Retail Trade as well as Financial Intermediation. Overall we have to notice that the competition in the service sector has not

---

29    Note that the higher values of the iSHEN in 2005 than in 1970 for domestic services as well as for Health & Social Work seem to be due to the fact that these industries grew fast over the observation period, therefore the heterogeneity in both cases is likely to be overestimated in 2005.

risen as much as in the manufacturing sector – this is due to the lower mobility of consumers and employees. Moreover, the completion of the internal market program with respect to services has not yet been realized (Molle 2006).

From Table 38 we also learn that industry-weighted heterogeneity indices are generally smaller than in the manufacturing sector and that we find both convergence and divergence processes over time. Turning to the developments of the service industries individually, we obtain the following picture:

*Table 39: Highest and Lowest Concentration Values in the Service Sector*

| Industry | Lowest SHE 1970 | Highest SHE 1970 | Lowest SHE 2004 | Highest SHE 2004 |
|---|---|---|---|---|
| Domestic Services | UK (-.022) | ESP (.095) | SWE(-.032) | ITA (.062) |
| Hotels & Restaurants | DK (-.033) | PRT (.079) | BEL (-.045) | PRT (.066) |
| Wholesale & Retail Trade | GRC (-.065) | ITA (.071) | ESP (-.042) | PRT (.126) |
| Transport & Storage | FRA (-.026) | GRC (.106) | PRT (-.018) | GRC (.031) |
| Post & Telecommunication | NLD (-.013) | BEL (.015) | PRT (-.008) | IRL (.018) |
| Financial Intermediation | BEL (.017) | SWE (-.023) | FIN (-.022) | IRL (.037) |
| Real Estate | GRC (-.011) | FIN (.013) | GRC -.016) | FIN (.013) |
| Business Services | PRT (-.069) | FRA (.041) | PRT (-.095) | BEL (.046) |
| Education | BEL (-.048) | SWE (.098) | GRC (-.053) | SWE (.109) |
| Health & Social Work | ESP (-.027) | BEL (.041) | NLD (-.019) | SWE (.056) |

Source: EU KLEMS Database, March 2007

The development in Domestic Services is driven by two countries: On the one hand, by the de-specialization of Spain, on the other hand by the increasing specialization of Italy. The more advanced economies are, the lower the employment level in Domestic Services in general. Thus, the development in Spain seems to represent the economic upgrade of this economy towards EU-average levels. Altogether, convergence occurs in this industry since the one-country specialization of Italy has never become as strong as the former one-country specialization of Spain.

Countries benefiting from comparative advantage due to natural (sun & beach) and cultural resources are relatively specialized into hotels; surprisingly, the hotel business as well as restaurants benefited much from the upgrade and upswing of the Irish economy, bringing many foreigners to the country from the mid-1980s onwards.

In Transport & Storage, the employment level of Greece converges toward all other countries from the 1980s onwards. We interpret this as a sign of technological catch-up in Greece, leading to rationalization and automation, reducing employment. Thus, Greece did not lose competitiveness but even increased competitiveness while reducing employment. A similar picture arises in Wholesale & Trade: At the beginning of the investigation period countries with high employment shares were mainly low-productivity countries such as Portugal and Italy. Greece and Spain increasingly "specialized into" this industry, but again this is more likely to be due to a failure to catch-up in productivity than real specialization due to competitiveness. All other remaining countries retained low employment shares and were even converging slightly.

In Post & Telecommunication we observe general convergence until the early 1990s. From then onwards, divergence processes set in. It is mainly Ireland and Germany driving these processes. This could be due to the fact that the internationalization of mobile phone companies, rationalization and automation processes outweigh catch-up effects of lagging countries.

The striking development in Financial Intermediation was the continuous rise of employment in Ireland. Back in the 1970s, this industry was underrepresented compared to the EU-average, but a steady increase in competitiveness caused Ireland to become the relatively most specialized country in Financial Intermediation from the early 1990s onwards. Greece also was able to specialize into Financial Intermediation from the 1980s onwards, but starting off from the lowest employment shares in Western Europe, thus undergoing a "normal" catch-up process. Finland, on the other hand, lost competitiveness from the early 1990s onwards, becoming the least specialized country from the late 1990s onwards. Potential for more concentration is to be expected in financial intermediation due to major changes in the economic environment due to capital market integration.

Economic integration is expected to have little influence on an industry such as Real Estate. Since this is a mere national industry that cannot be easily transferred from one country to another, it is expected that national differences with regard to employment patterns continue to exist. In Business Services, some sub-branches have to be located close to consumers whereas others are easily transferrable between countries. Therefore, concentration processes are higher than in Real Estate.

In Education, the differences among countries continued to exist; no catch-up of lagging countries occurred. Instead, three sub-groups accrued: On the one hand, Denmark, Finland and Sweden remained the countries that invest most in

Education and even increased their lead; on the other hand, the Southern European Countries retained their exceptionally low levels of employment in Education. In Health and Social Work, Sweden retained his leadership over the whole investigation period, thus exemplifying its reputation as a welfare state. To a lesser degree, this is also true for Denmark. Lagging countries such as Spain and Portugal were able to catch up but are still lagging far behind.

To summarize, the development in services was mainly driven by the persistence of national differences due to the need for proximity between producer and consumer. In industries, where reallocation of production is possible, concentration occurred. True concentration due to competitive specialization occurred in financial intermediation, whereas specialization due to unproductive employment occurred in several industries where Greece or other Southern European Countries seem to be the most specialized.

## 4.5.5 Estimation Results for the Manufacturing Sector

Building on the descriptions given above, we analyze inter-industry convergence and divergence using time-series and panel data methods (for $\sigma$- and $\beta$-convergence tests, respectively), starting with the manufacturing sector.

As Table 40 shows, we find both $\sigma$-convergence and $\sigma$-divergence in the manufacturing sector. Significant convergence over the entire observation period is found for the food, drink and tobacco industry, the manufacturing of wood products and the fabricated metal industry. In the former two branches, convergence seems to result from the de-specialization of one country, as the low coefficient of $iSHE^{N-1}$ shows: Ireland and Finland, which in the 1970s had particularly high shares in the FDT and wood industries, respectively, shifted towards the emerging and ICT-related industries over time. This finding confirms the results of Brülhart et al. (1998b) and Midelfart-Knarvik et al. (2000) who discuss at length the outstanding phenomenon of structural change in Finland and Ireland.

Regarding $\sigma$-divergence, the results might be interpreted in line with our hypothesis regarding the role of economies of scale and forward and backward linkages: the chemical, rubber and plastics, and transport equipment industries diverge significantly over the observation period. With the exception of transport equipment, employment shares have been rising in these industries, implying that some countries increased employment more than others, exploiting their competitive potential. Similarly, the influence of intra-industry linkages can also be seen as an explanation for the significant divergence of textile, leather and footwear production (see Midelfart-Knarvik et al. 2000) as well as (partly) of the manufacturing of non-metal mineral products. Note that employment shares in these industries have been shrinking over the observation period. This implies that some countries reduced employment more slowly than others. In particular, in the textile and leather industries, the strength of Southern European countries (like Italy, Spain, and especially Portugal) may be driven by the lower wage level, due to which these countries could hold production sites longer than Northern Europe and were able to avoid productivity increases until jobs finally had to be cut in the mid-nineties (as can be seen more clearly from the $\beta$-convergence test below). That means that in the case of the leather and textile industries, instead of specialization in Southern European countries, we observe a delayed restructuring process towards the EU-average. This might be due to the liberalization of trade via world-wide agreements and the establishment of the WTO.

In emerging industries, such as the ICT-related branches, we find $\sigma$-divergence. In four industries (recycling, accounting and computing machines, communications equipment, and precision instruments) the results can be interpreted as one-country-specialization, given the insignificant or slightly positive time trends of the $iSHE^N$, combined with significant and positive coefficients of the *max deviation*. The countries which specialize in these emerging industries are Ireland for Accounting and Computing Machines and for Precision Instruments, Finland for Communications Equipment and the Netherlands for the recycling industry. We attribute this phenomenon to the existence of first-mover advantages in combination with technological externalities. The specialization in Precision Instruments as well as in Communications Equipment only started in the 1990s, which is in line with the technological development in these branches.

*Table 40: σ-convergence in Manufacturing Industries*

| | time trend $\ln iSHE_s^N$ | | time trend $\ln iSHE_s^{N-1}$ | | time trend *max deviation* | |
|---|---|---|---|---|---|---|
| Food, Drink & Tobacco | -.011 ** | (.005) | -.00987 | (.007) | -.019 ** | (.009) |
| Textile | .010 *** | (.003) | .011 ** | (.004) | .008 | (.005) |
| Leather | .014 ** | (.006) | .012 ** | (.006) | .019 * | (.011) |
| Wood | -.001 ** | (.005) | -.007 * | (.004) | -.020 * | (.011) |
| Paper | -.007 | (.006) | -.005 | (.007) | -.008 | (.011) |
| Printing & Publishing[1] | .016 *** | (.005) | .020 *** | (.007) | -.006 | (.011) |
| | -.022 *** | (.008) | -.019 * | (.011) | | |
| Coke & Fuel | .000 | (.012) | -.003 | (.016) | .006 | (.019) |
| Chemicals | .012 ** | (.006) | .007 * | (.004) | .037 *** | (.012) |

| | | | | | | |
|---|---|---|---|---|---|---|
| Rubber & Plastic | .019 *** | (.006) | .021 *** | (.006) | .006 | (.010) |
| Non-metal Mineral Products[2] | -.022 * | (.012) | -.198 | (.022) | -.008 | (.014) |
| | .019 ** | (.009) | .021 ** | (.009) | | |
| Basic Metals[5] | -.004 | (.003) | -.004 | (.002) | -.024 *** | (.009) |
| Fabricated Metals | -.009 * | (.005) | -.011 * | (.006) | .005 | (.024) |
| Machinery | .002 | (.003) | .002 | (.004) | .011 | (.007) |
| Accounting & Computing Machines | .019 | (.016) | .003 | (.013) | .039 * | (.020) |
| Electrical Engineering | -.005 | (.004) | -.007 * | (.004) | .008 | (.007) |
| Communications Equipment[3] | .005 | (.014) | -.003 | (.016) | -.010 | (.010) |
| | | | | | .115 * | (.061) |
| Precision Instruments[4] | .003 | (.005) | -.004 | (.003) | -.006 | (.011) |
| | | | | | .083 ** | (.034) |
| Transport Equipment | .011 * | (.006) | .011 * | (.006) | .010 | (.011) |
| Recycling | .008 * | (.005) | .002 | (.004) | .019 ** | (.009) |

***/**/* significant at the 1/5/10 percent level; standard errors in parentheses.
1 structural break in 1993/1994; 2 structural break in 1984/1985; 3 structural break in 1994/1995; 4 structural break in 1991/1992. In all cases, the first sub-period is in the upper line. 5 No logarithm. For details regarding the Augmented Dickey-Fuller test and the ARIMA-results, see Appendix.
Source: EU KLEMS Database, March 2007

The Food, Beverages and Tobacco (FBT) industry was characterized by one-county specialization of Ireland for over two decades. Over this period of time, Ireland de-specialized immensely due to the fact that the catch-up in productivity led to reductions in employment which is the reason why we find a strong convergence trend. On the other hand, the second most specialized country – Greece - did not show any sign of convergence with the other countries, which is why it now exhibits the widest gap from the EU average. Thus, while both Greece and Ireland were structurally lagging countries at the beginning of the investigation period, Ireland succeeded in de-specializing out of this low-tech and low-wage industry while Greece did not.

In both Electrical Engineering and in Coke & Fuel we find stable, continuous one-country specialization. The reasons might be quite diverse, however. Whereas in Electrical Engineering it is likely that we observe "real" specialization due to specific skills of German employees in the Coke & Fuel case it is more likely that the relative specialization of Greece is due to under-proportional labour productivity. The over-proportional employment shares are thus not a sign of real specialization but more so of low competitiveness in this industry.

In Transport Equipment, Belgium, Germany and Sweden increased their relative concentration immensely over time – at the expense of France and the UK (Midelfart-Knarvik et al. 2000 obtain similar results). Overall, we see that there are some big players in this industry, while the other countries continuously lose market shares. This process cannot only be attributed to high increasing returns to scale but has to do with consumer preferences for goods in sub-branches, i.e. while the demand for French and Italian cars declined, consumers' desired more Swedish and German cars.

For Accounting & Computing, our results contradict the results of Midelfart-Knarvik et al. (2000). Whereas they claim that strong de-concentration occurred between 1991 and 1997 due to the break-up of the German dominance in this field, our data show that relative concentration mainly occurred and continued to do so until the late 2000 in Ireland. During the 1990s we even observe the highest increases in relative concentration due to one-country specialization. A similar development occurs in Communications Equipment, where Finland is able to take the lead from the 1990s onwards, resulting in enormous one-country specialization effects. The reason for the contradicting results can result from the following reasons: We use the Krugman Index rather than the Gini Index, we use a different data sample – but what we believe to be most relevant is that we take into account structural breaks and calculated the indices for every year in the investigation period rather than only for four short time intervals.

We can already conclude that it is necessary to analyze the evolution of concentration patterns of each industry individually since on the one hand these patterns occur at different stages of time and on the other hand we can identify different forms of convergence (and divergence respectively): general convergence or one-country (one-club) developments. This distinction is relevant not only for economic policy but also gives hints for the evaluation of the competitiveness of individual countries in certain industries. Our data point towards one-country-divergence in the Chemical, Machinery, Office and Computing Machines and Recycling industries, whereas classical divergence obtains regarding printing and publishing, transport equipment, rubber and plastics, textile and leather. It is notable that one-country-divergence is found mainly in high technology industries which are assumed to be both dynamically developing and highly path-dependent. Contrastingly, more mature and less technology intensive branches exhibit rather classical divergence. We interpret this as a hint that path-dependency and the stadium of the industry lifecycle of an industry influence its development, while bearing in mind that the distinction between the two divergence types is vague.

For the estimations of β-convergence, we divided the observation period into sub-periods to account for a structural break if necessary; this was the case in 12 of the 19 manufacturing industries, with the others exhibiting a steady development over time. When comparing the sub-periods across industries it can be seen that the timing of the structural breaks is industry-specific rather than linked to European and worldwide economic integration.

Going into detail, the findings again show convergence of mature industries with high labour-, energy- and (natural) resource-intensities such as FDT, Wood, Paper, Basic and Fabricated Metals. The significant convergence of the paper and basic metals industries is not unexpected in respect of our hypotheses, yet of relevance nonetheless, given the insignificant σ-coefficients. As mentioned above, the results show a change from divergence to convergence in the textile and leather industries in the mid-nineties, caused by restructuring in South European countries. We also find divergence of industries with economies of scale (in the chemical industry, Rubber & Plastics, Transport Equipment, Recycling and Precision Instruments), mainly in the second half of the observation period. The results regarding the ICT-industries (i.e. Communications Equipment, and Accounting and Computing Machines) are remarkable: When single countries lead the development, we find divergence in the early stages of emerging industries, followed by convergence when countries catch up. This convergence trend in the last few years of the observation period was not detected by the time series analysis.

*Table 41: β-convergence in Manufacturing Industries*

|  | period | β | wald chi$^2$ | period | β | wald chi$^2$ |
|---|---|---|---|---|---|---|
| Food, Beverages & Tobacco | 1970-2004 | -.0082 ** (.005) | 2.87 | - | | |
| Textile | 1970-1993 | .012 *** (.003) | 15.42 | 1994-2004 | -.009 ** (.004) | 3.97 |
| Leather | 1970-1994 | .020 *** (.005) | 17.00 | 1995-2004 | -.016 *** (.006) | 8.03 |
| Wood | 1970-2004 | -.017 *** (.004) | 19.42 | - | | |
| Paper | 1970-2004 | -.009 *** (.003) | 14.21 | - | | |
| Printing & Publishing | 1970-1993 | .004 (.007) | 0.37 | 1994-2004 | -.032 ** (.013) | 5.99 |

| | period | β | wald chi² | period | β | wald chi² |
|---|---|---|---|---|---|---|
| Coke & Fuel | 1970-2000 | -.012 ** (.006) | 3.86 | 2001-2004 | .040 ** (.019) | 4.30 |
| Chemicals | 1970-2004 | .014 ** (.006) | 5.65 | - | | |
| Rubber & Plastic | 1970-1983 | -.012 (.014) | 0.73 | 1984-2004 | .012 * (.007) | 2.78 |
| Non-metal Mineral Products | 1970-1984 | -.018 ** (.008) | 5.30 | 1985-2004 | .003 (.008) | 0.12 |
| Basic Metals | 1970-2004 | -.022 *** (.004) | 27.50 | - | | |
| Fabricated Metals | 1970-1987 | -.012 * (.007) | 2.91 | 1988-2004 | -.004 (.008) | 0.26 |
| Machinery | 1970-2004 | -.001 (.004) | 0.05 | - | | |
| Accounting & Computing Machines | 1970-2001 | .048 *** (.005) | 76.08 | 2002-2004 | -.114 *** (.028) | 16.66 |
| Electrical Engineering | 1970-2004 | -.002 (.005) | 0.11 | - | | |
| Communications Equipment | 1970-2000 | .055 *** (.010) | 31.64 | 2001-2004 | -.061 ** (.025) | 5.73 |
| Precision Instruments | 1970-2000 | .008 (.007) | 1.41 | 2001-2004 | .060 *** (.017) | 12.85 |
| Transport Equipment | 1970-1993 | -.003 (.008) | 0.11 | 1994-2004 | .017 ** (.008) | 4.64 |
| Recycling | 1970-1980 | .011 (.011) | 1.02 | 1981-2004 | .012 ** (.006) | 4.14 |

***/**/* significant at the 1/5/10 percent level; standard errors in parentheses.
Source: EU KLEMS Database, March 2007.

## 4.5.6 Estimation Results for the Service Sector

In traditional industries in the service sector we do not find any significant changes in $SHE_s^N$ over time, as shown in table 9. In consumer-oriented industries like Domestic Services, Hotels & Restaurants and Health & Social Work this might particularly be due to their local boundedness and low rationalization possibilities. Significant changes in heterogeneity are found in three industries only, all of which are classified as standardized service industries: The Transport & Storage branch converges significantly over the observation period. Post and telecommunication services converge until 1988, which we attribute at least to a certain degree to technological and organizational developments resulting in productivity convergence across European countries. From 1989 onwards, Post and Telecommunications diverge. The same pattern of development can be detected in financial intermediation services after 1994. These trends of increasing concentration appear to be one-country specialization phenomena, caused by the specialization of Ireland.

Interestingly, no significant divergence is found for business services, which we expected to be characterized by economies of scale and a strong dependence on manufacturing industries. Yet due to the high aggregation level of our data the heterogeneity of Business Services subsumed in this branch might be too high, so that convergence and divergence trends within the business services industry may level each other out.

The financial sector was strongly affected by the price decrease in telecommunication and computer technology revolution. Information on financial markets anywhere in the world is now instantly available anywhere else, thus fostering agglomeration processes. The increasing concentration processes that occurred after 1993 are therefore no surprise. It is Ireland that benefited the most from the free movement of capital, which is reflected in one-country specialization.

Table 42: σ-convergence in Service Industries

| | time trend | $\ln iSHE_s^N$ | time trend | $\ln iSHE_s^{N-1}$ | time trend max deviation | |
|---|---|---|---|---|---|---|
| Domestic Services[1] | -.017 | (.014) | .007 | (.005) | -.042 ** | (.017) |
| | .010 | (.007) | | | .028 | (.025) |
| Hotels & Restaurants | .003 | (.002) | .004 | (.007) | -.006 | (.017) |
| Wholesale & Retail Trade | .004 | (.007) | .000 | (.008) | .016 | (.012) |
| Transport & Storage | -.019 ** | (.009) | -.012 * | (.006) | -.033 | (.023) |
| Post & Telecommunication[2] | -.024 *** | (.005) | -.026 ** | (.010) | -.013 | (.023) |
| | .011 * | (.006) | .006 | (.007) | .023 * | (.012) |
| Financial Intermediation[3] | -.006 | (.016) | .001 | (.021) | -.011 | (.018) |
| | .016 ** | (.007) | .002 | (.011) | .084 *** | (.032) |
| Real Estate | .003 | (.007) | .005 | (.011) | .001 | (.016) |
| Business Services | .009 | (.009) | .009 | (.009) | .004 | (.017) |
| Education | -.002 | (.010) | -.007 | (.017) | .009 | (.006) |
| Health & Social Work | .007 | (.006) | .008 | (.007) | .003 | (.006) |

***/**/* significant at the 1/5/10 percent level; standard errors in parentheses.
1 structural break in 1981/1982 for iSHEN, in 1990/1991 for the most deviating country; 2 structural break in 1988/1989; 3 structural break in 1993/1994. In all cases, the first sub-period is in the upper line.
Source: EU KLEMS Database, March 2007.

Applying the β-convergence test to service industries, we find convergence in several branches, but no case of divergence (see table 43). It is surprising and contradicts the results of the σ-convergence test that six out of ten service industries significantly converge, albeit not necessarily over the entire observation period.

A surprisingly sharp discrepancy between σ and β convergence is found in Financial Intermediation: We find significant σ-divergence from the 1990s onwards, which stands in contrast to the highly significant β-convergence in the same sub-period. The reason for this development is that all countries converge – with the exception of Ireland, which rapidly specializes into Financial Intermediation. In the σ-convergence test, we identify this phenomenon as one-country-specialization, while in the β-convergence test the outlier Ireland is concealed by other countries' convergence.

*Table 43: β-convergence of Service Industries*

| | period | β | wald chi² | period | β | wald chi² |
|---|---|---|---|---|---|---|
| Domestic Services | 1970-2004 | -.002 (.009) | 0.08 | - | | |
| Hotels & Restaurants | 1970-1987 | .006 (.004) | 1.83 | 1988-2005 | -.014 * (.008) | 3.17 |
| Wholesale & Retail Trade | 1970-2005 | -.014* (.008) | 3.00 | - | | |
| Transport & Storage | 1970-2005 | -.021*** (.005) | 21.33 | - | | |
| Post & Telecommuni-cation | 1970-2005 | -.004 (.008) | 0.18 | - | | |
| Financial Intermedia-tion | 1970-1990 | .002 (.007) | 0.08 | 1991-2005 | -.053*** (.018) | 9.21 |
| Real Estate | 1970-1988 | -.026*** (.007) | 12.33 | 1989-2005 | -.011 (.012) | 0.75 |
| Business Services | 1970-2005 | .001 (.006) | 0.03 | - | | |
| Education | 1970-1990 | -.015* (.008) | 3.30 | 1991-2005 | -.002 (.009) | 0.06 |
| Health & Social Work | 1970-2005 | .000 (.004) | 0.00 | - | | |

***/**/* significant at the 1/5/10 percent level; standard errors in parentheses.
Source: EU KLEMS Database, March 2007

It is also interesting to note that we are only able to reproduce the significant convergence and divergence found in the $\sigma$-convergence test in the transport & storage industry. This implies that the significant changes of the differences between countries cannot be attributed to a general convergence pattern which would become visible in the country-level analysis given by the $\beta$-convergence test. This is especially true for industries such as post & telecommunication, where both converging and diverging trends within sub-branches of this industry seem to level each other out. This confirms our view that both tests produce an incomplete picture, so that a combination of both is required for a reliable and comprehensive analysis.

# 4.6 Conclusion

A summary of our findings is given in Table 44, which compares the results of the $\sigma$- and $\beta$-tests. It can be seen that the first group, the converging industries, are mainly mature manufacturing industries and standardized service industries, respectively. On the other hand, divergence is found mainly in industries with medium to high technology intensity, economies of scale and growth potentials. Employment shares have been growing over the observation period in all industries in this group. Notably, we do not find divergence in service industries. The interpretation is difficult for the next two groups, switching from convergence to divergence and vice versa. In the case of emerging high-tech industries, such as the production of accounting and computing machines and communications equipment, the convergence after 2000 could be caused by the technological catch-up of follower countries. In contrast, the divergence-convergence pattern of mature industries like the textile and leather production seems to be caused by the delayed restructuring of Southern European countries, which reduced employment in these industries later than the other European countries. The convergence of employment in Hotels and Restaurants after 1987 is also interesting. We regard it as a hint towards converging lifestyles (although we cannot verify this hypothesis with our data and methods). In a number of countries, finally, heterogeneity does not change to a significant extent. This is particularly notable in the case of Business Services, in which employment has risen considerably, but apparently to a similar extent in all countries. The constancy of two classical manufacturing industries, Machinery and Electrical Engineering, regarding both employment and country specialization, is also intriguing.

*Table 44: Convergence and Divergence Patterns of Industries*

| | Growth* | Convergence** | | Divergence** | |
|---|---|---|---|---|---|
| | | $\Sigma$ | $\beta$ | $\sigma$ | $\beta$ |
| Food, Beverages & Tobacco | + | + | + | | |
| Fabricated Metals | + | + | + | | |
| Wood | (+) | + | + | | |
| Paper | (-) | | + | | |
| Basic Metals | - | + | + | | |
| Transport & Storage | - | + | + | | |
| Wholesale & Retail Trade | - | | + | | |
| Chemicals | (+) | | | + | + |
| Rubber & Plastic | + | | | + | + (after 1984) |
| Precision Instruments | + | | | + (after 2000) | + (after 2000) |

| | Growth* | Convergence** | | Divergence** | |
|---|---|---|---|---|---|
| Transport Equipment | (+) | | | + | + (after 1993) |
| Recycling | + | | | + | + (after 1980) |
| Accounting & Computing Machines | (+) | | + (after 2001) | + | + (until 2001) |
| Communications Equipment | (-) | | + (after 2000) | + | + (until 2000) |
| Textile | - | | + (after 1993) | + | + (until 1993) |
| Leather | - | | + (after 1994) | + | + (until 1994) |
| Hotels and Restaurants | (+) | | + (after 1987) | | |
| Printing & Publishing | + | + (until 1993) | + (until 1993) | + (after 1993) | + (after 1993) |
| Non-metal Mineral Products | (-) | + (until 1984) | | + (after 1984) | |
| Coke & Fuel | - | | + (until 2000) | | + (after 2000) |
| Post & Telecommunication | - | + (until 1988) | | + (after 1988) | |
| Education | + | | + (until 1990) | | |
| Real Estate | (+) | | + (until 1988) | | |
| Domestic Services | + | | | | |
| Business Services | + | | | | |
| Health & Social Work | + | | | | |
| Machinery | (+) | | | | |
| Electrical Engineering | (+) | | | | |
| Financial Intermediation | - | | + (after 1990) | + (after 1993) | |

* Growth of employment share in the EU 1970-2004: + growing, (+) slightly growing, (-) slightly shrinking, + shrinking. ** Significant $\sigma/\beta$ value found in the estimation.

# 5 Specialization Patterns of European Countries

## 5.1 Introduction

At the beginning of our observation period, the European Economic Community (EEC) only comprised the six founding members, i.e. Belgium, France, Germany, Italy, Luxembourg and the Netherlands. These countries created a costums union that comprised a large number of industries and also set up common agricultural and trade policies (Molle 2006).[30] Although intra-European quotas and tariffs were abolished, many non-tariff barriers continued to exist due to differences in national regulations (e.g. with regard to product standards, licensing procedures, indirect taxation), however, which likely hindered the expansion of trade and specialization. Moreover, at that time the mobility of labour was restricted as different school and university degrees were not easily recognized in all other member states. In the first half of the 1980s the European Commission aimed to complete the integration of product (for both goods and services) and factor (both capital and labour) markets thereby setting an end to the fragmentation of Western European economies; the object was to complete the internal market by 1992 as being laid out in the Single European Act of 1986. As stated in Article 159 EC, the objectives are the following: higher competiveness via speeding up structural change and altering the specialization profile of countries towards high-wage and high-growth industries; easing the exploitation of both economies of scale and scope (also by fostering co-operations among firms). With regards to the free movement of goods and capital, full market integration has been realized whereas the free movement of services and workers has not yet been realized even though a free internal labour market via the harmonization of social security, residence permits, diploma recognition, working as well as health and safety conditions has been achieved  (Commission of European Communities 1997). Thus the level of both permanent and temporary migration has constantly remained at three percent of the European labour force since the 1970s and is behind expectations (Molle 2006). This low level of mobility (as has been already described in chapter 2) implies that workers have not yet taken full advantage of the benefits of free movement – i.e. better opportunities to cap-

---

30  At the same time the European Free Trade Association (EFTA) was established as an alternative to the EEC and included some later EEC member countries such as Denmark, United Kingdom (both left EFTA to join EEC in 1973), Portugal (which became a member of EEC in 1986) as well as Austria, Finland and Sweden (which are members of EEC since 1995).

italize special qualifications via higher wages –nor have employers been able to optimize the choice of factor-input-mix since national segmented labour markets still support a mis-match between the skills required by expanding industries and the skills obtained by employees in declining industries. Thus structural change should be slower than theory predicts and the degree to which specialization patterns of countries have changed should have remained low. The adoption of a common currency in 1999 as well as the enlargement of the European Union into Central and Eastern Countries in 2004 has led to a further removal of institutional and non-tariff barriers within Europe and unified former segmented national markets (for a more comprehensive historical overview see Watts 2008). Above all, the introduction of the Euro should further deepen the production market integration since exchange rate uncertainties no longer hinder exports. Moreover, the wage differentials between Western and Eastern European countries has put many labour-intensive industries under pressure, in some industries shifts of production sites were remarkable.

European integration has led to a remarkable increase in trade flows among the European countries as expected by the European Commission. Krugman (1991a and 1991b) however pointed out, that it is quite likely that economic integration does foster inter-industry trade implying also the specialization of countries. Thus, trade specialization could be the starting point for further economic specialization such that countries take more benefit of their comparative advantages. The EC (1993) on the other hand believed that increased integration would only increase intra-industry trade, leading to less specialization, and contribute to the convergence of economies, with asymmetric shocks occurring less frequently.

The majority of factors described above imply that the advantages and disadvantages of countries become more evident, giving firms more incentives to relocate production to more favourable destinations implying increased specialization on the one hand and leading to changes in the demand patterns of costumers for domestic and foreign goods on the other hand. Given these developments, we aim to shed light on the development of industry structures in Western Europe. In particular the question is whether lagging countries were able to change their economic structures such that structural convergence in the sense of catch-up to the technologically leading countries in Western Europe was attained leading to de-concentration processes. Divergence of production structures between countries is of great relevance, as low labour mobility is not able to offset the negative effects of asymmetric shocks (OECD 1999). Countries would therefore be more vulnerable to shocks that create divergence in the labour market, with rising unemployment and falling wages in some countries and labour shortages and inflationary pressures in other countries (Braunerjelm et al. 2000).

As a start, we report the results for absolute specialization values over the observation period 1970 to 2005 employing the Hirschman-Herfindahl Index (as being described in section 3.4.1.1). We show the values for the beginning and the end period as well as for 1992, when the internal market was realized in Europe. According to economic theory, decreasing trade barriers should have reinforced the specialization patterns.

*Table 45 Absolute Specialization (HHI) in Western Europe*

| Country | 1970 | 1992 | 2005 |
|---|---|---|---|
| Austria | .0537 | .0611 | .0713 |
| Belgium | .0497 | .0614 | .0803 |
| Denmark | .0584 | .0804 | .0876 |
| Finland | .0562 | .0579 | .0576 |
| France | .0529 | .0643 | .0770 |
| Germany | .0470 | .0534 | .0663 |
| Greece | .0668 | .0679 | .0791 |
| Ireland | .0639 | .0639 | .0691 |
| Italy | .0572 | .0590 | .0608 |
| Netherlands | .0559 | .0708 | .0871 |
| Portugal | .0677 | .0640 | .0697 |
| Spain | .0612 | .0674 | .0680 |
| Sweden | .0575 | .0772 | .0811 |
| UK | .0476 | .0658 | .0806 |

Source: EU Klems database March 2008

Looking at absolute specialization in Table 45, we find that specialization increased in almost all countries over the investigation period. It is only Portugal, which shows de-specialization tendencies until the 1990s and a delayed start of specialization occurring from then onwards. If we look at Finland, there is de-specialization taking place beginning in the 1990s. Last but not least, Ireland is an exception since specialization sets in quite late in the 1990s. It is not the aim of this book to study the origins of these processes in detail. We have to point out, however, that - as has been already stressed in the former chapter - both Finland and Ireland underwent major restructuring processes from the 1990s onwards also implying a change in specialization patterns that are changing in different ways than in other countries of Europe (see a more detailed discussion in Helg et al. 1995, Midelfart-Knarvik 2002, 2003 and Brülhart 2001a).

Since we are interested to what degree the economic structures of European countries deviate from one another, we furthermore investigate the relative specialization patterns of Western European Countries for the period 1970 to 2005 in depth. Particularly we focus on changes that occurred due to transformations in the economic environment following both European and worldwide economic integration. Another aim is to highlight similarities between the economic developments of individual countries by assigning similar countries to clubs. So far, only specialization patterns of individual countries have been studied in depth. Differences between countries have been of major interest, whereas the similarities between countries (in the sense that they can form a club of similar economic structures) have not been fully recognized. Many studies such as the work by Midelfart-Knarvik et al. (2001, 2002, 2003) focus on the heterogeneity of countries from the EU average. Additionally, Midelfart-Knarvik et al. (2001) formed clubs according to the date of entrance to the European Union and found that the six founding countries exhibited lowest degree of specialization. The highest level of specialization was reported for the groups that joined during the 1970s and 1980s. All clubs reported increasing specialization patterns from the 1980s onwards.

# 5.2 Methodological Issues and Data

## 5.2.1 Data

The empirical analysis in this chapter is based on macro data of 14 EU member states (EU 15 without Luxembourg), covering the observation period of 1970-2005. Similar to the preious chapters, data is drawn from the KLEMS database (see Timmer et al. 2007). We thus include 19 manufacturing industries and 15 service industries, according to the NACE classification. Some industries are not included in the analysis: Data for Utilities (Electricity, Gas and Water Supply), Public Administration and Community Services - like public waste disposal or cultural activities - is partly missing or available only at a highly aggregated level. The agricultural sector has been excluded as it would bias the results towards strong convergence in line with the three-sector-hypothesis, since employment in all Western European countries shifted from the agricultural to the manufacturing and services sectors over the investigation period (see Chapter 4). To eliminate this well-known trend, we excluded the entire sector. Again, we rely on employment data, captured in total yearly hours worked by employed persons, which is the most comprehensive and (for our purposes) robust measure of industry shares available for the time horizon of 1970 to 2005.[31]

## 5.2.2 Indices

In the following we will focus on both heterogeneity as well as similarities between Western European Countries. As Baumol (1986) and Barro and Sala-i-Martin (1992) hypothesized that convergence could rather hold within groups of countries that share similar characteristics (Azariadis and Drazen 1990) than across all countries alike, we will analyze this empirically. Thus we will focus on the issue of "club convergence" with respect to the specialization features of Western European economies. Moreover, we are interested whether we find both conditional and unconditional convergence, i.e. convergence across or within clubs. Since Aiginger et al. (1999) showed that factor endowments of European countries converged during the 1980s and 1990s as lagging countries were able to accumulate more capital as they offered higher returns on capital, especially with respect to R&D capital, this could have led to overall economic convergence. For our analysis we use variations of the Krugman Specialization Index as described in section 3.4.2.1. In its original form, this index measures the differences between two countries $A$ and $B$ (Krugman 1991b):

$$K_{A,B} = \sum_{i=1}^{I} | b_i^A - b_i^B |$$

where $b_i^A, b_i^B$ are the employment shares of industry $i$ in country $A$ and $B$, respectively. We use this index for a pair wise comparison of all countries for each year in the observation period. Based on the original Krugman Index of Specialization, $K$, we then generalize the index to more than two countries, summing up the differences of a country's employment shares from the average employment share of a country group $\bar{b_i}$ :

---

31    Total annual hours worked are preferable to the number of employees, which can be biased by national and inter-temporal differences in working hours and the share of part-time workers. A drawback of employment data is a productivity bias: Countries with particularly low productivities in an industry appear more specialized in this industry when focusing on employment data rather than on output data. This could lead to a systematic underestimation of specialization if high productivity and specialization are correlated. To overcome this problem, output-oriented indicators such as value added or exports could be used, but the availability of reliable data on these variables over the entire observation period of 1970 to 2005 is limited due to exchange rate problems; moreover the valuation of services is critical.

$$\hat{K}_A = \sum_{i=1}^{I} |b_i^A - \bar{b}_i|$$

Similarly, we sum up the index values of all countries of a country group with $a$ countries in order to measure the total heterogeneity within this group:

$$\hat{K} = \frac{1}{a} \sum_{\alpha=1}^{a} \sum_{i=1}^{I} |b_i^\alpha - \bar{b}_i|$$

In this case, we divide the index by the number of countries to make the values comparable for varying numbers of countries within the country groups. Comparing these indices over time, we can interpret diminishing values as a sign of, first, convergence of two countries towards each other ($K_{A,B}$), second, of a country towards the country group ($\hat{K}_A$), or third, of the entire country group towards its average ($\hat{K}$). Similarly, increasing values are a sign for divergence within the country group.

In order to analyze which industries are the drivers of convergence or divergence, the index can also be constructed such that it focuses only on one industry $i$. In this case, we sum up the differences between the employment shares of all countries compared to the average employment share in that industry and then weight it by the number of countries.

$$\hat{K}_i = \frac{1}{A} \sum_{a=1}^{A} |b_i^a - \bar{b}_i|$$

Obviously, the differences between countries are likely to be larger for large industries than for small (niche) industries, since we analyze absolute values instead of, for instance, percentages of the average employment share of the industry. Caution is therefore advised when interpreting the values and their development over time, since in many cases decreasing index values might be accompanied by decreasing employment shares (i.e. heterogeneity between countries diminishes over time in an industry, while at the same time the importance of the industry itself declines).

## 5.2.3 Identification of Country Clubs

We contend that European countries are clustered in country groups due to their industry structure. We base our argument on the pair wise Krugman Specialization Indices in 1970, and on whether a further converging trend has appeared until 2005. Thus, we cluster countries which have low $K$ values compared to each other and high $K$ values compared to countries outside the club, so that heterogeneity within the club is minimized, as shown in Table 46. On the upper right of the main diagonal, we plot the values of the pair wise Krugman Specialization Indices in 1970. We can thus interpret the initial values of heterogeneity between two countries. The lower the level, the more similar the economic structures of the two countries with respect to each other were at the beginning of the observation period. On the lower left side of the main diagonal, we plot the relative development of the respective $K$ values, comparing the absolute values of 1970 to 2005. A decline hints towards convergence, whereas a rise is a sign of growing heterogeneity between two countries.

*Table 46: Assigning Countries to Clubs*

|  | AUT | BEL | DK | FIN | FR | GER | GRC | IRL | ITA | NL | PRT | ESP | SWE | UK |
|---|---|---|---|---|---|---|---|---|---|---|---|---|---|---|
| **AUT** | x | 0.318 | 0.327 | 0.331 | 0.292 | 0.280 | 0.375 | 0.375 | 0.337 | 0.352 | 0.352 | 0.280 | 0.373 | 0.301 |
| **BEL** | -0.087 | x | 0.384 | 0.431 | 0.405 | 0.300 | 0.507 | 0.454 | 0.421 | 0.388 | 0.479 | 0.337 | 0.471 | 0.353 |
| **DK** | -0.058 | -0.164 | x | 0.310 | 0.281 | 0.357 | 0.475 | 0.301 | 0.435 | 0.226 | 0.479 | 0.396 | 0.343 | 0.366 |
| **FIN** | 0.142 | -0.004 | 0.251 | x | 0.357 | 0.400 | 0.478 | 0.377 | 0.381 | 0.437 | 0.417 | 0.334 | 0.401 | 0.421 |
| **FR** | -0.231 | -0.451 | 0.000 | 0.077 | x | 0.276 | 0.450 | 0.357 | 0.303 | 0.275 | 0.483 | 0.400 | 0.360 | 0.208 |
| **GER** | -0.308 | -0.091 | -0.140 | -0.073 | -0.376 | x | 0.497 | 0.444 | 0.338 | 0.346 | 0.508 | 0.413 | 0.370 | 0.224 |
| **GRC** | 0.051 | 0.049 | 0.223 | 0.070 | 0.051 | -0.011 | x | 0.481 | 0.419 | 0.511 | 0.421 | 0.364 | 0.645 | 0.498 |
| **IRL** | -0.238 | -0.187 | 0.219 | 0.268 | -0.070 | -0.317 | -0.123 | x | 0.389 | 0.358 | 0.506 | 0.348 | 0.453 | 0.438 |
| **ITA** | -0.161 | 0.074 | 0.094 | -0.164 | 0.276 | 0.078 | -0.117 | 0.161 | x | 0.452 | 0.335 | 0.311 | 0.495 | 0.363 |
| **NL** | -0.241 | -0.410 | 0.240 | 0.070 | -0.347 | -0.209 | 0.049 | 0.063 | -0.045 | x | 0.489 | 0.459 | 0.395 | 0.338 |
| **PRT** | 0.325 | 0.265 | 0.329 | 0.324 | 0.172 | 0.111 | -0.174 | 0.064 | 0.117 | 0.183 | x | 0.352 | 0.622 | 0.590 |
| **ESP** | 0.266 | 0.342 | 0.239 | 0.038 | 0.010 | -0.006 | -0.153 | 0.094 | -0.143 | 0.119 | -0.062 | x | 0.536 | 0.445 |
| **SWE** | -0.019 | -0.151 | -0.411 | -0.157 | -0.027 | -0.091 | 0.046 | 0.034 | 0.053 | -0.012 | 0.131 | -0.047 | x | 0.350 |
| **UK** | -0.219 | -0.303 | -0.053 | -0.020 | -0.104 | 0.075 | -0.033 | -0.378 | 0.135 | -0.367 | -0.013 | -0.056 | 0.197 | x |

Source: EU KLEMS database, March 2008.

Based on Table 46, we identify three clubs – one containing mainly the Central European countries (Austria, Belgium, France, Germany, Ireland, the Netherlands and the UK), a second group consisting of Southern Europe (Greece, Italy, Portugal and Spain) and a third club containing Scandinavian Countries (Denmark, Finland and Sweden).

This classification method is somewhat arbitrary, since we do not use a fixed limit for the $K$ values. Besides, there is not a "natural" number of country clubs, so that alternative patterns would be possible as well. To validate our classification we therefore calculate the index $\hat{K}_A$ of each country $A$ to each of the country clubs we identified, excluding the country from the construction of each club as we do so, in order to avoid a bias towards the club where we allocated the country. The country should be part of the club where $\hat{K}_A$ is lowest.

In Table 47, we display the Krugman Specialization Indices calculated by comparing each country with each club. The lower the value, the higher is the similarity between the country and the club. The minimum values are marked in bold. In most cases, the decision about club affiliation is unambiguous, as both the pair wise comparisons and the comparison of the country with the club return the same result. It can be seen that - with some few exceptions - the classification is identical in 1970 and in 2005. Remarkably, with the exception of Portugal and the UK, all countries converge towards their own club in the period from 1970 to 2005, thus moving closer to the other countries within the same club. There are, however, some exceptions: Austria, Ireland and the Netherlands, which we have all assigned to the Central European club, are more similar to Scandinavia or - in the case of Austria - to South Europe, in 1970. These three countries are characterized by a switch in the club they fit in best as is shown below. A more delicate case is Finland a will be discussed below.

*Table 47: Krugman Indices - Assignment of Countries to Clubs*

|  | 1970 | | | 2005 | | |
|---|---|---|---|---|---|---|
|  | Central Europe | South Europe | North Europe | Central Europe | South Europe | North Europe |
| AUT | .258 | **.256** | .293 | **.182** | .278 | .296 |
| BEL | **.318** | .356 | .396 | **.224** | .437 | .316 |
| DK | .295 | .385 | **.254** | .281 | .464 | **.236** |
| FIN | .352 | .330 | **.323** | .377 | **.328** | .335 |
| FRA | **.201** | .314 | .269 | **.122** | .369 | .263 |
| GER | **.213** | .334 | .320 | **.177** | .365 | .290 |
| GRC | .449 | **.371** | .514 | .473 | **.314** | .582 |
| IRL | .386 | .355 | **.329** | **.289** | .390 | .397 |
| IT | .306 | **.262** | .393 | .361 | **.250** | .430 |
| NL | .298 | .401 | **.284** | **.202** | .452 | .304 |
| PRT | .508 | **.304** | .482 | .565 | **.333** | .627 |
| ESP | .389 | **.277** | .402 | .390 | **.220** | .434 |
| SWE | .336 | .505 | **.319** | .351 | .516 | **.224** |
| UK | **.165** | .380 | .323 | **.202** | .398 | .363 |

Source: EU KLEMS database, March 2008.

Even though we base the decision which club a country belongs to on the pair wise Krugman Specialization Indices calculated for the beginning and the end of the investigation period only, we are aware of the fact that the developments over the whole period are relevant. For this reason we present a more detailed and more elaborate analysis for the countries that switch the club they fit best into in Figure 9 to Figure 11. Thereby we check whether the assignment to a club is rather stable over time even for those countries. As can also be seen from these figures, however, these countries' switch to Central Europe occurred at an early stage of the observation period. For the sake of simplicity, we there-

152

fore decide to add these three countries to Central Europe for the whole observation period. For Finland the situation is more difficult as the country more often switches between being assigned to the North and the South Club. As in the majority of the years under study, Finland is closer to North, we assign it to North. The problem of Finland and Ireland – changing the economic structure from a latecomer to a technological fore-runner or a country that attracts many international investors to locate their headquarters in Ireland, makes it difficult to assign these countries to any club.

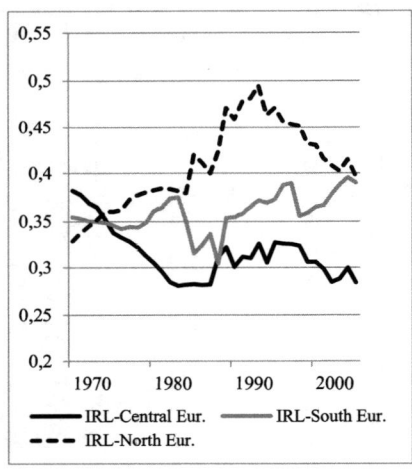

Figure 9:    Club Deviation of Ireland

Source: EU KLEMS database, March 2008.

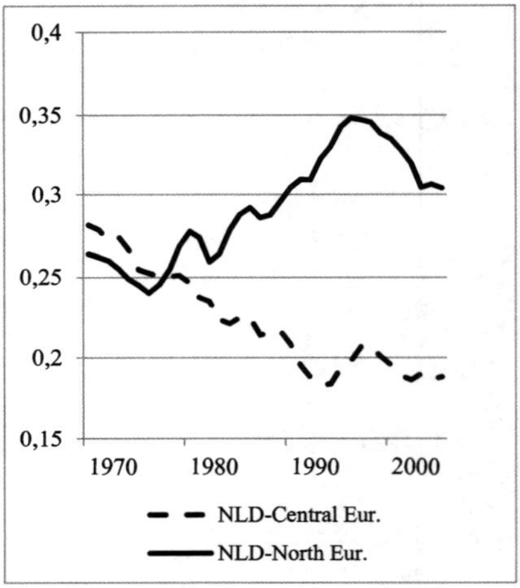

Figure 10:    Club Deviation of the Netherlands

Source: EU KLEMS Database, March 2008.

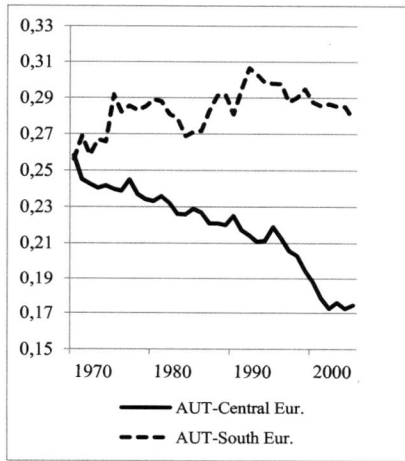
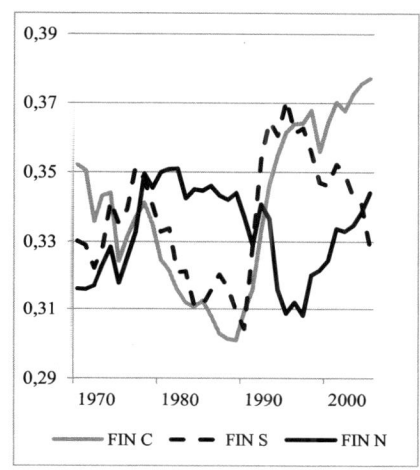

*Figure 11:   Club Deviation of Austria*
Source: EU KLEMS database, March 2008.

*Figure 12:   Club Deviation of Finland*
Source: EU KLEMS Database, March 2008.

# 5.3   Empirical Results

In a next step, we analyze the development of specialization patterns for the three country clubs and compare the differences across clubs as well as within clubs. In order to find out why the clubs developed as they did and which countries and industries were the driving forces of economic development within the clubs, we then focus on the country and industry levels for each club separately.

## 5.3.1  Heterogeneity between and within Country Clubs

From Table 47, we can see that in the majority of cases countries do not reduce heterogeneity towards other clubs over the investigation period from 1970 to 2005. More generally, we portray this phenomenon in Figure 13, which makes clear that the three clubs do not become more similar over time. Thus we do not find pan-European convergence - the heterogeneity of industry structures across European countries remains largely constant over the whole investigation period, or even rises. Quite the contrary, the differences between North, Central, and South Europe even rise slightly over the investigation period. Not surprisingly, the economic structures of the Southern Countries compared to the North Countries are the most diverse, starting from a level of 0.363 and almost steadily increasing to 0.450 in the mid-nineties, before slight convergence trends set in, which most likely were initiated by catching-up processes in lagging South European Countries.

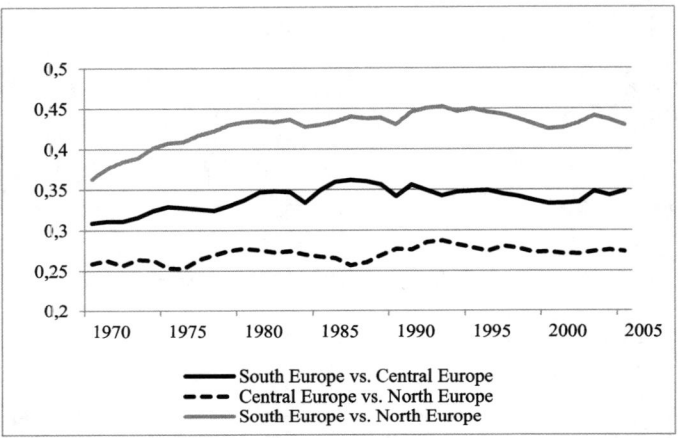

*Figure 13: Heterogeneity between Clubs 1970 – 2005*
Source: EU KLEMS database, March 2008.

Focusing on the heterogeneity of the countries *within* individual clubs instead of the differences between clubs, the picture is quite different: In all clubs the countries became more homogenous over time, as Figure 14 shows. Yet, as the clubs are drifting apart, overall heterogeneity in Europe as a whole (or between Western European Countries in general) has hardly declined since 1970 (see the upper line "Europe" in Figure 14). It also implies that the heterogeneity across all Western European Countries is higher than the heterogeneity within each of the clubs, which comes as no surprise if we postulate that clubs must be characterized by the fact that countries within a club share similar economic structures and in order to have more than one club there must be differences in economic structures as well.

If we look at the heterogeneity within clubs, the lowest initial level of heterogeneity is found for the club North Europe, while the convergence path is steepest for Central Europe which is the most homogenous club at the end of the observation period. Interestingly, both the North and the South club exhibit diverging trends from the 1990s onwards.

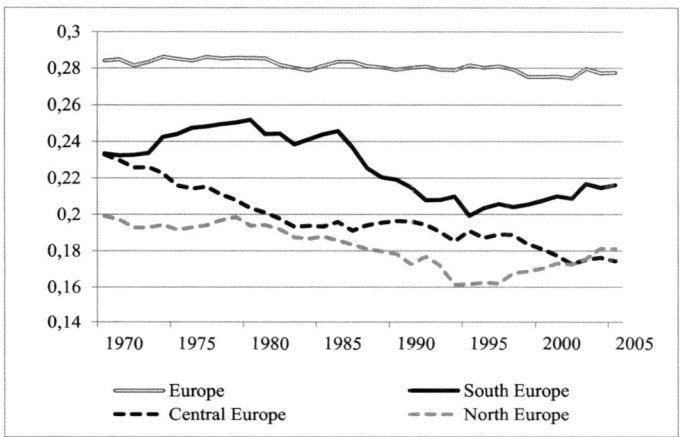

*Figure 14: Heterogeneity within clubs*
Source: EU KLEMS database, March 2008.

## 5.3.2 Specialization Patterns and Structural Change of Country Clubs

The degree to which these three country clubs differ from each other can be seen in detail below, where the employment shares per industry and club, both in 1970 and 2005 are on display. In order to have a reference level, we also show the EU average employment shares.

The largest industries in all clubs - both in 1970 and 2005 - are traditional low and medium low-tech manufacturing industries as well as low-skill and social branches. For the manufacturing sector this manifests itself in high employment shares in Food, Textiles, Machinery and Metal Fabrication; the service sector is dominated by industries such as Retail Trade, Transport, Wholesale Trade, Education and Health & Social Work. There are patterns of structural change occurring, though: Employment has decreased in all manufacturing industries, in particular in low-technology industries and there above all in the production of Textiles. At the same time, tertiarization took place; the fastest growing industry by far has been Business-related Activities. These patterns can be found in all clubs to a certain degree, although some degree of specialization of the clubs relative to the European average values remains.

*Table 48: Employment in European Clubs*

|  | 1970 | | | 2005 | | |
|---|---|---|---|---|---|---|
|  | Central | South | North | Central | South | North |
| FBT | .047 | **.052** | .048 | .029 | **.031** | .024 |
| Textiles | .054 | **.085** | .036 | .007 | **.029** | .004 |
| Leather | .008 | **.018** | .005 | .001 | **.008** | .001 |
| Wood | .011 | .022 | **.025** | .006 | .010 | **.012** |
| Pulp & Paper | .012 | .007 | **.022** | .005 | .004 | **.011** |
| Printing & Publishing | .020 | .014 | **.027** | .014 | .011 | **.015** |
| Coke | **.003** | .003 | .001 | .001 | **.001** | .001 |
| Chemicals | **.025** | .021 | .014 | **.012** | .010 | .012 |
| Rubber & Plastics | **.014** | .010 | .012 | **.011** | .009 | .009 |
| Mineral Products | .021 | **.028** | .018 | .008 | **.014** | .007 |
| Basic Metals | **.025** | .015 | .019 | .007 | .007 | **.009** |
| Fabricated Metal | **.043** | .042 | .027 | .023 | **.031** | .025 |
| Machinery | **.051** | .030 | .044 | .023 | .023 | **.033** |
| Accounting & Computing Machines | **.002** | .002 | .002 | **.002** | .001 | .001 |
| Electrical Engineering | **.020** | .014 | .012 | **.010** | .008 | .008 |
| Communication Equipment | **.012** | .008 | .009 | .005 | .004 | **.010** |
| Precision Instruments | **.015** | .006 | .007 | **.008** | .004 | .007 |
| Motor Vehicles | **.025** | .016 | .016 | **.015** | .009 | .014 |
| Transport Equipment | **.013** | .012 | .013 | .006 | .005 | **.006** |
| Recycling | .019 | **.024** | .017 | .011 | **.017** | .012 |
| Motor Vehicles & Fuel | .033 | .034 | **.036** | .032 | **.034** | .027 |
| Wholesale Trade | .063 | .059 | **.072** | .062 | .064 | **.071** |
| Retail Trade | .106 | **.140** | .107 | .102 | **.125** | .080 |
| Hotels & Restaurants | .041 | **.070** | .040 | .058 | **.094** | .039 |
| Transport | .068 | .072 | **.077** | .063 | .068 | **.072** |
| Post & Telecommunication | **.024** | .018 | .022 | .019 | .016 | **.021** |
| Financial Intermediation | **.032** | .021 | .024 | **.045** | .028 | .027 |
| Real Estate | .007 | .005 | **.012** | .016 | .008 | **.021** |
| Renting of Machinery | **.003** | .001 | .001 | **.005** | .003 | .004 |
| IT-related Activities | **.005** | .003 | .004 | .024 | .023 | **.026** |

|  | 1970 | | | 2005 | | |
|---|---|---|---|---|---|---|
|  | Central | South | North | Central | South | North |
| R&D | **.004** | .001 | .003 | .007 | .002 | **.010** |
| Business Activities | **.050** | .024 | .032 | **.147** | .096 | .090 |
| Education | .051 | .052 | **.077** | .076 | .072 | **.105** |
| Health & Social Work | .067 | .049 | **.103** | .131 | .068 | **.169** |
| Domestic Services | .007 | **.023** | .014 | .013 | **.061** | .018 |

Source: EU Klems database, March 2009

The employment structures of the clubs, as shown in Table 48, show interesting patterns: South European countries are characterized by the most pronounced specialization in low-tech and low-skill industries of all three clubs, especially comparative advantages prevail in Textiles, Leather and Hotels & Restaurants. This is true for the whole investigation period. Even though employment rates in these low-tech industries decreased remarkably – especially the employment share in textiles dropped from 3.5 to 2.9 per cent – comparative advantages due to lower wage costs still seem to prevail. At the same time, the low employment level of South Europe in the health & social work industry is notable, whereas low-wage services are the most prominent with domestic services even almost tripling in size.

In contrast, North European countries exhibit a strong social sector (i.e. high employment shares in Education and Health & Social Work) and even increase their lead over time. Notable as well is the specialization in the wood and paper industries in the 1970s due to comparative advantages in natural resources that continued over time even though employment levels in the respective industries declined by 50 per cent. Thus comparative advantages and specialization patterns seem to be rather sticky over time even for countries that operate close to the production possibility frontier and have undergone remarkable technological change. In line with the technological upgrade of employment structures in North European Countries, employment shares dropped not only in the wood and paper production but in all major low-tech and low-skill industries, however. The employment shares in medium-high and high-tech industries remained largely stable. In the service sector employment shares in high-skill industries such as Education, R&D or IT-related activities rose significantly.

Specialization patterns of the Central European club are less pronounced than in the other two clubs. It seems that Central European countries have had competitive advantages in traditional medium- and high-tech industries such as Electrical Engineering and Machinery. Remarkably, the structural change from manufacturing towards the service sector is stronger than for the other clubs: This is above all driven by increasing specialization in IT-related and business-related services like Renting of Machinery or R&D, as well as by a higher level of specialization in Financial Intermediation and de-specialization in low-tech and medium-low tech industries such as Textiles. Caused by tertiarization as well as by catch-up processes, the differences between the clubs are diminishing over time in most manufacturing industries - above all in low-tech industries. Exceptions to this tendency are found in two emerging industries: Divergence occurs in the office and accounting industry due to the strong specialization of Ireland, and in the communication equipment industry due to the specialization of Finland. An interesting development is also found for the chemical industry, where employment drops by more than fifty per cent both in Central and South Europe, but with different consequences: whereas in Central Europe a - over-proportional - high employment share shifts towards EU average levels, em-ployment in South Europe was already below average in 1970 and has declined even further. Similarly, employment in Machinery and Motor Vehicles decreas-es significantly, with the strongest decline in Central Europe which might be giving up its specialization in these industries. However, caution is advised when interpreting these shifts, as the developments may be caused also by au-tomation and rationalization processes or by outsourcing trends (leading to a shift from e.g. Machinery to Engineering Services). In this respect, the rise of Chinese exports has had an enormous impact on the textile industry in Western Europe, where Portugal and Italy have been facing difficulties in keeping up with the increasing low-wage competition from South Asian countries (European Commission 1993).

Regarding the service industries, the three clubs drifted apart from one an-other in particular in the social sector (i.e. with regard to Education, Health and Social Work) as well as in Hotels and Restaurants. The former has been growing in all clubs, but at different speeds. Remarkably, the growth rate in North Euro-pean countries - which were already characterized by a large social sector in 1970 -was the highest, implying structural divergence across the clubs. This is not surprising since the goals of public policy are heterogeneous across the clubs. A similar picture arises in the hotels and restaurants industry, where South European countries - which already had a high share of employment in this in-dustry in 1970 - grew most quickly, whereas Central Europe proved unable to catch up to the leading countries. Surprisingly, in South Europe employment levels of domestic workers are high from 1970 onwards, growing steadily over time. This trend seems to parallel the Central and North European growth in the social sector, so that it might be due to institutional differences in the sense that in South Europe social services are taken over by domestic workers.

Summarizing the effects from above by assigning industries to industry classes, we obtain the following picture as shown in Table 49.

*Table 49: Employment Shares by Industry Characteristics*

| Industry characteristic | Central Europe 1970 | Central Europe 2005 | South Europe 1970 | South Europe 2005 | North Europe 1970 | North Europe 2005 |
|---|---|---|---|---|---|---|
| Low tech | .152 | .061 | .198 | .092 | .163 | .067 |
| Med-low tech | .089 | .038 | .085 | .053 | .064 | .042 |
| Med-high tech | .126 | .067 | .094 | .065 | .104 | .074 |
| High tech | .074 | .036 | .051 | .028 | .043 | .038 |
| Low skill | .324 | .346 | .404 | .455 | .3589 | .328 |
| High skill | .236 | .453 | .169 | .308 | .267 | .452 |

Source: EU Klems database, March 2009

South Europe has the highest level of low-tech employment over the whole investigation period, even though it is declining in all clubs. Central Europe was the leader in medium-low tech industries in 1970 but employment fell by more than 50 per cent which is equivalent to the lowest employment share of all clubs in that category in 2005. Similar developments can be reported for the medium-high tech and the high-tech industries. Employment in low-tech industries declined on average by 2.1 per cent annually in South Europe, by 2.4 per cent in North Europe and even by 2.5 per cent in Central Europe, where low-tech industries in 2005 accounted for the lowest level compared to the other clubs. It is above all remarkable that employment in medium low tech industries in Central Europe declined twice as much as in the other two clubs over the investigation period, i.e. a fall of 2.4 per cent per annum compared to a decline of 1.2 per cent in the other two clubs. There is also wide variation in the decline of employment levels – whereas almost two per cent employment is lost in Central Europe and 1.7 per cent in South Europe, the loss in North Europe is only 0.3 per cent per annum. The highest rate of employment creation is in Central Europe for high-skill jobs. The employment levels of Central and North Europe have become more similar for all industry groups over time, implying overall convergence between these two clubs.

Compared to the European average, South European countries were characterized by strong specialization in the production of low-tech and low-skill industries over the whole investigation period. This becomes especially visible if we compare the employment shares of Textiles, Leather, Retail Trade, Transport and Hotels & Restaurants with the other clubs or with the Western European average. At the same time, the persisting backwardness of South Europe relative to the other two clubs in the health & social work industry is notable. Additionally, this club lacks competitiveness in high-tech and high-wage industries such as Chemicals, Electrical Engineering and Transport Equipment, where employment drops by more than 50 per cent over the investigation period.

In contrast, Scandinavian countries exhibit a strong social sector (i.e. high employment shares in Education and Health and Social Work) from 1970 onwards and can even increase the lead in these industries compared to the other two clubs. Thus the importance of the social welfare state has even increased over the course of time, implying an increase in both absolute and relative specialization in Health and Social Work. Moreover, we find relative specialization in more traditional industries such as the wood and paper industries at the beginning of the observation period due to comparative advantages in natural resources. In line with the technological upgrade of North European Countries, the specialization in these industries has not been kept up since employment in all major low-tech and low-wage industries has fallen by almost 50 per cent over the investigation period. The employment shares in medium-high and high-tech industries in general remained largely stable. In the service sector a similar picture arises: Whereas North European countries once were heavily specialized in Retail Trade, this club managed to upgrade economic structures and so these countries are now characterized by over proportional employment shares in high-skill industries such as Education or IT-related activities.

In contrast to the two clubs described above, the Central European club is not as deeply specialized in some few industries only. In general, employment levels in low-tech industries were already low in 1970 and continued to decrease further. It seems that Central European countries have had no competitive advantages in this kind of industries, while employment in traditional medium- and high-tech industries such as Electrical Engineering and Machinery was high at the beginning of the investigation period. The structural change from manufacturing towards the service sector is the strongest for this club: while in 1970 the manufacturing sector was largest in Central Europe with the service sector being the smallest, specialization patterns changed so much that in 2005 Central Europe has the smallest manufacturing and the largest service sector of all three clubs. This is above all driven by increasing specialization in IT-related and Business-related Services like Renting of Machinery or R&D, as well as by a higher level of specialization in Financial Intermediation. It has to be noted that the developments in this club are mainly driven by the economic structures of the big countries belonging to it, i.e. Germany, France and the UK.

Taking these findings together, we can say that the three clubs follow similar paths of structural change. They are characterized by an increasing importance of the service sector – in particular high-skill service industries and industries associated with the welfare state show rising employment shares– while manufacturing industries – in particular low-tech industries – are shrinking. The speed of this process however differs between the clubs, such that South Europe has not been able to catch up to the other European regions with respect to emerging, technology-intensive manufacturing industries and high-skill service industries.

### 5.3.3 Convergence and Divergence within Central Europe

As has been described above, the Central European club is characterized by a strong trend of within-club convergence over the investigation period, contradicting the results of pair wise comparisons in Midelfart-Knarvik et al. (2002). The reason for the differences in results could be due to the fact that the authors only report pair wise Krugman Specialization Indices for two periods in time (i.e. 1980-1983 and 1994-1997) and report the heterogeneity of individual countries in comparison to the large economies of Germany, France and the UK only, thus suppressing important information regarding the development of economic structures.

We can elaborate on our results in more detail, presenting the development of the pair wise Krugman Specialization Indices calculating the differences between the employment shares of a given country and the average employment shares of the club it belongs to. The results are displayed in Figure 15. As can be seen there, nearly all Central European countries converged towards the club average over the course of time. An exception is the UK which was close to the Central European average from the beginning. Taking a closer look, we can even identify two sub-clubs for 1970: there are the big players France, Germany and the UK, which tend to be relatively less specialized than the other group, consisting of the smaller countries Austria, Belgium and the Netherlands. We could attribute this either to a higher degree of specialization of smaller countries compared to larger countries (see Chapter 2), or it could be a result of a mere calculation effect, where larger countries obtain more weight in the club-average and thus should be closer to the average than smaller countries, which get less weight in the club average.

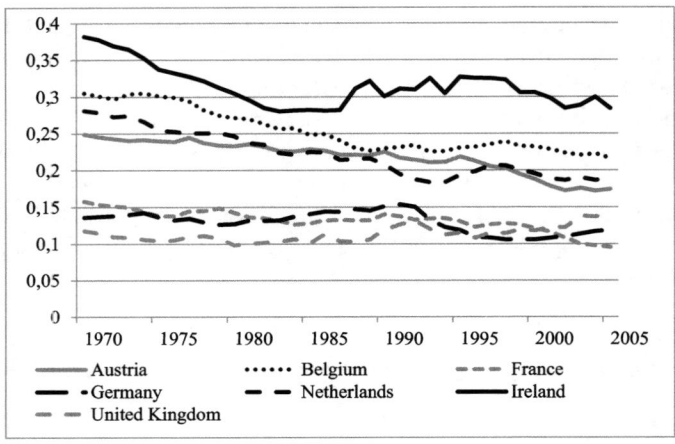

*Figure 15: Heterogeneity of Central European Countries*
Source: EU KLEMS database, March 2008.

We find a convergence trend between these two sub-clubs starting at the beginning of the 1990s such that until 2005 the differences between the small and big countries have largely vanished. This suggests that economic integration may have different effects on the two groups: While relative specialization levels of small countries were reduced, heterogeneity of the larger countries was low and remained roughly unchanged. Obviously, Ireland deviates from both sub-clubs. However, it is found to be the most converging country – which is in line with the literature about the Irish catch-up process (Midelfart-Knarvik et al. 2003) – followed by strong relative de-specialization patterns in Belgium and the Netherlands. Since we are interested in the reasons for structural heterogeneity, we take a closer look at the differences at the industry level and how they evolve for each country over time in Table 50.

*Table 50: Deviation from Central Club by Industry Characteristic*

|  | Low tech 1970 | Low tech 2005 | Med-low tech 1970 | Med-low tech 2005 | Med-high tech 1970 | Med-high tech 2005 | High tech 1970 | High tech 2005 | Low skill 1970 | Low skill 2005 | High skill 1970 | High skill 2005 |
|---|---|---|---|---|---|---|---|---|---|---|---|---|
| AUT | .029 | .017 | .021 | .008 | .055 | .018 | .029 | .012 | .067 | .067 | .048 | .052 |
| BEL | .029 | .010 | .040 | .008 | .052 | .018 | .028 | .021 | .082 | .091 | .075 | .068 |
| FR | .013 | .008 | .013 | .004 | .014 | .010 | .025 | .009 | .044 | .027 | .050 | .036 |
| GER | .014 | .008 | .005 | .009 | .031 | .029 | .017 | .015 | .028 | .015 | .042 | .043 |

| | Low tech 1970 | Low tech 2005 | Med-low tech 1970 | Med-low tech 2005 | Med-high tech 1970 | Med-high tech 2005 | High tech 1970 | High tech 2005 | Low skill 1970 | Low skill 2005 | High skill 1970 | High skill 2005 |
|---|---|---|---|---|---|---|---|---|---|---|---|---|
| IRL | .072 | .023 | .045 | .017 | .058 | .026 | .023 | .037 | .094 | .073 | .090 | .108 |
| NL | .052 | .014 | .031 | .009 | .052 | .030 | .026 | .011 | .058 | .057 | .063 | .068 |
| UK | .020 | .012 | .012 | .010 | .029 | .017 | .002 | .009 | .031 | .035 | .023 | .059 |

Source: EU KLEMS database, March 2008.

The figures show that with regard to low-tech and medium-high tech industries, all countries in this club are converging. In medium-low tech industries, all countries but Germany are converging which is due to the fact that almost all countries are de-specializing whereas Germany prolongs its lead in certain industries. In high-tech industries, all countries but Ireland are converging. This is mainly due to the structural upgrade of Ireland since the 1990s and its ability to attract multinational firms to relocate their headquarters to Dublin. For service industries, the results are mixed – whereas in the manufacturing industries, there is an overall trend towards convergence – apart from few exceptions, the developments in the service sector are more complex with a lot of deviation occurring especially in the high skill industries.

From Table 51 we gain more evidence that specialization patterns tend to be sticky over time: despite the convergence tendencies in many industries, the most specialized countries - i.e. the countries with comparative advantages – remain in their leading role over the whole period of time. This is, for instance Austria for Wood, Germany for Pulp & Paper, Electrical Apparatus and Machinery, Ireland for Accounting & Computing Machines and Food, and Belgium in the chemical industry and in metal production. Path-dependency thus seems to occur mainly in mature industries and in industries with large economies of scale, whereas in industries that are characterized by rapid technological progress (such as Communications Equipment, Precision Instruments or Rubber & Plastics), specialization patterns are likely to be unstable over time since new competitors can easily gain ground, thus shifting employment opportunities from one country to another. In the service sector, we find stickiness of one-country-specialization patterns as well, e.g. for Belgium in Post & Telecommunication, for France in R&D and for the UK in Renting of Machinery. In these cases, institutional and legal differences between the countries may play an important role by leading to the outsourcing of R&D or the Renting of Machinery to other countries.

Turning to the question of which industries were the drivers of convergence, we have to focus on heterogeneity within the Central European club for each industry separately. From Table 51 it can be seen that the main drivers of convergence are the low-tech industries, in particular the production of food, textiles and basic metals. Interestingly, Machinery also exhibits a high degree of convergence, which is a remarkable parallel with our finding that Central Europe de-specializes in this industry. In contrast, divergence occurs only in service industries, mainly in high-skill areas like Business-related Services. Interestingly, employment in Hotels & Restaurants also diverges, which could be due to the fact that people tend to undertake more international journeys today than in 1970. Back then, people tended to spend more holidays in their home and in neighbouring countries whereas nowadays (also due to declining transport costs) countries such as Austria benefit and specialize in tourism (Janger and Wagner 2004).

Table 51: Industry-specific Heterogeneity in Central Europe ($\hat{K}_i$)

|  | 1970 | 2005 | $\Delta\hat{K}_i$ | Development relative to 1970 |
|---|---|---|---|---|
| FBT | .078 | .037 | -.041 | -.530 |
| Textiles | .068 | .013 | -.055 | -.812 |
| Leather/Footwear | .022 | .003 | -.019 | -.848 |
| Wood | .022 | .015 | -.007 | -.310 |
| Pulp & Paper | .013 | .007 | -.006 | -.465 |
| Printing & Publishing | .026 | .017 | -.010 | -.365 |
| Coke | .009 | .003 | -.006 | -.670 |
| Chemicals | .034 | .037 | .003 | .084 |
| Rubber & Plastics | .019 | .015 | -.004 | -.199 |
| Mineral Products | .030 | .015 | -.016 | -.518 |
| Basic Metals | .087 | .024 | -.063 | -.720 |
| Fabricated Metal | .049 | .026 | -.023 | -.464 |
| Machinery | .128 | .058 | -.071 | -.551 |
| Accounting & Computing Machines | .021 | .016 | -.005 | -.232 |
| Electrical Engineering | .048 | .025 | -.023 | -.475 |
| Communication Equipment | .021 | .011 | -.010 | -.462 |
| Precision Instruments | .027 | .027 | .000 | -.014 |
| Motor Vehicles | .064 | .048 | -.016 | -.249 |

| | 1970 | 2005 | $\Delta \hat{K}_i$ | Development relative to 1970 |
|---|---|---|---|---|
| Transport Equipment | .037 | .010 | -.027 | -.736 |
| Recycling | .034 | .015 | -.019 | -.551 |
| Motor Vehicles & Fuel | .021 | .024 | .003 | .163 |
| Wholesale Trade | .066 | .071 | .005 | .069 |
| Retail Trade | .087 | .049 | -.038 | -.437 |
| Hotels & Restaurants | .100 | .117 | .017 | .170 |
| Transport | .030 | .031 | .001 | .019 |
| Post & Telecommunication | .033 | .033 | .000 | -.004 |
| Financial Intermediation | .030 | .038 | .008 | .272 |
| Real Estate | .018 | .019 | .002 | .093 |
| Renting of Machinery | .011 | .012 | .001 | .053 |
| IT-related Activities | .015 | .027 | .012 | .825 |
| R&D | .017 | .021 | .004 | .224 |
| Business Activities | .103 | .182 | .078 | .759 |
| Education | .065 | .053 | -.012 | -.187 |
| Health & Social Work | .114 | .069 | -.045 | -.396 |
| Domestic Services | .082 | .053 | -.029 | -.354 |

Source: EU KLEMS database, March 2008.

For some industries with remarkable changes in specialization patterns, we can generally distinguish between two groups of developments: Either the development is driven by Ireland, or by the largest economy in this club, i.e. Germany. Regarding the first group, the catch-up and structural upgrade of the Irish economy over the whole investigation period has strongly shaped major developments. Whereas in 1970 Ireland was a country characterized by low labour productivity and a strong relative specialization in low-tech and low-wage industries such as the food industry, by 2005 it had profited dramatically from European Integration, which attracted large amounts of foreign direct investment by multinationals. Turning to the industries in detail, we see that even though Ireland remained the single most specialized country in Food, a strong trend of de-specialization is notable. This is consistent with the results obtained in section 4.5.5 (see Table 40). Concentrating on Central European Countries only, the effect is even larger than reported for the whole sample that contains Greece and Italy; two countries that were far more relatively specialized in Food than any other Central European Country. The Netherlands and the UK turned from countries producing food into import-dependent countries as employment figures dropped significantly (Aiginger 2000).

Taking one more look at Ireland,it is worth noting that the country that once was known as the poorhouse of the European Community benefited heavily from structural funding for lagging regions. These huge investments helped to transform the country from being heavily specialized in the production of food to one of the fastest growing countries, characterized by over proportional employment shares in fast growing, high-tech industries such as Accounting & Computing Machines or Communications Equipment. This development can be attributed to Ireland's success in attracting foreign firms in this field. The structural turnaround was strongly influenced by Ireland's industrial policy, which promoted the opening of many (US-American) subsidiary firms of international headquarters in these industries such as Intel, Yahoo, Microsoft, HP, Apple, Google, or Amazon.com.

Ireland was characterized by a strong specialization in Accounting and Computing Machines already in the 1970s. As Since other countries could not catch-up, the one-country specialization of Ireland remained a fairly stable pattern in that industry until Ireland lost considerable employment beginning in the late 1990s, leading to one-country convergence (see the explanation in section 4.5.3 or 4.5.5). It is notable, that there is no other industry in which heterogeneity is as large and in which no other country had the chance to catch-up. As has already been laid out, we have to be careful in interpreting this result, since it is not merely the competitiveness of Irish workers or Irish firms that are responsible for that development. It is mainly foreign firms driving the process, which invested in Ireland due to a favourable tax regime.

The development in Communications Equipment is different from the former industries since Ireland's one-country specialization only set in at a very late stage of the observation period, i.e. in the mid-1990s. Earlier than that, Ireland had for a long time been the country characterized by the lowest employment shares in Communications Equipment of all Central European countries.

Thus, it is not initial advantages that lead to this path-dependent result; on the contrary, Belgium and the Netherlands, which were the relatively most specialized countries, experienced massive losses in employment shares over the course of time. It is again the strategy of Ireland's (and to a certain degree the UK's) industrial policy to attract foreign firms – but it seems that Ireland was the most successful in attracting foreign capital in this particular industry (Koski et al. 2002).

We now turn to the group of industries in which development is mainly driven by the persisting strong position of Germany. This is the case for Machinery, Electrical Engineering and Motor Vehicles, which all belong to the group of medium-high or high tech industries. In both Machinery and Electrical Engineering, Germany is characterized by a strong lead in the 1970s. Even though we have to recognize a steady decline of the employment shares since the 1970s, leading to a remarkable convergence trend in this industry, Germany remains the single most important countries in producing these goods in our country sample.

As such, this is not only a sign of a dissipating competitive advantage of Germany but a sign of structural change. Apart from Austria all countries in the sample have moved out of Machinery, which comes as no surprise due to the shift from an industrial to a service society occurring in all advanced economies, decreasing the need for new machinery in the traditional sense.

The production of motor vehicles is scale-intensive (Pratten 1988), thus employment share should over proportionally be found in large and central places. This is true for the beginning of the observation period, when France, Germany and the UK had the largest employment shares. At the same time, small, non-integrated countries such as Austria and Ireland had small employment shares in line with the results of Brülhart (1998b). From the 1980s onwards, a different picture arises, since employment levels in France and the UK decreased dramatically. Germany has always had a strong tradition in the production of Motor Vehicles. Thus, while other countries already specialized out of Motor Vehicles, employment has kept constant in Germany (Aiginger 2000). On the contrary, there is almost a complete collapse visible in that industry in the UK. Tylecote and Vertova (2007) attribute this to the superior system of production of Germany and the US that was much more inspired by the fordist production than the UK model. The development of Austria is also noteworthy, since the need of economies of scale would imply that little countries have competitive disadvantages compared to larger countries. The employment share in Motor Vehicles increased remarkably in Austria however, especially from the early 1990s onwards. This is due to the success of Austrian's proactive cluster policy for car component suppliers.

Regarding the service sector, remarkable patterns are found for Retail Trade, Hotels & Restaurants and Financial Intermediation. In many cases, Ireland is also found to be the single most important country driving convergence process within Central European service industries. This is for instance true for Retail Trade, where the change in employment patterns in Ireland is driving the convergence process.

The tremendous rise in foreign investment has already been identified as a major contributor to the structural catch-up and high economic growth rates in Ireland since the 1980s. Along with attracting foreign firms that invest in Ireland, we see employment in Financial Intermediation more than tripling over the investigation period. Especially, establishing the Single Market triggered increases in FDI flows as well as the economic boom in the US ensured abundance of US capital outflow (Dunning 1997 a, 1997b). The low degree of financial regulation combined with a favorable tax system for international investors and multinational firms attracted many foreign banks and made employment rise from the lowest figures in the sample to the highest employment shares by the beginning of the 1990s. The development is even more remarkable if we compare the development to other countries. Even though the Single Market Program benefited all countries, we even identify employment decreases in all countries but Ireland from the early 1990s onwards. On the one hand, this is due to the demand of international investors for the Irish market, but on the other hand the growing demand of the Irish population for loans to finance their houses – an effect that should not be underestimated. This kind of specialization proved to be successful during the last decade, but was one of the reasons why Ireland was hit so hard by the economic crisis in 2008.

To summarize the structural development in Central Europe, the convergence trend of Ireland is outstanding. This comes as no surprise, however, since it was the single most deviating country at the beginning of the period, which implies a larger catch-up potential. At the same time, the development is astonishing since Ireland could also have remained a traditional cohesion country such as Greece or Portugal, or it could have converged more towards the Scandinavian countries, which was the club Ireland was closest to in 1970. Several studies highlighted the turnaround of Ireland from Europe's poorhouse to the "Celtic Tiger" (Sweeney 1998), attributing the high growth rates to a favourable industrial policy and the effects of EU structural spending. It must be noted however, that only at first glance does Ireland seem to be so heavily specialized in skill- and research-intensive industries. In economic reality, however, it is often the case that the major part of employment in Ireland in these industries carries out non-research intensive tasks. The proper high-tech activities and work on research and development is mostly carried out in multinational firms' home countries, i.e. above all in the US. Nevertheless, Ireland – both its economic structure and its economic growth – doubtlessly benefited from international investments.

Turning to the other countries of Central Europe, the convergence of larger and smaller countries is remarkable. This shows that fears that economic integration could favour larger countries and maks smaller countries worse off is unwarranted for the Central European case. All in all, we also find "stickiness" of industry structures: Only in rare cases does industrial leadership change from one country to another. However, all countries are characterized by structural change which affects them in similar ways, so that persisting specialization patterns in manufacturing industries are reduced. which is found to be the main driver of Central European convergence.

## 5.3.4 Convergence and Divergence within South Europe

In contrast to the clear findings for the Central European club, we only find diminishing indices for Greece and Spain. Portugal seems to diverge even more from the average - in particular in the first half of the observation period, before a period of convergence sets in in the late 1980s until the mid-1990s (see Figure 16). From the mid-1990s onwards, the picture changes: the convergence trends of Greece, Spain and Portugal vanish, while Italy starts diverging from the other countries. Taken together, the Club-Krugman is growing from the mid-1990s on (see Figure 13), caused by the development of Italy. We will argue below that these patterns can be understood as catch-up processes of Portugal and Greece, while Italy is taking the technological lead. In general, it can be said that Italy and Spain are specialized in medium-technology and more skill-intensive industries than Greece and Portugal, which supports the results obtained by Midelfart-Knarvik et al. (2002).

*Table 52: Employment Shares in South Europe (technology classes)*

| | Low tech 1970 | Low tech 2005 | Med-low tech 1970 | Med-low tech 2005 | Med-high tech 1970 | Med-high tech 2005 | High tech 1970 | High tech 2005 | Low skill 1970 | Low skill 2005 | High skill 1970 | High skill 2005 |
|-----|------|------|------|------|------|------|------|------|------|------|------|------|
| GRC | .065 | .033 | .024 | .018 | .043 | .029 | .025 | .013 | .139 | .149 | .048 | .046 |
| ITA | .025 | .009 | .014 | .007 | .013 | .012 | .013 | .006 | .039 | .051 | .026 | .041 |
| PRT | .036 | .058 | .025 | .015 | .031 | .020 | .021 | .009 | .124 | .127 | .029 | .073 |
| ESP | .047 | .019 | .021 | .005 | .011 | .013 | .011 | .007 | .065 | .049 | .038 | .054 |

Source: EU KLEMS database, March 2008.

Looking at Table 52, we see that Greece was highly dependent on low-tech employment in the 1970s – almost two-third of overall jobs was to be found in these industries. Even though the level of employment in low-tech industries decreased, still one third of all manufacturing jobs were still in low-tech – and most often – low-wage industries in 2005. Portugal on the other hand is the only country in the South European club, where low-tech employment rose during the observation period up from one third to almost 60 per cent of all employment in the manufacturing sector. The level of high-tech employment remains low throughout the whole investigation period for all four countries. On the contrary, employment shares in high-tech industries declined in all countries and are on average below 0.10. Regarding low- and high-skill employment, Portugal could increase employment above all in high-skill industries; the same is to some extent also true for Italy and Spain whereas Greece was not able to offer many more jobs in high-skill industries.

The overall picture of within-club convergence can be seen in Figure 16: The large countries Italy and Spain are closest to the club over the whole investigation period. Be aware that this can be also due to the fact that large countries get higher weights in the calculation of the club employment shares for every industry. It is remarkable, however, that the economic structure of Portugal becomes more diverse from the club until the 1980s, only then the specialization patterns become closer to that of the whole club. Yet, starting in the early 1990s, small divergence trends start again. For Greece, the development is similar to that of Portugal. These developments can be explained by delayed structural catch-up in the 1980s, yet from the 1990s onwards, European integration and globalization processes put both Greece and Portugal under pressure.

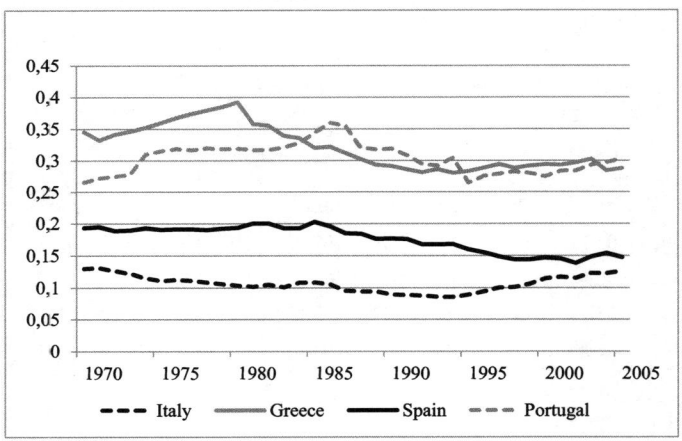

*Figure 16: Heterogeneity of Southern European Countries*
Source: EU KLEMS database, March 2008.

As in the Central European club, the manufacturing industries are converging, yet with two exceptions: Heterogeneity in the leather industry remains constant over time and it has even grown slightly in the rubber & plastics production as we can see from Table 53.

Table 53: Industry-Specific Heterogeneity in Southern Europe ($\hat{K}_i$)

|  | 1970 | 2005 | $\Delta\hat{K}_i$ | Development relative to 1970 |
|---|---|---|---|---|
| FBT | .066 | .029 | -.037 | -.566 |
| Textiles | .066 | .058 | -.007 | -.113 |
| Leather/Footwear | .016 | .016 | .000 | .004 |
| Wood | .013 | .012 | -.002 | -.144 |
| Pulp & Paper | .003 | .002 | -.001 | -.455 |
| Printing & Publishing | .009 | .003 | -.005 | -.611 |
| Coke | .006 | .004 | -.002 | -.374 |
| Chemicals | .017 | .007 | -.010 | -.575 |
| Rubber & Plastics | .006 | .007 | .001 | .214 |
| Mineral Products | .013 | .011 | -.002 | -.129 |
| Basic Metals | .022 | .006 | -.016 | -.726 |
| Fabricated Metal | .049 | .028 | -.020 | -.417 |
| Machinery | .038 | .036 | -.002 | -.051 |
| Accounting & Computing Machines | .004 | .002 | -.002 | -.560 |
| Electrical Engineering | .021 | .012 | -.009 | -.414 |
| Communication Equipment | .014 | .006 | -.008 | -.603 |
| Precision Instruments | .014 | .008 | -.006 | -.442 |
| Motor Vehicles | .024 | .017 | -.006 | -.263 |
| Transport Equipment | .011 | .005 | -.006 | -.561 |
| Recycling | .013 | .005 | -.008 | -.617 |
| Motor Vehicles & Fuel | .019 | .023 | .004 | .228 |
| Wholesale Trade | .094 | .070 | -.024 | -.254 |
| Retail Trade | .057 | .087 | .031 | .541 |
| Hotels & Restaurants | .053 | .050 | -.003 | -.063 |
| Transport | .091 | .050 | -.041 | -.453 |
| Post & Telecommunication | .009 | .013 | .004 | .482 |
| Financial Intermediation | .010 | .016 | .006 | .618 |
| Real Estate | .016 | .021 | .005 | .314 |
| Renting of Machinery | .002 | .003 | .001 | .736 |

| | 1970 | 2005 | $\Delta \hat{K}_i$ | Development relative to 1970 |
|---|---|---|---|---|
| IT-related Activities | .010 | .056 | .046 | .596 |
| R&D | .001 | .002 | .001 | 2.864 |
| Business Activities | .043 | .051 | .008 | .178 |
| Education | .037 | .049 | .012 | .317 |
| Health & Social Work | .029 | .023 | -.006 | -.219 |
| Domestic Services | .036 | .074 | .038 | 1.039 |

Source: EU KLEMS database, March 2008.

The convergence in the textile industry (as the largest industry in this club) is relatively slow. This is contrary to the result for Central Europe, where a high degree of convergence was detected. It should be noted, however, that even though employment in Textiles fell in all Southern European countries, the levels remain quite heterogeneous. With regard to economic structures, we should pay additional attention to the fact that employment in this low-tech industry in Italy is far more high-skilled than in the other countries, since Italy focuses on the quality segment of this industry and has high-value added segments where design, research and development are important competitive factors (Aiginger 2000). In contrast, the other South European countries are in more direct rivalry with Asian countries, since they tend to produce more similar products, i.e. standardized mass products of lower quality. Due to the fact that the textile industry is characterized by the fact that modern technology can be relatively easily adopted at low costs even in poor, low-tech countries, South European Countries are struggling, since they cannot cope with the cost competition from South-Asian countries. This tendency has been strengthened after the removal of quotas, tariffs and other forms of protectionism in the textile industry by the WTO in 1995 (Jimenez Cortes 1997). Moreover, the decrease in transportation costs made the fragmentation of the production of textiles even more profitable (Hummels et al. 2001), thus leading to a relocation of unskilled, labour-intensive tasks to labour-abundant places in developing countries. The reason for the low degree of convergence across South European countries above all seems to be the delayed structural change of Portugal. In more detail, we can attribute the high degree of heterogeneity to the fact that Portugal holds high employment levels in low-tech industries such as the textile production until the mid-1990s (when protectionism was set to end by the WTO) before a reduction process similar to the other South European countries began. A similar development can be observed in the leather industry, where Portugal even increased employment shares in the first half of the investigation period, before it started reducing it in line with the other countries. Thus, starting in the mid-1990s, we observe a remarkable decline of employment shares in textiles, leading to convergence initiated by one-country de-specialization of Portugal.

In the service sector, the most strongly converging industry is Transport, which is mainly caused by the employment reduction of Greece. In Retail Trade, Computer Services and Private Households, heterogeneity strongly increases at the same time. The developments in Retail Trade and Computer Services can be interpreted as a hint regarding the special role Italy plays within the South European club: While at the beginning of the 1970s, employment levels were highest in Spain and Italy, Retail Trade was of minor importance in Greece and Portugal. Since the early 1980s, developments started to change, however. Whereas employment dropped by almost 40 per cent in Italy, and remained roughly unchanged in Spain, this low-skill industry continued to create new employment possibilities in Greece and Portugal. Thus, while Italy specialized out of this industry, the structurally more lagging countries gain more and more employment in this industry - above all after establishing the Single Market. This process has lead not only to increasing heterogeneity within the South European club but also implies distortions against the structurally leading countries in Central and Northern Europe. We interpret the one-country de-specialization of Greece in Transport as a sign of technological catch-up by Greece, leading to rationalization and automation and reducing employment from the 1980s onwards. Thus, Greece did not lose competitiveness, but rather increased competitiveness while reducing employment in this industry. At the same time, employment in the skill-intensive computer services industry has been growing more strongly in the Italian economy than in the other three countries, where the development sets in later and remains less dynamic.

In general, we conclude that structural change towards a qualitative upgrade of South European economic structures has only partly occurred. Catch up processes compared to the economic development of Ireland, for instance, were especially weak in Greece in Portugal. These two economies still are characterized by the majority of employment possibilities being found in low-tech, low-skill and low-wage industries. This is a particular problem due to the increased competitive pressures from outside Europe. The main problems of these two countries are lacking a large home market and are characterized by a peripheral geographical location such that they have difficulties in attracting foreign investors. In contrast to Ireland, Greece and Portugal moreover have disadvantages with respect to their mother tongue, the corporate tax system and the fact that the South cohesion countries protected their labour markets from international competition (above all in the production of textiles and leather) which likely made inefficiently operating firms in business for a too long period of time. The lack of foreign investors, an inflexible labour market and the shelter of uncompetitive industries have hindered structural change, leading to a gradual loss of competitiveness and rising unemployment as production is now relocated to more favorable countries.

The specialization patterns in Italy are characterized by strong path dependency, too. Italy's economic structure is mainly determined by its comparative advantages in low-tech, low-wage industries dating back to the 1950s and to the dynamic economies of scale, which imply that Italian firms have increased productivity and thus cost-efficiency in the production of goods they have been producing for decades (De Benedictis and Padoan 1999 or Epifani 1999). There are differences compared to Greece and Portugal, however. As already pointed out with regard to employment in Textiles, even though Italy seems to appear strongly specialized in a low-tech industry, the tasks are high-skill and high-tech and thus the textile industry in Italy should be regarded as much more competitive than the respective industries in Greece or Portugal. We do however see a convergence of employment patterns of Italy with other European countries that is absent for Greece and Portugal. As a sign of this development, occupations within an industry get more similar, i.e. the share of management workers increases while the share of unskilled workers decreases. Italy and Spain on the other hand, managed the process of structural change better – implying within-club divergence as being captured in Figure 16. This is at least what the national figures imply. We must note, however, that the inter-regional disparities within these two countries pose problems of their own.

## 5.3.5 Convergence and Divergence within North Europe

In our third country group, Scandinavia, we find only slight convergence, caused by the fact that Denmark and Sweden were already similar in economic structures at the beginning of the investigation period – thus the potential for further convergence was rather low. On the other hand, we already tackled the problem of the poor fit of Finland with the club. Finland was never able to catch up to the two other countries. Whereas Denmark did not converge further to the club-average over the period of time however, the economic structure of Sweden becomes more similar to the club. It thus becomes evident, that the within-club convergence of North European countries is only due to the development of the Swedish economy (see Figure 17).

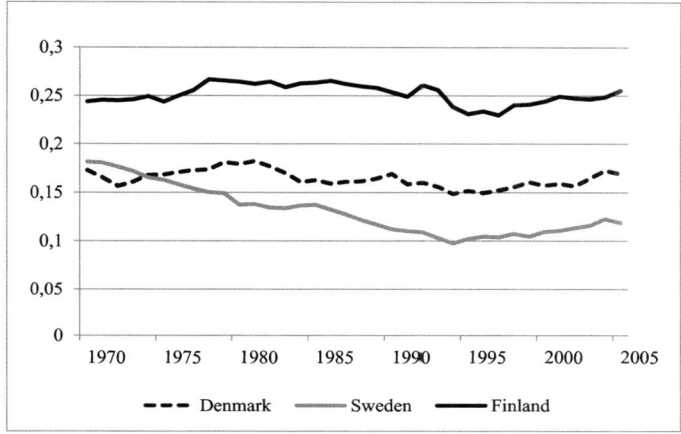

*Figure 17: Heterogeneity of North European Countries*
Source: EU KLEMS database, March 2008.

Taking a closer look at the developments regarding structural change, all three countries reduced their employment shares in the low-tech industries significantly. Whereas Denmark and t some degree Finland increased employment in high-tech industries, Sweden decreased jobs in these kind of industries dramatically. With regard to the service sector, there are relevant differences between the countries. Whereas both Denmark and Sweden reduce low-skill work, Finland increases employment. With regard to high-skilled labour in the service sector, the levels of Sweden stay constant over time; whereas Denmark and Finland are able to increase employment shares by about 40 per cent (see Tabke 54).

*Table 54: Employment Shares in North Europe (technology classes)*

|  | Low tech 1970 | Low tech 2005 | Med-low tech 1970 | Med-low tech 2005 | Med-high tech 1970 | Med-high tech 2005 | High tech 1970 | High tech 2005 | Low skill 1970 | Low skill 2005 | High skill 1970 | High skill 2005 |
|---|---|---|---|---|---|---|---|---|---|---|---|---|
| DK | .049 | .022 | .017 | .010 | .021 | .020 | .007 | .011 | .045 | .032 | .033 | .075 |
| FIN | .060 | .018 | .017 | .005 | .019 | .017 | .014 | .015 | .063 | .091 | .070 | .109 |
| SWE | .025 | .009 | .020 | .006 | .023 | .016 | .023 | .004 | .059 | .040 | .044 | .044 |

Source: EU KLEMS database, March 2008.

Investigating the patterns of structural convergence on the industry level, we see that the countries converged in all industries of the manufacturing sector apart from Communications Equipment and Precision Instruments (see Table 55). In contrast, there are both convergence and divergence trends occurring in the service sector. In particular, we don't find any high-skill industry or any traditional service industry converging, whereas the picture with regard to low-skill, hybrid and standard industries is mixed.

*Table 55: Industry-specific Heterogeneity in North Europe ($\hat{K}_i$)*

|  | 1970 | 2005 | $\Delta\hat{K}_i$ | Development relative to 1970 |
|---|---|---|---|---|
| FBT | .048 | .024 | -.024 | -.509 |
| Textiles | .036 | .004 | -.031 | -.875 |
| Leather | .005 | .001 | -.005 | -.892 |
| Wood | .025 | .012 | -.013 | -.514 |
| Pulp & Paper | .022 | .011 | -.011 | -.486 |
| Printing & Publishing | .027 | .015 | -.012 | -.453 |
| Coke | .001 | .001 | .000 | -.161 |
| Chemicals | .014 | .012 | -.002 | -.127 |
| Rubber & Plastics | .012 | .009 | -.003 | -.280 |
| Mineral Products | .018 | .007 | -.011 | -.598 |
| Basic Metals | .019 | .009 | -.011 | -.551 |
| Fabricated Metal | .027 | .025 | -.002 | -.081 |
| Machinery | .044 | .033 | -.011 | -.257 |
| Accounting & Computing Machines | .002 | .001 | -.001 | -.528 |
| Electrical Engineering | .012 | .008 | -.003 | -.283 |
| Communication Equipment | .009 | .010 | .001 | .121 |
| Precision Instruments | .007 | .007 | .000 | .014 |
| Motor Vehicles | .016 | .014 | -.002 | -.142 |
| Transport Equipment | .013 | .006 | -.007 | -.525 |
| Recycling | .017 | .012 | -.006 | -.318 |
| Motor Vehicles & Fuel | .036 | .027 | -.009 | -.238 |
| Wholesale Trade | .072 | .071 | -.002 | -.022 |
| Retail Trade | .107 | .080 | -.027 | -.251 |
| Hotels & Restaurants | .040 | .039 | -.001 | -.025 |
| Transport | .077 | .072 | -.005 | -.069 |
| Post & Telecommunication | .022 | .021 | -.001 | -.053 |

| | 1970 | 2005 | $\Delta \hat{K}_i$ | Development relative to 1970 |
|---|---|---|---|---|
| Financial Intermediation | .024 | .027 | .004 | .148 |
| Real Estate | .012 | .021 | .009 | .705 |
| Renting of Machinery | .001 | .004 | .002 | 1.680 |
| IT-related Activities | .004 | .026 | .021 | 4.985 |
| R&D | .003 | .010 | .006 | 1.859 |
| Business Activities | .032 | .090 | .058 | 1.788 |
| Education | .077 | .105 | .029 | .376 |
| Health & Social Work | .103 | .169 | .066 | .637 |
| Domestic Services | .014 | .018 | .004 | .266 |

Source: EU KLEMS database, March 2008.

Turning to the most significant developments, the convergence in low-tech industries is noteworthy. All three countries soon began to de-specialize in Textiles and Leather, i.e. in industries the Northern European countries have no competitive advantage in. Even more remarkable is the sharp drop in employment shares in Wood as well as in Pulp & Paper; industries in which Finland and Sweden were characterized by comparative advantages due to an abundance of natural resources. Because of the technological upgrade of Finland's economic structure, de-specialization and thus convergence processes can be identified in line with the results presented in 4.5.5.

The turnaround in Finland's structure towards employment in high-tech industries is best illustrated by looking at the development in Communications Equipment. Despite the dynamic growth from the 1990s onwards, the countries' employment shares in these emerging high-technology industries are still relatively small, so that these specialization (and divergence) patterns do not strongly affect heterogeneity. Hence, focusing on the manufacturing sector only, the Scandinavian club is converging over time, caused mainly by the structural change of Finland.

In the service sector, again the employment structure of Finland and its differences to the club average is the main cause for any divergence trends, whereas developments in the Danish economy are drivers of convergence, as is outlined by the following examples: At the beginning of the observation period Finland's service sector was dominated by employment in the retail trade and transport industries, i.e. mainly industries with low knowledge intensity, while in Denmark and even more so in Sweden knowledge-intensive industries such as

Health & Social Work dominated. We identify convergence in low-skill industries whenever both Danish - and Finnish employment shares were shrinking over time such as in Retail Trade or in Transport.

In Health & Social Work, the differences between Sweden and Denmark on the one hand and Finland on the other hand were already large in the 1970s and have since then been growing over time. This can be explained by the fact that even though employment shares in Denmark and Sweden were already remarkably higher than in Finland, the steadily higher growth rates in the former two countries prohibited any catch up by Finland until the 1990s. Interestingly, we find a growing share of employment in private households in Finland which cannot be observed for Denmark and Sweden. This could be interpreted as a hint that social services are partly being taken over by privately employed caretakers in Finland instead of social institutions, as might be common in Sweden and Denmark. However, to verify this hypothesis a more disaggregated data set would be required.

Altogether, Finland is – similar to Ireland – a good example for successful structural change. Finland turned from a country based on the production of low-tech products to a high-tech country. From the early nineties onwards, Finland developed its medium-high and high-tech industries – above all Machinery and Communications Equipment – such that in 2005 employment in these industries is far above the European average, while in the wood and pulp & paper industries, employment decreased over this period. The turnaround in the service sector is less remarkable. Finland's economy was dominated by low-skill industries such as Retail Trade or Transport and mainly continued to be so – especially if we compare Finland to the other two Scandinavian countries. We must not overlook the rise in employment in high-skill industries such as Education, however, while the share of low-skill industries has been shrinking. As these developments are parallel to the shift in the average, Finland remains relatively specialized in Retail Trade and Transport instead of Education. Studying the Finnish economic structure in such detail also makes clear why this country so badly fits with any club. On the one hand, specialization patterns in the manufacturing sector are close to the Northern club: The strong wood and pulp & paper industries in the 1970s are typical for the densely wooded Scandinavian countries. On the other hand, in the service sector the specialization on Retail Trade and Transport instead of education and Health and Social Work makes Finland's economy resemble the Southern European club. Thus, while Finland's manufacturing sector is "typically North European", its service sector, and in particular the health and social sector, seems to be less developed and thus shifts the country close to the South European countries in our analysis.

# 5.4 Conclusion

To summarize, all Western European Countries are characterized by significant changes in their economic structures due to the decline of traditional low-tech and low-skill industries as opposed to the rise of more skill and technology intensive industries. Even though the economic structures tend to be persistent and quite heterogeneous across Europe, there are some common trends: Technological progress lead to an overall decrease of manufacturing industries and a rise in service industries. Moreover, the qualifications needed for employment in all industries have risen. This increased the difficulty for lower qualified people to find adequate employment. In this context, the danger of structural unemployment should not be underestimated (Berthold et al. 2002), especially in an environment such as the European, where labour market institutions are very rigid. Unemployment could increase in cases where the skills offered do not fit the skills needed in the prosperous industries and where traditional industries are unable to face the international cost competition. This could above all pose a danger to Greece and Portugal, which face strong competition from Asian countries in low-tech industries, where their relative specialization levels are still high. The problem of these countries seems to be that they have not yet developed enough to cope with the effects of liberalization in their for a long time sheltered (unproductive) industries – above all Textiles and Leather. They need to pursue industrial policies in order to properly upgrade their economic structures towards high-tech and high-skill industries. In contrast to these two Cohesion countries, Finland and Ireland have successfully upgraded their economic structures from an unfavorable exposure to low-tech and low-skill industries in the 1970s into fast growing high-tech industries. According to Barry (2000, 2001), one necessary feature for the upgrade of Ireland's economic structure was the increase in well-educated labour supply due to the net inflow of immigrants and the rise in FDI. By contrast, immigration and foreign direct investment are much lower in Greece and Portugal. Moreover, the earlier membership of Ireland in the European Community lead to abandoning protectionist policies much sooner, thus the pressure to adjust economic structures occurred at a much earlier stage of economic development (Barry 1996).

Overall however, we identify that specialization patterns in Europe are fairly sticky, i.e. specialization patterns only change slowly. The abundance of natural resources led to a long-lasting specialization pattern of Northern European countries in the pulp & paper and wood industries, the abundance of knowledge in the steel and chemical industries to a specialization of Germany in the respective industries. The mismatch of required labour skills and cost-disadvantages are the reasons for the ever declining employment shares in the textile industry in Central and North European Countries from the 1970s onwards. Declining transportation costs and increasing international division of labour put the Southern European countries under pressure only since the 1990s, when cost-advantages vanished. It thus holds true that countries specialize in industries where they have a cost- or skill-advantage.

# Literature

Acar, W. and K. Sankaran (1999), The Myth of the Unique Decomposability: Specializing the Herfindahl and Entropy Measures? in: *Strategic Management Journal,* Vol. 20, 969-975.

Aiginger, K. (2000), Specialization of European Manufacturing, in: *Austrian Economic Quarterly,* vol. 2, 81-92.

Aiginger, K.; Böheim, M.; Gugler, K.; Peneder, M. and M. Pfaffermayr (1999), Specialisation and (Geographic) Concentration of European Manufacturing, Working paper 1, DG Enterprise, European Commission, Brussels.

Aiginger, K. and St. Davies (2004), Industrial specialization and geographic concentration: two sides of the same coin? Not for the European Union, in: *Journal of Applied Economics*, vol. 12, 231-248.

Aiginger, K. and W. Leitner (2002), Regional Concentration in the United States and Europe: Who Follows Whom? in: *Weltwirtschaftliches Archiv,* vol. 138, 652-679.

Aiginger, K. and M. Pfaffermayr (2004), The Single Market and Geographic Concentration in Europe, in: *Review of International Economics*, vol. 12, 1-11.

Alonso-Villar, O. (2005), The Effects of Transport Costs Revisited, in: *Journal of Economic Geography,* vol. 5, 589–604.

Amiti, M. (1998), New Trade Theories and Industrial Location in the EU: A Survey of Evidence, in: *Oxford Economic Review,* vol. 14, 45-53.

Amiti, M. (1999), Specialisation Patterns in Europe, in: *Review of World Economics,* vol. 573-593.

Anderton, R.; Barrell, R. and J.W. Veld (1992), Macroeconomic Convergence in Europe: Achievements and Prospects, in: Barrell, R. (ed.) *Economic Convergence and Monetary Union in Europe*, 1–30.

Appelbaum, E. and R. Schettkat (1997), *Labour market adjustments to structural change and technological progress*, New York.

Appelbaum, E. and Schettkat, R. (1999), Are prices unimportant? The changing structure of the industrialized economies, in: Journal ofPost Keynesian Economics, vol. 21, 387–398,

Arndt, S.W. and H. Kierzkowski (2000), *Fragmentation: New Production Patterns in the World Economy,* New York.

Arrow, K. (1962), The Economic Implications of Learning by Doing, in: *Review of Economic Studies,* Vol. 29, 155-173.

Arthur, W.B. (1988), Self-reinforcing mechanisms in economics, in: Anderson, P.; Arrow, K. and D. Pines (eds.),*The economy as an evolving, complex system*, 9-31.

Arthur, W.B. (1989), Competing technologies, increasing returns, and "lock-in" by historical Events, in: *Economic Journal,* vol. 99, 116-31.

Arthur, W.B. (1994), *Increasing returns and path dependence in the economy*, Ann Arbor.

Atkinson, A.B. (1970), On the Measurement of Inequality, *in: Journal of Economic Theory,* vol. 2, 244-263.

Attaran, M. and M. Zwick (1987), Entropy and Other Measures of Industrial Diversification, in: *Quarterly Journal of Business and Economics,* vol. 26, 17-35.

Azariadis, C. and A. Drazen (1990), Threshold externalities in economic development, in: *Quarterly Journal of Economics,* vol. 105, 501-26.

Bahl, R.W.; Firestine, R. and D. Phares (1971), Industrial Diversity in Urban Areas: Alternative Measures and Intermetropolitan Comparisons, in: *Economic Geography*, vol. 47, 414-425.

Balassa, B. (1963), An empirical demonstration of classical comparative cost theory, in: *Review of Economics and Statistics,* vol. 4, 231-238.

Baldwin, R. (2012), Global supply chains: Why they emerged, why they matter, and where they are going, CEPR Discussion Papers 9103, CEPR Discussion Papers.

Baldwin, R., Forslid, R., Martin, P., Ottaviano, G.I.P. and F. Robert-Nicoud (2003). *Economic Geography and Public Policy*, Princeton University Press.

Barro, R.J. and X. Sala-i-Martin (1992), Convergence, in: *Journal of Political Economy,* vol. 100, 223-251.

Barro, R.J. and X. Sala-i-Martin (1995), *Economic Growth,* New York.

Barry, F. (1996), Peripherality in economic geography and modern growth theory. Evidence from Ireland's adjustment to free trade, in: *World Economy,* vol. 19, 345-65.

Barry, F. (2000), The Celtic Tiger Era: delayed convergence or regional boom?, in: *ESRI Quarterly Economic Commentary*, 36-42.

Barry, F.; Bradley, J. and A. Hannan (2001), The Single Market, the Structural Funds and Ireland's Recent Economic Growth, in: *Journal of Common Market Studies*, vol. 39, 537-552.

Barry, F. (2003), Irish Economic Development over Three Decades of EU Membership, in: *Czech Journal of Economics and Finance*, Vol. 53, 394 – 412.

Barth, D. (2001), *Liberalising international trade in services: the European perspective*, The World Trade Organization millennium round.

Baumol, W.J. (1967), Macroeconomics of Unbalanced Growth: The Anatomy of Urban Crisis, in: *American Economic Review*, vol. 57, 415-426.

Baumol, W.J. (1986) Productivity growth, convergence and welfare: what the long run data show, in: *American Economic Review*, vol. 76, 1072-1085.

Baumol, W.J. (2001), Paradox of the Services: Exploding Costs, Persistent Demand, in: Raa, T. and R. Schettkat (eds.), *The Growth of Service Industries: The Paradox of Exploding Costs and Persistent Demand*, Northampton, MA and Cheltenham, UK, 3-28.

Baumol, W.J and E.N. Wolff (1988), Productivity Growth, Convergence and Welfare: Reply, in: *American Economic Review*, vol. 78, 1155-1159.

Behrens, K.; Duranton, G. and F. Robert-Nicoud (2010) Productive cities: Sorting, selection and agglomeration, CEPR Discussion Papers Nr. 7922.

Behrens, K.; Lamorgese, A.R.; Ottaviano, G. and T. Tabuchi (2009), Beyond the home market effect: Market size and specialization in a multi-country world, in: *Journal of International Economics*, vol. 79, 259-265.

Beine, M. and S. Coulombe (2007), Economic integration and the diversification of regional exports: evidence from the Canadian-U.S. Free Trade Agreement, in: *Journal of Economic Geography*, vol. 7, 93-111.

Bentolila, S. and J. Dolado (1991), Mismatch and internal migration in Spain, 1962-1986, in: Padoa Schioppa, F. (ed), *Mismatch and Labour Mobility*, Cambridge University Press, 182-234.

Bentivogli, C., and P. Pagano (1999), Regional disparities and labour mobility; the Euro-11 versus the USA, in: *Labour,* vol. 13, 737–760.

Bernard, A. and S. Durlauf (1995), Convergence in International Output, in: *Journal of Applied Econometrics*, vol. 10, 9-108.

Berthold, N.; Fehn, R. and E. Thode (2002), Falling Labour Share and Rising Unemployment: Long-Run Consequences of Institutional Shocks? in: *German Economic Review*, vol. 4, 431-459.

Bickenbach, F.; Bode, E. and Ch. Krieger-Boden (2010), Structural Cohesion in Europe: Stylized Facts, Working Papers, Kiel Institute for the World Economy, No. 1669.

Böhning, W.R. (1979), International Migration in Western Europe, Reflections on the Last Five Years, in: *International Labour Review,* vol. 118, 401-415.

Bordo, M.D.; Eichengreen, B. and D.A. Irwin (1999), Is globalization today really different than globalization a hundred years ago? NBER Working Paper, No. 7195.

Borts, G.H. and J.L. Stein (1964), *Economic growth in a free market*, New York.

Boschma, R.A. and K. Frenken (2003), Evolutionary economics and industry location, in: *Review for Regional Research*, vol. 23, 183-200.

Bourguignon, F. (1979), Decomposable income inequality measures, in: *Econometrica*, vol. 47, 901-920.

Brakman, St.; Garretsen, H and Ch. van Marrewijk (2009), *The New Introduction to Geographical Economics*, Cambridge.

Braunerhjelm, P.; Faini, R.; Norman, V.; Ruane, F. and P. Seabright (2000), *Integration and the Regions of Europe: How the Right Policies Can Prevent Polarization*. Monitoring European Integration 10, Centre for Economic Policy Research, London.

Brown, D.J. and J. Pheasant (1985), A Sharpe Portfolio Approach to Regional Economic Analysis, in: *Journal of Regional Science*, vol. 25, 51-63.

Brülhart, M. (1998a), Economic Geography, Industry Location and Trade: The Evidence, in: *The World Economy*, vol. 21, 775-801.

Brülhart, M. (1998b), Trading places: Industrial specialisation in the European Union, in: *Journal of Common Market Studies*, vol. 36, 319-346.

Brülhart, M. (2001a), Growing alike or growing apart? Industrial specialisation of EU Countries, in: C. Wyplosz (ed.), The Impact of EMU on Europe and the Developing Countries, Oxford University Press, 169-194.

Brülhart, M. (2001b), Evolving Geographical Specialisation of European Manufacturing Industries, in: *Weltwirtschaftliches Archiv*, vol. 137, 215-243.

Brülhart, M.; McAleese, D. and M. O'Donnell (1998), Ireland, in: Brülhart, M. and R.C. Hine (eds.), *Intra-Industry Trade and Adjustment: The European Experience*, London.

Brülhart, M. and F. Trionfetti (2004), Public expenditure, international specialisation and agglomeration, in: *European Economic Review*, vol. 48, 851-881.

Brülhart, M. and J. Torstensson (2007), Regional Integration, Scale Economies and Industry Location in the European Union, in: Jovanovic, M.N. (ed.), *Economic Integration and Spatial Location of Firms and Industries, Vol. I*, Cheltenham.

Brülhart, M. and R. Traeger (2005), An account of geographic concentration patterns in Europe, in: *Regional Science and Urban Economics*, vol. 35, 597-624.

Buigues, P.; Ilzkovitz, F. and J.F. Lebrun (1990), *The Impact of the Internal Market by Industrial Sector*. Special Issue of European Economy and Social Europe, Brussels.

Busse, M. (2001), Transaktionskosten und Wettbewerbspolitik, HWWA Discussion Paper No. 116.

Cave, W. and E. Giovanni (2007), The Statistical Measurement of Services: Recent Achievements and Remaining Challenges, in: *Metroceconomica*, Vol. 58, 479-501.

Chenery H.B. (1960), Patterns of Industrial Growth, in: *The American Economic Review*, vol. 50, 624-654.

Chenery, H.B. and M. Syrquin (1989), Three Decades of Industrialization, in: *World Bank Economic Review*, vol. 3, 145-181.

Chirot, D. (ed.) (1989), *The Origins of Backwardness in Eastern Europe*, Berkeley, University of California Press.

Chisholm, M. (1968), *Rural Settlement and Land Use. An Essay in Location*, Chicago.

Chisholm, M. and J. Oeppen (1973), *The Changing Pattern of Employment. Regional Specialisation and Industrial Location in Britain*, London.

Clark, C. (1940), *The Conditions of Economic Progress*, Macmillan.

Cohen, S.S. and J. Zysman (1987): *Manufacturing Matters: The Myth of the Post-industrial Economy*, Basic Books, New York.

Combes, P.-P. and H.G. Overman (2004), The spatial distribution of economic activities in the European Union, in: Henderson, J.V. and J.F. Thisse (eds), *Handbook of Regional and Urban Economics*, ed. 1, vol. 4, chapter 64, 2845-2909, North Holland.

Commission of the European Communities (2003), *The future of the textiles and clothing sector in the enlarged European Union*, Communication from the Commission to the Council, the European Parliament, the European Economic and Social Committee and the Committee of the Regions.

Commission of the European Communities (1993), Growth, Competitiveness and Employment. The Challenges and Ways Forward to the 21$^{st}$ Century, in: *Bulletin of the European Communities*, vol. 6

Commission of the European Communities (1997), Commission Action Plan on the Free Movement of Workers, COM 586, Brussels.

Conkling, E.C. (1964), Measurement of Diversification, in: Manners, G. (ed.), South Wales in the Sixties, Studies in Industrial geography, Pergamon, 161-183.

Conkling, E.C. (1963), South Wales: A Case Study in Industrial Diversification, in: *Economic Geography*, vol. 39, 258-272.

Conroy, M.E. (1975a), *Regional Economic Diversification*, New York.

Conroy, M.E. (1975b), The concept and measurement of regional industrial diversification, in: *Southern Economic Journal*, vol. 41, 492-505.

Cowell, F. A. (1980), On the structure of additive inequality measures, in: *Review of Economic Studies*, vol. 47, 521.31.

Cowell, F.A. (1995), *Measuring Inequality*, London.

Crozet, M. and F. Trionfetti (2008), Trade costs and the Home Market Effect, in: *Journal of International Economics*,

Cuadrado-Roura, J.R.; Garcia-Greciano, B. and J.L. Raymond (1999), Regional Convergence in Productivity and Productive Structure: The Spanish Case, in: *International Regional Science Review*, vol. 22, 35-53.

Dagum, C. (1997), A New Approach to the Decomposition of the Gini Income Inequality Ration, in: *Empirical Economics*, vol. 22, 515-531.

Dalton, H. (1920), The Measurement of Inequality of Incomes, in: *The Economic Journal*, vol. 30, 348-361.

David, P.A. (1985), Clio and the economics of QWERTY, in: *American Economic Review*, vol. 75, 332-337.

David, P.A. (1986), Understanding the economics of QWERTY: The necessity of history, in: Parker, W.N. (ed.), *Economic History and the Modern Economics*, 30-49. Oxford, U.K.

David, P.A. (1988), Path dependence: Putting the past into the future of economics. Economic Series Technical Report 533, Institute for Mathematical Studies in the Social Sciences, Stanford.

David, P.A. (1992), Heros, herds and hysteresis in technological history, in: *Industrial and Corporate Change*, vol. 1, 129-79.

David, P.A. (1993a), Path dependence and predictability in dynamic systems with local network externalities: A paradigm for historical economics, In: Foray, D. and C. Freeman (eds.), *Technology and the wealth of nations*, 187-216.

David, P.A. (1993b), Historical economics in the long run: Some implications of path dependence, In: Snooks, G.D. (ed.), *Historical analysis in economics*, 29-40.

David, P.A. (1994), Why are institutions the "carriers of history"? Path dependence and the evolution of conventions, organisations and institutions, in: *Structural Change and Economic Dynamics*, vol. 5, 205-20.

Davies, S.W. and B.R. Lyons (1996), *Industrial Organisation in the European Union: Structure, Strategy and the Competitive Mechanism*, Oxford.

Davis, D.R. (1998), The Home Market, Trade, and Industrial Structure, in: *American Economic Review,* vol. 88, 1264-1276.

Davis, R.D. and D.E; Weinstein (1997), Increasing Returns and International Trade: An Empirical Confirmation, mimeo, Harvard University.

De Benedictis, L. and P.C. Padoan (1999), Dynamic scale economies, speciali-zation, and the cost of the single currency, in: *International Journal of Development Planning Literature*, vol. 14, 549-560.

De Bandt, J. (1999), The Concept of Labour and Competence Requirements in a Service Economy, in: *The Service Industries Journal*, vol. 19.

Decressin, J. and A. Fata' s (1995), Regional labour market dynamics in Europe, in: *European Economic Review*, vol. 39, 1627–1655.

Dedrick, J. and K. Kraemer (2002), *Globalization of the Personal Computer In-dustry: Trends and Implications'*, Paper 254 Center for Research on In-formation Technology and Organizations. University of California, Irvine.

De Grauwe, P. (2009), *Economics of monetary union*, 8.th ed, Oxford.

De la Fuente, A. (1997), The empirics of growth and convergence: a selective review, in: *Journal of Economic Dynamics and Control*, vol. 21, 64-75.

De la Fuente, A. (1999), La dinamica territorial de la poblacion Espanola: un paranoma y algunos resultados provisionales, in: *Revista de Economia Aplicada*, vol. 7, 53-108.

De Menil, G. (1999), Real capital market integration in the EU: how far has it gone? What will the effect of the Euro be? In: *Economic Policy*, vol. 28, 165–201.

Devereux, M.P.; Griffith, R. and H. Simspon (2004), The geographic distribu-tion of production activity in the UK, in: *Regional Science and Urban Economics*, vol. 34, 533-564.

Dobrinsky, R. and M. Landesmann (1995), *Transforming Economies and Euro-pean Integration*, Edward Elgar Publishing.

Dosi, G.; Pavitt, K. and L. Soete (1990), *The economics of technical change and international trade*, New York.

Dunning, J. (1997a), The European Internal Market Programme and Inbound Foreign Direct Investment, Part 1, in: *Journal of Common Market Studies*, vol. 35, 1-30.

Dunning, J. (1997b), The European Internal Market Programme and Inbound Foreign Direct Investment, Part 2, in: *Journal of Common Market Studies*, vol. 35 189-223.

Duranton, G. and H.G. Overman (2005), Testing for Localization Using Micro-Geographic Data, in: *Review of Economic Studies*, vol. 72, 1077-1106.

Durlauf, St. and P.A. Johnson (1995), Multiple Regimes and Cross-CountryGrowth Behavior, in: *Journal of Applied Econometrics*, vol. 10, 365-384.

Duro Moreno, J.A. (2001), Cross-country inequalities in aggregate welfare: some evidence, in: *Applied Economic Letters*, vol. 8, 403-406.

188

Easterlin, R.A. (1960), Interregional Differences in Per Capita Income, Population, and Total Income, 1840-1950, in: NBER Studies in Income and Wealth, (eds.), *Trends in The American Economy in the Nineteenth Century*, Princeton.

Ekholm, K. and R. Forslid (2001), Trade and Location with Horizontal and Vertical Multi-region Firms, in: *Scandinavian Journal of Economics*, vol. 103, 101-118.

Egger, P.; Gruber, St.; Larch, M. and M. Pfaffermayr (2007), Knowledge-capital meets new economic geography, in: *The Annals of Regional Science,* vol. 41, 857-875.

Eichengreen, B. (1993), Labour Markets and European Monetary Unification, in: Masson, P. and M. Taylor (eds.), *Policy Issues in the Operation of Currency Unions*, Cambridge University Press, Cambridge, 130–162.

Elfring, T. (1989), New evidence on the expansion of service employment in advanced economies, in: *Review of Income and Wealth*, vol. 35, 409–440.

Ellison, G. and Glaeser, E. (1997), Geographic Concentration in US Manufacturing Industry: a Dartboard Approach, in: *Journal of Political Economy*, vol. 105, 889-927.

Emerson, M.; Aujean, M.; Catinat, M.; Goybet, P. and A. Jacquemin (1988), *The Economics of 1992: The E.C. Commission's Assessment of the Economic Effects of Completing the Internal Market*, Oxford.

Epifani P. (1999), Sulle determinanti del modello di specializzazione internazionale dell'Italia, in: *Politica Economica*, vol. 15, 195-224.

European Commission (2002), *The future of the textiles and clothing sector in the enlarged European union*, Communication from the Commission to the Council, the European Parliament, the European Economic and Social Commitee and the Committee of the Regions.

Evans, P. and G. Karras (1996), Convergence revisited, in: *Journal of Monetary Economics,* vol. 37, 249-265.

Ezcurra, R. and P. Pascual (2007), Spatial Disparities in Productivity in Central and Eastern Europe, in: *Eastern European Economics,* vol. 45, 5-32.

Fagerberg, J., Verspagen, B. and N. von Tunzelmann, (1994), *The Dynamics of Technology, Trade and Growth*, Aldershot: Edward Elgar.

Fagerberg, J. (2000), Technological progress, structural change and productivity growth: a comparative study, in: *Structural Change and Economic Dynamics*, vol. 11, 393-411.

Faini, R.; Galli, G.; Gennari, P. and F. Rossi (1997), An empirical puzzle. Falling migration and growing unemployment differentials among Italian regions, in: *European Economic Review,* vol. 41, 571-579.

Falvey, R.E. and N. Gemmell (1996), Are services income-elastic? Some new evidence, in: *Review of Income and Wealth*, vol. 42, 257-269.

Fisher, A.G.B. (1939), Production, Primary, Secondary and Tertiary, in: *The Economic Record*, vol. 15, 22-38.

Fisher, A.G.B. (1952), A Note on Tertiary Production, in: *Economic Journal*, vol. 62, 820-834.

Florence, P.S. (1948), *Investment, Location, and Size of Plant*, Cambridge.

Forslid, R.; Haaland J.I. and K.H. Midelfart-Knarvik (2002), A U-Shaped Europe? A simulation study of industrial location, in: *Journal of International Economics*, vol. 57, 273-297.

Forslid, R. and G. Ottaviano (2003), An Analytically Solvable Core-periphery Model, in: *Journal of Economic Geography*, vol. 3, 229-240.

Fourastié J. (1949), *Le Grand Espoir du XXe Siècle: Progrès Technique – Progrès Economique – Progrès Social*, Paris.

Friedman, M. (1994), Do Old Fallicies Ever Die? In: *Journal of Economic Literature*, vol. 30, 2129-2132.

Fuchs, V.R. (1968), *The Service Economy*, New York, National Bureau of Economic Research.

Fuchs, V.R. (1969), *Production and Productivity in the Service Industries*, New York, National Bureau of Economic Research.

Fuchs, V.R. (1980). Economic Growth and the Rise of Service Employment, National Bureau of Economic Research, NBER Working Paper No. W0486.

Fujita, M.; Krugman, P. and A.J. Venables (1999), *The Spatial Economy*, MIT Press.

Fujita, M. and F.L. Rivera-Batiz (1988), Agglomeration and heterogeneity in space: Introduction, in: *Regional Science and Urban Economics*, vol. 18, 1-5.

Galor, O. (1996), Convergence? Inferences from Theoretical Models, in: *The Economic Journal*, vol. 106, 1056-1069.

Gao, T. (1999), Economic geography and the department of vertical multinational production, in: *Journal of International Economics*, vol. 48, 301-320.

Gersbach, H. and A. Schmutler (2000), Declining costs of communication and transportation: what are the effects on agglomeration, in: *European Economic Review*, vol. 44, 1745-1763.

Gershuny, J. and I. Miles (1983), *The new service economy: The transformation of employment in industrial societies*, London.

Gini, C. (1912). Variabilità e mutabilità, Reprinted in: Pizetti, E. and T. Salveini (eds.) *Memorie di metodologica statistica*, 1955, Rome.

Gini, C. (1921), Measurement of Inequality of Incomes, in: *The Economic Journal*, vol. 31, 124 -126.

Görgens, E. (1975), Die Drei-Sektoren-Hypothese, in: *Wirtschaftsstudium*, 287-292.

Gratton, C. (1979), Industrial Diversification in New Towns, in: *Urban Studies*, vol. 16, 157-164.

Gregory,M., Salverda,W. And R. Schettkat (eds.), 2006, *The US-European Gap in Service Demand and Employment*.

Grilliches, Z. (1992) *Output Measurement in the Service Sectors*, University of Chicago Press.

Grömling, M., Lichtblau, K. and A. Weber (1998), *Industrie und Dienstleistungen im Zeitalter der Globalisierung*, Köln.

Grossman, G.M. (1992), *Imperfect Competition and International Trade*, Cambridge.

Gugler, K. and M. Pfaffermayr (2004), Convergence in Structure and Productivity in European Manufacturing?, in: *German Economic Review*, vol. 5, 61-79.

Haaland, J.I.; Kind, H.J.; Midelfart-Knarvik, K.H. and J. Torstensson (1999), What determines the economic geography of Europe, CEPR Discussion Paper, No. 2072.

Hackbart, M.W. and D.A. Anderson (1975), On Measuring Economic Diversification, in: *Land Economics,* vol. 51, 374-378.

Hall, M. and N. Tideman (1967), Measures of Concentration, in: *Journal of the American Statistical Association*, vol. 62, 162-168.

Hammar, T. (ed.), *(1985), European immigration policy –A comparative study.* Cambridge u.a.

Hamilton, C. and L.A. Winters (1992), Opening up international trade with Eastern Europe, in: *Economic Policy*, Vol. 14, 77-116.

Hannah, L.and Kay, J. A. (1977), *Concentration in Modern Industry. Theory, Measurement and the UK Experience*, London.

Head, K., Mayer, T. and J. Ries (2002), On the pervasiveness of home market effects. *Economica*, vol. 69, 371–390.

Helpman, E. and P.R. Krugman (1985), *Market Structure and Foreign Trade*, Cambridge, Mass.

Herfindahl, O. C. (1950). Concentration in the Steel Industry, Ph. D. thesis, Columbia University.

Hill, Ch. (2007), *International Business: Wettbewerb auf dem globalen Markt,* New York.

Hill, B.E. and K.A. Ingersent (1982), *The Economic Analysis of Agricultural Trade*, London.

Hirschman, A.O. (1958), *The Strategy of Economic Development*, New Haven, Yale University Press.

Hirschman, A.O. (1964), The Paternity of an Index, in: *The American Economic Review*, vol. 54, 761-762.

Hoekman, B.M. and M. Kostecki (1996), *The Political Economy of the World Trading System: from GATT to WTO*, Oxford.

Holmes, T.J. (1999), Localization of Industry and Vertical Disintegration, in: *The Review of Economics and Statistics*, vol. 81, 314-325.

Hoover, E.M. (1936), The Measurement of Industrial Localization, in: *The Review of Economics and Statistics*, vol. 18, 162-171

Hoover, E.M. (1948), *The Location of Economic Activity*, New York.

Hotelling, H. (1929), Stability in Competition, in: *The Economic Journal*, vol. 39, 41-57.

Hummels, D., Ishii, J., and K.M.Yi (2001), The nature and growth of vertical specialization in world trade, in: *Journal of International Economics* vol. 54, 57-73.

Isard, W. (1960), *Methods of Regional Analysis: an Introduction to Regional Science*, Cambridge, Mass.

Islam, N. (2003), What have we learnt from the convergence debate? In: *Journal of* Economic Surveys, vol. 17, 309-362.

Jackson, R.W. (1984), An evaluation of alternative measures of regional diversification, in: *Regional Studies*, vol. 18, 103-112.

Janger, J. and K. Wagner (2004), Sectoral Specialization in Austria and in the EU-15, in: *Monetary Policy & The Economy*, Quarter 2.

Jimenez Cortes, C. (1997), *GATT, WTO and the Regulation of International Trade in Textiles*, Portland, Or.

Jones, R. and H. Kierkowski (1990), The role of services in production and international trade: A theoretical framework, in: Jones, R. and A. Krueger (eds.), The political economy of international trade, 31-48.

Jones, R. and H. Kierkowski (2001), A framework for fragmentation, in: Arndt, S. and H. Kierzkowski (eds.), Fragmentation: New production patterns in the world economy, 17-34.

Kalemli-Ozcan, S.; Sørensen, B.E. and O. Yosha (2003), Risk Sharing and Industrial Specialization: Regional and International Evidence in: *American Economic Review*, vol. 93, 903-918.

Kang, J. S. (2000), The services sector in output and international trade, in: Findlay, C., and T. Warren (eds), *Impediments to Trade in Services: Measurement and Policy Implications*, Routledge, London and New York, 18–41.

Katouzian, M.A. (1970), The Development of the Service Sector: A New Approach, in: Oxford Economic Papers, vol. 22.

Keeble, D.E. and D.P. Hauser (1971), Spatial analysis of manufacturing growth in outer South-East England 1960-1967, in: *Regional Studies*, vol. 5, 229-262.

Keller, W. (2002), Geographic Localization of International Technology Diffusion, in: *American Economic Review*, Vol. 92, 120-142.

Kim, S. (1995), Expansion of markets and the geographic distribution of economic activities: the trends in US regional manufacturing structure 1860-1987, in: *Quarterly Journal of Economics,* vol. 10, 881-908.

Klepper, St. (1996), Entry, Exit, Growth, and Innovation over the Product Cycle, in: *American Economic Review,* vol. 86, 562-583.

Kolm, S.C. (1969), The optimal production of social justice, in Margolis, J. and H. Guitton (eds.), *Public Economics*, 145-200.

Koski, H.; Rouvinen, P. and P. Ylä-Anttila (2002), ICT clusters in Europe, The great central banana and the small Nordic potato, in: *Information Economics and Policy*, vol. 14, 145-165.

Krieger-Boden, Ch. and I. Traistaru-Siedschlag (2008), Regional structural change and cohesion in the enlarged European Union: An Introduction, in: Krieger-Boden, Ch.; Morgenroth, E. and G. Petrakos (eds), *The Impact of European Integration on Regional Structural Change and Cohesion*, Routledge.

Krugman, P. (1980), Scale Economies, Product Differentiation, and the Pattern of Trade, in: *American Economic Review*, vol. 70, 950-959.

Krugman, P. (1991a), *Geography and Trade*, MIT Press.

Krugman, P. (1991b), Increasing returns and economic geography, in: *Journal of Political Economy*, vol. 99, 183-199.

Krugman, P. (1995), *Development, Geography, and Economic Theory*, The MIT Press Cambridge Mass.

Krugman, P. and A.J. Venables (1995), Globalisation and the Inequality of Nations, NBER Working Paper.

Kuznets, S. (1972), *Economic growth of nations. Total output and production structure,* Cambridge M.A.

Jennequin, H. (2008), The Evolution of the Geographical Concentration of Tertiary Sector Activities in Europe, in: *The Service Industries Journal*, Vol. 28, 291-306.

Laafia, I. (1999), Beschäftigung im Hochtechnologiebereich, in: Eurostat (eds.), *Statistik kurz gefasst, Thema 9, Forschung und Entwicklung*, Luxembourg.

Landesmann, M. (2000), Structural change in the Transition Economies 1989-1999, in: *Economic Survey of Europe*, vol. 2, 95-123.

Leser, C. (1949), Changes in level and diversity of employment in regions of Great Britain 1937-47, in: *Economic Journal*, vol. 59, 326-342.

Longhi, S.; Nijkamp, P and I Traistaru (2004), Economic Integration and Regional Structural Change in a Wider Europe: Evidence from New EU and Accession Countries, in: *Journal for Institutional Innovation, Development & Transition,* vol. 8, 48-55.

Los, B. and B. Verspagen (2006), The Evolution Of Productivity Gaps And Specialization Patterns, in: *Metroeconomica*, vol. 57, 464-493.

Lucas, R.E. (1988), On the Mechanics of Economic Development, in: *Journal of Monetary Economics*, vol. 22, 3-42.

Maasoumi, E. (1993), A compendium to information theory in economics and econometrics, in: *Econometric reviews*, vol. 12, 137-181.

Markusen; J. and A. Venables (1998), Multinationa firms and the new trade theory, in: *Journal of International Economics,* vol. 46, 183-203.

Markusen, J. and A. and Venables (2000), The theory of endowment, intra-industry and multi-national trade, in: *Journal of International Economics,* vol. 52, 209-234.

Marshall, A. (1920): Principles of Economics, Macmillan, 8nd ed., London, First published 1890.

Marshall, N. (1988): *Services and Uneven Regional Development*, Oxford University Press, Oxford.

Martin, P. and H. Rey (2000), Financial integration and asset returns, in: *European Economic Review*, vol. 44, 1327–1350.

Martin, P. and H. Rey (2004), Financial super-markets: size matters for asset trade, in: *Journal of International Economics*, vol. 64, 335–361.

Martin, P. and C. Rogers (1995), Industrial location and public infrastructure, in: *Journal of International Economics*, vol. 39, 335–351

Maurel, F. and Sédillot, B. (1999), A measure of the geographic concentration in French manufacturing industries, in: *Regional Science and Urban Economics*, vol. 29, 575-604.

Maurel, F., Fontagné, L., Mouhoud, E. and P. Petit (1999), Scenario pour une nouvelle Geographie Economique de l'Europe. Comissariat General du Plan.

McCann, P. (2005), Transport costs and new economic geography, in: *Journal of Economic Geography*, vol. 5, 305-318.

McLaughlin, G.E. (1930), Diversification in American Cities, in: *The Quarterly Journal of Economics,* vol. 45, 131-149.

Melitz, M.J. and G. Ottaviano (2008), Market Size, Trade, and Productivity, in: *Review of Economic Studies*, vol. 75, 295-316.

Midelfart, K.; Overman H.G. and A.J. Venables (2003), Monetary Union and the Economic Geography of Europe, in: *Journal of Common Market Studies*, vol. 41, 847–868.

Midelfart-Knarvik, K.; Overman, H.G.; Redding, S.J. and A.J. Venables (2002), Integration and industrial specialization in the European Union, in: *Revue Économique,* vol. 53, 469-482.

Midelfart-Knarvik, K.; Overman, H.G.; Redding, S.J. and A.J. Venables (2000), The Location of European industry, in: European Commission (eds.), *European integration and the functioning of product market*, Brussels, 213-270.

Minondo, A. (2011), Does comparative advantage explain countries' diversification level? In: *Review of World Economics,* vol. 147, 507-526.

Molle, W. (2006), *The Economics of European Integration, Theory, Practice, Policy*, 4th ed, Aldershot.

Moore, L. (1999), *Britain's Trade and Economic Structure, The Impact of the European Union*, London.

Nelson, R.R. (2005), *Technology, Institutions and Economic Growth*, Harvard University Press.

Norman, V.D. and A.J. Venables (1995), International Trade, Factor Mobility, and Trade Costs, in: *The Economic Journal*, vol. 105, 1488-1504.

OECD (1999), *EMU, Challenges and Policies*, Paris.

OECD (2003), *Classification of manufacturing industries based on technology. OECD Science, Technology Scoreboard 2003 – Towards a knowledge-based economy,* Paris.

OECD (2005), *Guide to Measuring the Information Society*, Paris.

Ohlin, B. (1933) *Interregional and International Trade*, Cambridge.

Ottaviano, G. (2012), Agglomeration, trade and selection, in: *Regional Science and Urban Economics*, vol. 42, 987-997.

Ottaviano, G. and T. van Ypersele (2005), Market size and tax competition, in: *Journal of International Economics*, vol. 67, 25-46.

Ottaviano, G. and J.F. Thisse (2004), Agglomeration and economic geography, Handbook of Regional and Urban Economics, in: Henderson J.V. and J.F. Thisse (ed.), *Handbook of Regional and Urban Economics*, vol. 4, 2563-2608.

Ottaviano, G.; Tabucchi, T. and J.F. Thisse (2002), Agglomeration and Trade Revisited, in: *International Economic Review*, vol. 43, 409-435.

Ottaviano, G. (1999), Integration, geography and the burden of history, in: *Regional Science and Urban Economics*, vol. 29, 245-256.

Palan, N. and C. Schmiedeberg (2010), Structural Convergence of European Countries, in: *Structural Change and Economic* Dynamics, vol. 21, 85-100.

Palan, N. and A. Rainer (2013), *The dynamics of industry concentration with an application to the textile industry*, Graz Schumpeter Working Paper Series.

Pasinetti, L.L. (1981), *Structural Change and Economic Growth,* Cambridge.

Pasinetti, L.L. (1993), *Structural Economic Dynamics – A Theory of the Economic Consequences of Human Learning,* Cambridge University Press.

Peikmans, J. and L.A. Winters (1988), *Europe's domestic market*, Chatham House, London.

Percoco, M.; Dall'Erba, S. and G. Hewings (2005), Structural Convergence of the National Economies of Europe, MPRA Paper, No. 1380.

Peri, G. (2002), Globalization, rigidities and national specialization: a dynamic analysis, in: *Structural Change and Economic Dynamics,* vol. 13, 151-177.

Picard, P.M. and E. Toulemonde (2006), Firms agglomerations and unions, in: *European Economic Review,* vol. 50, 669-694.

Pigliaru, F. (2003), Detecting Technological Catch-Up in Economic Convergence, in: *Metroeconomica*, vol. 54, 161-178.

Porat, M.U. (1976), The Information Economy, vol. 1, UMI Dissertation Information Service.

Porter, M.E. (1998), *On competition*, Boston.

Posner, M.V. (1961), International Trade and Technical Change, in: *Oxford Economic Papers*, vol. 13, 323–341.

Pratten, C. (1988), *A Survey of the Economies of Scale. In: Commission of the European Communities. Research on the "Cost of Non-Europe",* vol. 2, Studies on the Economics of Integration, Luxembourg.

Preissl, B. (2007), The German Service Gap or: Re-organising the Manufacturing-Service Puzzle, in: *Metroeconomica*, vol. 58, 457-478.

Puga, D. (1999), The rise and fall of regional inequalities, in: *European Economic Review*, vol. 43, 303-334.

Puga, D. and A. Venables (1998), Trading Arrangements and Industrial Development, in: *World Bank Economic Review,* vol. 12, 221-249.

Quah, D. (1993). Galton's fallacy and tests of convergence hypothesis, in: *The Scandinavian Journal of Econometrics*, vol. 95, 9-19.

Quah, D. (1997), Empirics for Growth and Distribution: Stratification, Polarization, and Convergence Clubs, in: *Journal of Economic Growth*, vol. 2, 27-59.

Radelet, S. and J. Sachs (1998), Shipping costs, manufactured exports and economic growth,

Ricardo, D. (1817), *On the Principles of Political Economy and Taxation*, London.

Rivera-Batiz, F.L. (1988), Increasing returns, monopolistic competition, and agglomeration economies in consumption and production, in: *Regional Science and Urban Economics*, vol. 18, 125-153.

Rodgers, A. (1957), Some aspects of industrial diversification in the United States, in: *Economic Geography*, vol. 33, 16-30.

Romer, P.M. (1986), Increasing Returns and Long-Run Growth, in: *Journal of Political Economy*. Vol. 94, 1002–1037.

Rose, R. (ed) (1985), *Public Employment in Western Nations*, Cambridge, Mass.

Rossi-Hansberg, E. (2005), A spatial theory of trade, in: *American Economic Review*, vol. 95, 1464-1491.

Rothschild, M. and J. Stiglitz (1970), Increasing Risk I, in: *Journal of Economic Theory,* vol. 2, 225-243.

Samuelson P.A. (1952), The transfer problem and transport costs: the terms of trade when impediments are absent, in: *Economic Journal*, vol. 62, 278-304.

Samuelson, P.A. (1954) The Transfer Problem and Transport Costs, II: Analysis of Effects of Trade Impediments, in: *The Economic Journal*, vol. 64, 264–289.

Sapir, A. (1996), The Effects of Europe's Internal Market Program on Production and Trade: A First Assessment, in: *Weltwirtschaftliches Archiv,* vol. 132, 457-475.

Saunders, P. and F. Klau (1985), The Role of the Public Sector, Causes and Consequences of the Growth of Government, in: *OECD Economic Studies*, 1-239.

Scherer, F.M. (1990), *Industrial market structure and economic performance,* 3rd ed., Boston.

Schettkat, R. and L. Yocarini (2006): The shift to services employment: A review of the literature, in: *Structural Change and Economic Dynamics,* vol. 17, 127-147.

Sen, A. (1973), *On Economic Inequality*, New York.

Shannon, C.E. (1948), A mathematical theory of communication, in: *The Bell System Technical Journal*, vol. 27, 379-423.

Shapiro, C., Varian, H. (1998): *Information Rules. A Strategic Guide to the Network Economy*, Harvard Business School Press.

Schettkat, R. and L. Yocarini (2006): The shift to services employment: A review of the literature, in: *Structural Change and Economic Dynamics*, vol. 17, 127-147.

Shorrocks, A.F. (1980), The class of additively decomposable inequality measures, in: *Econometrica*, vol. 48, 613-625.

Shorroks, A.F. (1984), Inequality decomposition by population subgroups, in: *Econometrica*, vol. 52, 1369-1385.

Siegel, P.B.; Johnson, T.G. and J. Alwang (1995), Regional Economic Diversity and Diversification, in: *Growth and Change*, vol. 26, 261-284

Singelmann, J. (1978a), *From Agriculture to Services. The Transformation of Industrial Employment*, Beverly Hills.

Singelmann, J. (1978b): The sectoral transformation of the labour force in seven industrialized countries, 1920–1970 in: *American Journal of Sociology*, vol. 83, 1224-1234.

Smith, S.M. and C.M. Gibson (1988), Industrial Diversification in Nonmetropolitan Counties and Its Effect on Economic Stability, in: *Western Journal of Agricultural Economics*, vol. 13, 193-201.

Smith, A. and A.J. Venables (1988), Completing the internal market in the European community. Some Industry Simulations, in: *European Economic Review*, Vol. 32, 1501-1525.

Stigler, G.J. (1956), *Trends in Employment in the Service Industries*, PPrinceton University Press.

Stiroh, K.J. (2002), Information technology and the U.S. productivity revival: what do the industry data say? In: *American Economic Review*, vol. 92, 1559-1576.

Storper, M.; Chen, Y. and F. De Paolis (2002), Trade and the location of industries in the OECD and European Union, in: *Journal of Economic Geography*, vol. 2, 73-107.

Südekum, J. (2006), Concentration and Specialisation Trends in Germany since Re-Unification, in: *Regional Studies*, vol. 40, 861-873.

Summers, R. (1985), Services in the International Economy, in: Inman, R.P. (ed), *Managing the Service Economy, Problems and Prospects*, Cambridge.

Sweeney, P. (1998), *The Celtic Tiger: Ireland's Continuing Economic Miracle*, Oxfordshire.

Syrquin, M. (2010): Kuznets and Pasinetti on the study of structural transformation: Never the Twain shall meet? in: *Structural change and Economic Dynamics*, vol. 21, p.248-257.

Tabuchi, T. and J.-F. Thisse (2002), Taste heterogeneity, labour mobility and economic geography, in: *Journal of Development Economics*, vol. 69, 155-177

Tauer, L.W. (1992), Diversification of production activities across individual states, in: *Journal of Production Agriculture*, vol. 5, 210-214.

Theil, H. (1967), *Economics and Information Theory*, North Holland.

Thünen von J.H. (1826), *Der Isolirte Staat in Beziehung auf Landwirthschaft und Nationalökonomie, oder Untersuchungen über den Einfluss, den die Getreidepreise, der Reichtum des Bodens und die Abgaben auf den Ackerbau Ausüben.*

Thomas, G.B. (1967), *Manpower Problems in the Service Sector*, Paris, OECD.

Timmer, M., O'Mahony, M. and B. van Ark (2007), The EU KLEMS Growth and Productivity Accounts: An Overview, University of Groningen and University of Birmingham.

Tirole, J. (1988), *The Theory of Industrial Organization.* Cambridge.

Tress, R. C. (1938), Unemployment and the diversification of industry, in: *The Manchester School*, vol. 9, 140-152.

Tylecote, A. and G. Vertova (2007), Technology and institutions in changing specialization: chemicals and motor vehicles in the United States, United Kingdom, and Germany, in: *Industrial and Corporate Change*, vol. 16, 875–911.

UNCTAD (2013), GVCs and Development: Investment and Value Added Trade in the Global Economy.

Venables, A.J (1996), Equilibrium Locations of Vertically Linked Industries, in: *International Economic Review*, vol. 37, 341-59.

Vernon, R. (1966), International Investment and International Trade in the Product Cycle, in: *Quarterly Journal of Economics*, vol. 80, 191–207.

Wasylenko, M.J. and R.A. Erickson (1978), On Measuring Economic Diversification, Comment, in: *Land Economics*, Vol. 54, 106-109.

Waterson, M. (1984): The profitability-concentration relation: market power or efficiency? in: *Journal of Industrial Economics*, vol.32, 435-50.

Watts, D. (2008), *The European Union*, Edinburgh.

Weber, A. (1909), *Über den Standort der Industrien*, Tübingen.

White, T. (2001), *Investing in People: Higher Education in Ireland from 1960 to 2000*, Dublin.

Williamson, J.G. (1965), Regional Inequality and the Process of National Development: A Description of Patterns, in: *Economic Development and Cultural Change*, vol. 13, 1-45.

Witt, U. (2003), *The Evolving Economy - Essays on the Evolutionary Approach to Economics,* Aldershot.

Wodon, Qu. and S. Yitzhaki (2006), Convergence forward and backward? in: *Economic Letters*, vol. 92, 47-51.

Wolff, E.N. (2007), Measures of technical change and structural change in services in the USA: was there a resurgence of productivity growth in services, in: *Metroeconomica*, vol. 58, 368-395.

World Bank (2009), *Reshaping Economic Geography*, World Development Report 2009.

World Trade Organization (2008), Understanding the WTO, available under http://www.wto.org/english/thewto_e/whatis_e/tif_e/understanding_e.pdf

Yamamoto, K. (2002), Location of industry, market size, and imperfect international capital mobility, in: *Regional Science and Urban Economics*, vol. 38, 518-532.

Yu, Z. (2005), Trade, market size, and industrial structure: revisiting the home market effect, in: *Canadian Journal of Economics*, vol. 38, 255–272.

# Appendix

## Appendix A: Industry Classification

*Table A 1: Industry classification*

| Sectors | Classification | Industries | NACE |
|---|---|---|---|
| Agriculture | | Agriculture, hunting, forestry and fishing | 01, 02 |
| Manufacturing | Low technology | Food, Beverages and Tobacco | 15, 16 |
| | | Textiles and Textile Products | 17-18 |
| | | Leather and Footwear | 19 |
| | | Wood, Wood Products and Furniture | 20 |
| | | Pulp, Paper and Paper Products | 21 |
| | | Printing, Publishing, and Reproduction of Recorded Media | 22 |
| | Medium-low technology | Non-metallic Mineral Products (glass, ceramics, plaster) | 26 |
| | | Basic Metals Products | 27 |
| | | Fabricated Metal Products | 28 |
| | Medium-high technology | Coke, Refined Petroleum, and Nuclear Fuel | 23 |
| | | Rubber and Plastics Products | 25 |
| | | Machinery and Equipment, n.e.c. | 29 |
| | | Transport Equipment: Motor Vehicles, Aircraft and Spacecraft | 34,35 |
| | | Recycling; manufacturing n.e.c. | 36, 37 |
| | High technology | Chemical Industry | 24 |
| | | Office, Accounting and Computing Machines | 30 |
| | | Electrical Engineering | 31 |
| | | Communications Equipment | 32 |
| | | Medical, Precision and Optical Instruments | 33 |
| Services | Low knowledge intensity | Domestic Services | 95 |
| | | Hotels and Restaurants | 55 |
| | | Wholesale and Retail Trade | 50-52 |
| | | Transport and Storage | 60-63 |
| | | Real Estate | 70 |

| Sectors | Classification | Industries | NACE |
|---------|----------------|------------|------|
| | High knowledge intensity | Post and Telecommunication | 64 |
| | | Financial Intermediation | 65-67 |
| | | Business Services | 71-74 |
| | | Education | 80 |
| | | Health and Social work | 85 |

*Table A 2: Characteristics of Manufacturing Industries*

| | Increasing Returns to Scale | Inter- industry Linkages | Intra-industry Linkages |
|---|---|---|---|
| Food, Beverages & Tobacco | Low | High | Medium |
| Textile | Low | Low | High |
| Leather | Low | Low | High |
| Wood | Low | Medium | Medium |
| Paper | Medium | Low | High |
| Printing & Publishing | Medium | Low | High |
| Coke & Fuel | High | High | Low |
| Chemicals | High | Low | High |
| Rubber & Plastic | Low | High | Low |
| Non-metal Mineral Products | Medium | Medium | Medium |
| Basic Metals | Medium | Medium | Medium |
| Fabricated Metals | High | Medium | Medium |
| Machinery | Medium | Medium | Medium |
| Accounting & Computing Machines | Medium | High | Medium |
| Electrical Engineering | Medium | Medium | Medium |
| Communications Equipment | Medium | Low | Medium |
| Precision Instruments | Medium | Medium | Low |
| Transport Equipment | High | Medium | High |
| Recycling | Medium | Medium | Low |

*Table A3: Characteristics of Service Industries*

| Industry | Change in Labour productivity | Industry Characteristic |
|---|---|---|
| Domestic Services | Low | traditional |
| Hotels & Restaurants | medium | hybrid |
| Wholesale & Retail Trade | medium | hybrid |
| Transport & Storage | High | standard |
| Real Estate | medium | hybrid |
| Post & Telecommunication | High | standard |
| Business Services | High | standard |
| Health & Social Work | Low | traditional |
| Education | Low | traditional |

# Appendix B: Empirical results

*Table B 1: Augmented Dickey-Fuller test for manufacturing industries*

| | $\ln SHE_t^N$ | | $\ln SHE_t^{N-1}$ | | $\ln$ *max deviation* | |
|---|---|---|---|---|---|---|
| | d=0 | d=1 | d=0 | d=1 | d=0 | d=1 |
| Food, Beverages | -0.852 | -4.742 | -1.835 | -4.891 | 0.461 | -3.874 |
| Textile | -2.922 | -4.417 | -2.398 | -5.114 | -2.023 | -5.273 |
| Leather & Footwear | -2.759 | -3.737 | -3.036 | -3.822 | -1.189 | -4.311 |
| Wood | -1.608 | -4.089 | -1.427 | -5.148 | -1.655 | -5.000 |
| Paper | -1.037 | -3.995 | -1.779 | -5.359 | -0.645 | -5.443 |
| Printing & Publishing | -1.632 | -4.102 | -1.741 | -3.988 | -0.597 | -6.090 |
| Non-metal Mineral Products | -1.446 | -3.703 | -1.469 | -4.049 | -2.661 | -4.587 |
| Basic Metals | -0.468 | -5.101 | -1.245 | -5.067 | -1.644 | -3.884 |
| Fabricated Metals | 0.179 | -6.200 | 0.279 | -6.321 | -1.376 | -5.110 |
| Coke & Fuel | -0.512 | -3.569 | -0.241 | -4.042 | -1.543 | -5.394 |
| Rubber & Plastic | -1.330 | -3.826 | -1.641 | -3.599 | 0.58 | -6.157 |
| Machinery | -1.078 | -5.279 | -1.548 | -5.951 | -2.07 | -3.725 |
| Transport Equipment | -0.394 | -4.791 | -0.879 | -4.728 | -1.414 | -5.388 |
| Others; Recycling | -0.636 | -5.024 | -1.046 | -4.753 | -0.557 | -5.515 |
| Chemicals | -1.371 | -7.161 | -1.231 | -7.235 | -2.022 | -5.239 |
| Accounting & Computing Machines | -1.194 | -2.187 | -1.203 | -2.638 | 0.498 | -4.009 |
| Electrical Engineering | -0.250 | -4.309 | -2.055 | -5.396 | 2.606 | -2.523 |
| Communications Equipment | -0.468 | -4.127 | -0.980 | -4.354 | -0.194 | -5.227 |
| Medical, Precision & Optical instruments | 0.111 | -4.599 | -1.512 | -4.688 | -0.073 | -3.518 |

1%/5%/10% critical values: -3.689/-2.975/-2.619 (d=0); -3.696/-2.978/-2.620 (d=1).

*Table B 2: Augmented Dickey-Fuller test for service industries*

| | $\ln SHE_t^N$ | | $\ln SHE_t^{N-1}$ | | $\ln$ *max deviation* | |
|---|---|---|---|---|---|---|
| | d=0 | d=1 | d=0 | d=1 | d=0 | d=1 |
| Domestic Services | -0.596 | -5.630 | 0.006 | -5.767 | -2.270 | -6.041 |
| Hotels & Restaurants | -2.383 | -9.826 | -1.249 | -8.087 | -1.597 | -4.606 |
| Wholesale & Retail Trade | -2.034 | -5.449 | -1.359 | -4.634 | -2.539 | -8.004 |
| Transport & Storage | 1.348 | -5.279 | 0.302 | -6.238 | 0.852 | -5.894 |

|  | ln $SHE_t^N$ | | ln $SHE_t^{N-1}$ | | ln *max deviation* | |
|---|---|---|---|---|---|---|
|  | d=0 | d=1 | d=0 | d=1 | d=0 | d=1 |
| Real Estate | -2.380 | -4.946 | -2.684 | -5.253 | -1.207 | -3.365 |
| Post & Telecommunication | -1.711 | -5.457 | -1.899 | -6.065 | -1.174 | -5.468 |
| Financial Intermediation | -1.461 | -7.091 | -1.027 | -8.038 | -0.056 | -4.895 |
| Business Services | -0.636 | -4.032 | -0.548 | -4.187 | -1.577 | -2.769 |
| Health & Social Work | -2.629 | -4.347 | -2.529 | -4.391 | -1.926 | -4.83 |
| Education | -1.323 | -4.517 | -1.242 | -4.330 | -1.844 | -4.99 |
| Observations | 35 | 34 | 35 | 34 | 35 | 34 |
| 1% critical value | -3.682 | -3.689 | -3.682 | -3.689 | -3.682 | -3.689 |

1%/5%/10% critical values: -3.682/-2.972/-2.618 (d=0); -3.689/-2.975/-2.619 (d=1).

*Table B 3: ARIMA results: $SHE^N$ in manufacturing industries*

|  | constant | AR(1) | AR(2) | AR(3) | MA(1) | MA(2) |
|---|---|---|---|---|---|---|
| Food, Beverages & Tobacco | -0.0110 ** (0.0052) | -0.8182 *** (0.2410) | - | - | 1.1116 *** (0.2637) | 0.4358 ** (0.2050) |
| Textile | 0.0097 *** (0.0030) | - | - | - | - | - |
| Leather & Footwear | 0.0135 ** (0.0059) | -0.0095 (0.3936) | - | - | 0.4636 (0.3502) | - |
| Wood | -0.0097 ** (0.0047) | - | - | - | - | - |
| Paper | -0.0065 (0.0062) | 0.3044 (0.1353) | - | - | - | - |
| Printing & Publishing (structural break 1993/1994) | 0.0160 *** (0.0051) | - | - | - | -0.0876 (0.2328) | - |
|  | -0.0215 *** (0.0081) | 0.4501 (0.3335) | -0.5169 (0.4687) | - | - | - |
| Non-metal Mineral Products (structural break 1984/1985) | -0.0221 * (0.0122) | | | | | |
|  | 0.0188 ** (0.0086) | -0.8893 *** (0.2022) | - | - | 0.9905 *** (0.2780) | 0.2930 (0.2785) |
| Basic Metals | -0.0044 (0.0027) | 0.3004 * (0.1700) | 0.2937 (0.2602) | - | - | - |
| Fabricated Metals | -0.0091 * (0.0052) | - | - | - | - | - |
| Coke & Fuel | 0.0001 (0.0119) | 0.3259 (0.2650) | - | - | - | - |
| Rubber & Plastic | 0.0192 *** (0.0056) | -0.9524 (0.6912) | -0.4422 (0.7513) | -0.2954 (0.2134) | 0.8789 (0.6797) | 0.2001 (0.6706) |
| Machinery | 0.0022 (0.0031) | - | - | - | - | - |

| | constant | AR(1) | AR(2) | AR(3) | MA(1) | MA(2) |
|---|---|---|---|---|---|---|
| Transport Equipment | 0.0110 * (0.0061) | 0.3072 (0.1942) | - | - | - | - |
| Others; Recycling | 0.0081 * (0.0046) | 0.9357 * (0.4903) | -0.3041 (0.2303) | - | -0.7709 * (0.4308) | - |
| Chemicals | 0.0116 ** (0.0059) | - | - | - | - | - |
| Accounting & Computing Machines | 0.0194 (0.0163) | - | - | - | 0.1121 (0.2353) | - |
| Electrical Engineering | -0.0050 (0.0035) | - | - | - | -0.4579 *** ( 0.1535) | - |
| Communications Equipment | 0.0050 (0.0141) | - | - | - | 0.6350 *** (0.1182) | - |
| Medical, Precision & Optical instruments | 0.0033 (0.0047) | - | - | - | 0.3229 * (0.1805) | -0.2331 (0.1842) |

206

Table B 4: ARIMA results: SHEN-1 in manufacturing industries

| | constant | AR(1) | AR(2) | AR(3) | MA(1) | MA(2) |
|---|---|---|---|---|---|---|
| Food, Beverages & Tobacco | -0.0087 (0.0071) | -0.8331 *** (0.1297) | - | - | 1.4896 *** (0.1895) | 0.9194 *** (0.2205) |
| Textile | 0.0105 ** (0.0041) | - | - | - | - | - |
| Leather & Footwear | 0.0122 ** (0.0061) | -0.0332 (0.3298) | - | - | 0.5102 * (0.3030) | - |
| Wood | -0.0072 * (0.0044) | -0.0875 (0.2778) | -0.0080 (0.2899) | - | - | - |
| Paper | -0.0047 (0.0069) | 0.0180 (0.1698) | - | - | - | - |
| Printing & Publishing (structural break 1993/1994) | 0.0203 *** (0.0067) | - | - | - | - | - |
| | -0.0194 * (0.0114) | 0.7412 (0.4637) | -0.6332 *** (0.1964) | - | - | - |
| Non-metal Mineral Products (structural break 1984/1985) | -0.198 (0.0215) | 0.4498 * (0.2586) | - | - | - | - |
| | 0.0213 ** (0.0089) | -0.9459 ** (0.3776) | - | - | 0.9244 (0.5650) | 0.1017 (0.3010) |
| Basic Metals | -0.0036 (0.0023) | 0.3003 ** (0.1374) | 0.1411 (0.1498) | - | - | - |
| Fabricated Metals | -0.0106 * (0.0057) | - | - | - | - | - |
| Coke & Fuel | -0.0025 (0.0158) | -0.2329 (0.7247) | - | - | 0.5736 (0.6588) | 0.3112 (0.2927) |
| Rubber & Plastic | 0.0212 *** (0.0058) | -0.0544 (0.8166) | -0.2461 (0.2472) | - | -0.0892 (0.7846) | - |
| Machinery | 0.0016 (0.0035) | - | - | - | - | - |
| Transport Equipment | 0.0109 * (0.0064) | 0.2703 (0.2067) | - | - | - | - |
| Others; Recycling | 0.0019 (0.0043) | 1.4622 *** (0.1409) | -0.8896 *** (0.1570) | - | -1.5698 *** (0.2733) | 0.8202 *** (0.2549) |
| Chemicals | -0.0067 * (0.0037) | - | - | - | -0.3843 ** (0.1701) | -0.1182 (0.2140) |
| Accounting & Computing Machines | 0.0029 (0.0132) | -0.6367 * (0.3442) | - | - | 0.8203 *** (0.3116) | - |
| Electrical Engineering | -0.0065 * (0.0037) | - | - | - | -0.4693 *** (0.1497) | - |
| Communications Equipment | -0.0028 (0.0158) | - | - | - | 0.9047 *** (0.0824) | - |
| Medical, Precision & Optical instruments | -0.0035 (0.0031) | - | - | - | 0.1267 (0.1662) | -.4917 *** (0.1702) |

*Table B 5: ARIMA results: max. deviation in manufacturing industries*

| | constant | AR(1) | AR(2) | MA(1) | MA(2) | MA(3) |
|---|---|---|---|---|---|---|
| Food, Beverages & Tobacco | -0.0193 ** (0.0091) | - | - | 0.3448 *** (0.1055) | - | - |
| Textile | 0.0075 (0.0050) | - | - | - | - | - |
| Leather & Footwear | 0.0187 * (0.0106) | - | - | 0.1941 (0.1504) | - | - |
| Wood | -0.0195 * (0.0112) | 0.1217 (0.1721) | -0.3774 * (0.2226) | - | - | - |
| Paper | -0.0083 (0.0105) | - | - | 0.2091 (0.1643) | -0.0570 (0.1972) | 0.4099 ** (0.2004) |
| Printing & Publishing | -0.0057 (0.0106) | -0.0687 (0.1755) | 0.1400 (0.2090) | - | - | - |
| Non-metal Mineral Products | -0.0080 (0.0138) | - | - | - | - | - |
| Basic Metals | -0.0235 *** (0.0088) | - | - | - | - | - |
| Fabricated Metals | 0.0052 (0.0244) | - | - | 0.5850 *** (0.2206) | 0.4892 *** (0.1645) | - |
| Coke & Fuel | 0.0062 (0.0193) | -0.5194 * (0.2741) | - | 0.8919 *** (0.1433) | - | - |
| Rubber & Plastic | 0.0056 (0.0101) | - | - | - | - | - |
| Machinery | 0.0109 (0.0073) | -0.7674 *** (0.1822) | -0.7130 *** (0.1770) | 1.2787 *** (0.2243) | 0.5794 ** (0.2509) | - |
| Transport Equipment | 0.0103 (0.0113) | -0.6154 * (0.3182) | - | 0.8133 *** (0.2562) | - | - |
| Others; Recycling | 0.0188 ** (0.0089) | 0.4145 *** (0.1518) | - | - | - | - |
| Chemicals | 0.0373 *** (0.0115) | - | - | 0.4547 *** (0.1651) | - | - |
| Accounting & Computing Machines | 0.0387 * (0.0198) | - | - | - | - | - |
| Electrical Engineering | 0.0078 (0.0068) | 0.0835 (0.1704) | -0.2185 (0.1275) | - | - | - |
| Communications Equipment | -0.0099 (0.0103) | - | - | 0.0946 (0.2067) | - | - |
| | 0.1145 * (0.0614) | - | - | - | - | - |
| Medical, Precision & Optical instruments | -0.0057 (0.0107) | - | - | 0.0562 (0.2829) | - | - |
| | 0.0830 ** (0.0344) | - | - | - | - | - |

*Table B 6: ARIMA results: $SHE^N$ in service industries*

|  | constant | AR(1) | AR(2) | AR(3) | MA(1) |
|---|---|---|---|---|---|
| Domestic Services (structural break in 1981/1982) | -0.0168 (0.0138) | 0.5568 * (0.2983) | - | - | - |
|  | 0.0096 (0.0068) | - | - | - | - |
| Hotels & Restaurants | 0.0025 (0.0022) | -0.1322 (0.2436) | - | - | -0.4863 ** (0.2158) |
| Wholesale & Retail Trade | 0.0042 (0.0074) | -0.6853 (0.4620) | 0.0820 (0.2907) | 0.1968 (0.2445) | 0.7845 * (0.4383) |
| Transport & Storage | -0.0191 ** (0.0089) | 0.0529 (0.1975) | 0.2380 (0.2155) | - | - |
| Real Estate | 0.0038 (0.0074) | - | - | - | - |
| Post & Tele-communication (structural break in 19888/1989) | -0.0236 *** (0.0052) | - | - | - | -0.4013 * (0.2251) |
|  | 0.0105 * (0.0060) | -0.5492 (0.3920) | -0.4022 (0.4116) | - | - |
| Financial Intermediation (structural break in 1993/1994) | -0.0058 (0.0163) | - | - | - | - |
|  | 0.0160 ** (0.0072) | - | - | - | -0.1536 (0.3831) |
| Business Services | 0.0086 (0.0087) | - | - | - | 0.4059 *** (0.1538) |
| Health & Social Work | 0.0073 (0.0058) | 0.2431 (0.1822) | - | - | - |
| Education | -0.0023 (0.0097) | - | - | - | - |

*Table B 7: ARIMA results: SHE$^{N-1}$ in service industries*

|  | constant | AR(1) | AR(2) | MA(1) |
|---|---|---|---|---|
| Domestic Services | 0.0072 (0.0052) | - | - | - |
| Hotels & Restaurants | 0.0044 (0.0068) | -0.9343 *** (0.1487) | - | 0.7923 ** (0.3482) |
| Wholesale & Retail Trade | 0.0004 (0.0078) | 0.2420 (0.1945) | - | - |
| Transport & Storage | -0.0116 * (0.0060) | -0.1660 (0.7663) | -0.2183 (0.2317) | 0.0531 (0.8739) |
| Real Estate | 0.0052 (0.0114) | - | - | 0.2596 * (0.1495) |
| Post & Telecommunication (structural break in 1988/1989) | -0.0260 ** (0.0098) | - | - | - |
|  | 0.0056 (0.0074) | -0.4213 (0.2708) | - | - |
| Financial Intermediation (structural break in 1993/1994) | 0.0012 (0.0209) | - | - | 0.6706 ** (0.3112) |
|  | 0.0023 (0.0108) | 0.2854 (0.4288) | - | - |
| Business Services | 0.0090 (0.0093) | - | - | 0.4015 *** (0.1465) |
| Health & Social Work | 0.0082 (0.0065) | - | - | 0.2338 (0.1614) |
| Education | -0.0068 (0.0173) | 0.2492 (0.3009) | - | - |

*Table B 8: ARIMA results: max deviation in service industries*

|  | constant | AR(1) | AR(2) | MA(1) | MA(2) |
|---|---|---|---|---|---|
| Domestic Services (structural break in 1990/1991) | -0.0423 ** (0.0170) | - | - | - | - |
|  | 0.0279 (0.0253) | -0.0192 (0.4432) | - | - | - |
| Hotels & Restaurants | -0.0061 (0.0173) | - | - | 0.1506 (0.1725) | -0.3205 (0.2143) |
| Wholesale & Retail Trade | 0.0162 (0.0120) | -0.3245 ** (0.1342) | - | - | - |
| Transport & Storage | -0.0331 (0.0225) | 0.0083 (0.2103) | 0.3359 (0.2614) | - | - |
| Real Estate | 0.0007 (0.0156) | 0.1674 (0.4171) | - | 0.2643 (0.3625) | 0.4720 *** (0.1574) |
| Post & Telecommunication (structural break in 1988/1989) | -0.0132 (0.0227) | 0.3067 (0.3823) | - | - | - |
|  | 0.0233 * (0.0123) | -0.3459 * (0.1879) | - | - | - |
| Financial Intermediation (structural break in 1993/1994) | -0.0112 (0.0183) | - | - | 0.6312 ** (0.2569) | - |
|  | 0.0839 *** (0.0321) | -0.2533 (0.5193) | -0.7490 ** (0.3383) | - | - |
| Business Services | 0.0042 (0.0168) | - | - | 0.6331 *** (0.1943) | - |
| Health & Social Work | 0.0030 (0.0063) | - | - | - | - |
| Education | 0.0091 (0.0063) | - | - | - | - |

Table B9: Country Deviation by Industry in the Manufacturing Sector ($\times 10^{-2}$)

|  | AUT | BEL | DK | FIN | FRA | GER | GRC | IRL | ITA | NLD | PRT | ESP | SWE | UK |
|---|---|---|---|---|---|---|---|---|---|---|---|---|---|---|
| Food 1970 | 2.7 | 0.7 | 7.1 | 1.4 | 0.3 | -0.7 | 9.4 | 14.4 | -0.30 | 5.8 | 2.4 | 4.9 | -1.9 | -2.2 |
| Food 2004 | 0 | 1.3 | 4.3 | -4 | 3.7 | 0.1 | 7.6 | 6.6 | -3.4 | 1.3 | -1.8 | 0.7 | -5 | 0 |
| Textile 1970 | 0.4 | 1.4 | -4.7 | -0.5 | 0.6 | -3.2 | 9.5 | -1.8 | 6.6 | -6.4 | 16.4 | 2.6 | -7.6 | -2.3 |
| Textile 2004 | -3 | -1.7 | -5.7 | -4.7 | -2.9 | -5.6 | 12.3 | 5.6 | 7 | -5.9 | 21.2 | 2.9 | -6.7 | -3.8 |
| Leather & Footwear 1970 | 0.1 | -1.1 | -0.8 | -0.3 | 0.1 | -0.3 | 0.7 | -0.4 | 2.1 | -1.5 | 2.5 | 0.6 | -1.5 | -1 |
| Leather & Footwear 2004 | -0.6 | -1.1 | -1.4 | -1 | -0.6 | -1.2 | 1.3 | -1.3 | 2 | -1.3 | 4.8 | 0.7 | -1.4 | -1.2 |
| Wood 1970 | 1.6 | -1.3 | -0.1 | 7 | -0.6 | -0.5 | 1.5 | -0.7 | 1.8 | -1.7 | 3.6 | 1.1 | 3.9 | -1.6 |
| Wood 2004 | 2.6 | -1.1 | -0.2 | 3.6 | -0.9 | -0.8 | 2.4 | -0.3 | 0.5 | -1.5 | 2.3 | 0.3 | 2.2 | -0.6 |

| | AUT | BEL | DK | FIN | FRA | GER | GRC | IRL | ITA | NLD | PRT | ESP | SWE | UK |
|---|---|---|---|---|---|---|---|---|---|---|---|---|---|---|
| Paper 1970 | 0.6 | -0.2 | -0.3 | 7.7 | -0.2 | 0.1 | -0.8 | 0.3 | -1.2 | 0.2 | -1.1 | -0.8 | 4.5 | 0.3 |
| Paper 2004 | 0.4 | 0 | -0.6 | 5.7 | -0.2 | 0.3 | -1 | -0.5 | -0.6 | 0.2 | -1.2 | -0.6 | 3.3 | 0.2 |
| Printing & Publishing 1970 | -0.4 | -0.3 | 5 | 1.5 | 0.1 | 0.2 | 0.1 | 1 | -1.1 | 4.3 | -1.2 | -1.1 | 2 | -0.4 |
| Printing & Publishing 2004 | -1.6 | -0.6 | 2.3 | 1 | 0.2 | -0.8 | -0.6 | 1.7 | -1.9 | 3.6 | -2.4 | -0.5 | 0.1 | 4 |
| Non-metal Mineral Products 1970 | -0.3 | 0 | -0.5 | -0.2 | 0.4 | 0.2 | 0.9 | -0.5 | -0.1 | -0.2 | -0.5 | -0.1 | -0.4 | -0.3 |
| Non-metal Mineral Products 2004 | -0.2 | 0.6 | -0.3 | 0.2 | 0.3 | -0.2 | 1 | -0.3 | 0 | 0.2 | -0.4 | -0.2 | -0.1 | -0.2 |
| Basic Metals 1970 | -1.5 | 1.8 | -1.4 | -2.6 | -1.6 | 0.9 | -1.6 | 0.2 | -0.2 | 1.9 | -2.1 | 0.4 | -1.7 | 0.3 |
| Basic Metals 2004 | -1.3 | 6.8 | 1.9 | -1 | -1.4 | 0.8 | -1 | 5 | -1.1 | 2.2 | -3.1 | -0.2 | 0.2 | 0.9 |
| Fabricated Metals 1970 | 0.4 | -0.7 | 0.3 | 0.6 | 0.5 | -0.5 | -0.2 | -0.1 | -0.5 | -0.9 | -0.9 | -0.6 | 0.2 | 1.2 |
| Fabricated Metals 2004 | -0.3 | -0.4 | 0.7 | -0.9 | 1.2 | 0.6 | -2.2 | -0.5 | -0.9 | -0.9 | -2.2 | -0.8 | -1.3 | 1.5 |
| Coke & Fuel 1970 | 0.6 | 1.4 | 0.7 | -0.9 | -0.3 | -0.3 | -0.4 | 1.3 | 0.9 | -2.8 | 1.7 | 2.7 | -0.9 | -0.9 |
| Coke & Fuel 2004 | 0.6 | 0.5 | -0.9 | -1 | -1 | -1.3 | 0.5 | 0.6 | 1.9 | -1.5 | 2.1 | 1.8 | -2.4 | -1 |
| Rubber & Plastic 1970 | 3.3 | 6.1 | -3.4 | -2 | -1.2 | 0 | -2.6 | -3 | -2.1 | -2.4 | -3.3 | 0.6 | 1.7 | 2.2 |
| Rubber & Plastic 2004 | 2 | 2.7 | -1.7 | 0.5 | -0.2 | 0.9 | 0 | -2 | -0.8 | -0.7 | -2 | 0.8 | 1.9 | -0.9 |
| Machinery 1970 | -1.2 | -1.6 | -1.4 | -4.7 | 1.3 | -0.6 | -2.8 | -2.7 | 1.8 | 1.2 | -2.8 | -1.6 | -0.7 | 0.7 |
| Machinery 2004 | -0.5 | -0.1 | -0.4 | -0.9 | 2.2 | -0.8 | -3.8 | -4.4 | 1.3 | -0.3 | -2.9 | 0.2 | -0.4 | -0.1 |
| Transport Equipment 1970 | -2.5 | -4.1 | 2.1 | 0.7 | 0.1 | 3.6 | -5.6 | -5 | -2.5 | -2.7 | -6.2 | -4.5 | 2.7 | 0.2 |
| Transport Equipment 2004 | 2.5 | -3.6 | 4.8 | 3.8 | -1.4 | 3.8 | -4.4 | -5.2 | 0.6 | -0.8 | -6.1 | -3.9 | 3.6 | -1.5 |
| Others; Recycling 1970 | -0.3 | -0.3 | -0.3 | -0.3 | -0.3 | 0.1 | -0.5 | 1.4 | -0.1 | 0 | -0.5 | 0.1 | 0.2 | 0.2 |
| Others; Recycling 2004 | -0.4 | -0.4 | -0.2 | -0.4 | 0.1 | -0.2 | -0.5 | 5.4 | -0.2 | 0 | -0.5 | 0.2 | -0.2 | 0.3 |
| Chemicals 1970 | -1.7 | -0.2 | 0 | -1.5 | -1.3 | 1.6 | -2.9 | -1.6 | -0.2 | -2.7 | -1.4 | -1.6 | -1.3 | 0.6 |
| Chemicals 2004 | -0.2 | -0.3 | 1.2 | -0.6 | -0.2 | 2.1 | -3.5 | -0.6 | 0.1 | -3.1 | -1.8 | -1.3 | -0.6 | -0.4 |
| Accounting & Computing Machines 1970 | 1 | 1.6 | -0.3 | -1.2 | -0.1 | 0.2 | -2 | -1.3 | -0.7 | 2.4 | -1.5 | -0.9 | 1 | 0.3 |
| Accounting & Computing Machines 2004 | 1.3 | -0.1 | -0.3 | 6 | 0.3 | 0.1 | -2 | 0.9 | -0.3 | 1.5 | -1.2 | -0.9 | 1.8 | -0.1 |
| Electrical Engineering 1970 | -0.8 | -2.1 | -1 | -2 | 0.8 | 0.5 | -2.1 | -0.1 | -0.6 | 2.2 | -2.1 | -2.1 | -0.3 | 0.5 |
| Electrical Engineering 2004 | -0.4 | -1.7 | 0.8 | -0.3 | 0.5 | 1.1 | -2.1 | 5.8 | -0.5 | 0.9 | -2.3 | -1.8 | 0.4 | 0.5 |
| Communications Equipment 1970 | -4.4 | -2.8 | -3.1 | -2.4 | 1.7 | -1.1 | -3.6 | -1.9 | -1 | -1.4 | -4 | -0.6 | 0.7 | 3.6 |
| Communications Equipment 2004 | -2.9 | 1 | -5.1 | -4.2 | 1 | 3.6 | -5 | -4.4 | -3.7 | -2.9 | -4.7 | 0.6 | 5.1 | 1.5 |
| Medical, Precision & Optical instruments 1970 | 2.5 | 1.5 | 2.1 | -0.2 | -0.2 | -0.3 | 3.1 | 0.6 | 0.1 | 4.6 | 1 | 0.9 | -0.4 | -1.5 |

| | AUT | BEL | DK | FIN | FRA | GER | GRC | IRL | ITA | NLD | PRT | ESP | SWE | UK |
|---|---|---|---|---|---|---|---|---|---|---|---|---|---|---|
| Medical, Precision & Optical instruments 2004 | 1.9 | -1.6 | 0.6 | -1.9 | -0.8 | -2.5 | 0.9 | -0.7 | 0.1 | 9 | 2.1 | 2.1 | -0.4 | 0.5 |

Table B10: Country Deviation by Industry in the Service Sector

| | AUT | BEL | DK | FIN | FRA | GER | GRC | IRL | ITA | NLD | PRT | ESP | SWE | UK |
|---|---|---|---|---|---|---|---|---|---|---|---|---|---|---|
| Domestic Services 1970 | -1.8 | 3.3 | 0.5 | -1.6 | -1.5 | -1.4 | -1.3 | 0.2 | 0.7 | 2.7 | 1.6 | 9.5 | n.a. | -2.2 |
| Domestic Services 2005 | -2.9 | -1.2 | -2.4 | -2.7 | -1.1 | -1.4 | -0.2 | -2.3 | 6.2 | 0.3 | 1.6 | 2 | -3.2 | -2.7 |
| Hotels & Restaurants 1970 | 6.3 | -3.2 | -3.3 | -1.1 | -0.4 | -1.4 | 3.5 | 0.6 | 2.4 | -3.1 | 7.9 | 4.2 | -3.3 | -1.7 |
| Hotels & Restaurants 2005 | 2.3 | -0.45 | -4.1 | -2.9 | -2.2 | -1.4 | 4.6 | 2.3 | 2.2 | -3.9 | 6.6 | 5.1 | -4.2 | -0.8 |
| Wholesale & Retail Trade 1970 | -1.8 | -1.3 | -1.1 | 0.3 | -2.6 | 1.6 | -6.5 | 1.2 | 7.1 | -0.9 | 6.9 | -1.2 | -2.9 | -3.1 |
| Wholesale & Retail Trade 2005 | 0.6 | -3.2 | -2 | -2.5 | -3 | -0.4 | 5.8 | -2.7 | 1.2 | -0.9 | 12.6 | 4.2 | -4.2 | -1.6 |
| Transport & Storage 1970 | -0.1 | -0.3 | 0.1 | 1.6 | -2.6 | 1.2 | 10.6 | -1.3 | -1.3 | -1.4 | -1.9 | 1.5 | -1.6 | 0.8 |
| Transport & Storage 2005 | 0.9 | 0.6 | 0.5 | 2.5 | -0.3 | -0.1 | 3.1 | 0.1 | 1.2 | -0.4 | -1.8 | 0.2 | -0.5 | -1.1 |
| Real Estate 1970 | 0.5 | 1.5 | -0.5 | -0.3 | -0.5 | 0.1 | 0.4 | 1.4 | -0.7 | -1.3 | -1.2 | -0.9 | 0.3 | 1.3 |
| Real Estate 2005 | 0 | 1 | -0.6 | 0.7 | 0.2 | -0.7 | 0.2 | 1.8 | -0.4 | -0.3 | -0.8 | 0.2 | 0.4 | 0.6 |
| Post & Telecommunication 1970 | -0.3 | 1.7 | -0.1 | -1 | 0 | 1.6 | -1.2 | -1.7 | -1.7 | 0.5 | -1.3 | -1.1 | -2.3 | 0.1 |
| Post & Telecommunication 2005 | 0.1 | 0.5 | -0.4 | -2.2 | 0.1 | 1 | -0.2 | -3.7 | -1.1 | 0.7 | -1.9 | -1.2 | -1.7 | 0.8 |
| Financial Intermediation 1970 | 0.4 | -0.6 | 0.2 | 1.3 | 0.6 | -0.2 | -1.1 | -0.7 | -0.8 | 0 | 0.8 | -0.2 | 0.7 | 0.1 |
| Financial Intermediation 2005 | 0.3 | -0.8 | 0.6 | 1.3 | 0.1 | -0.3 | -1.6 | -0.1 | -1.1 | 0.2 | -1 | 0.4 | 0.5 | 0.6 |
| Business Services 1970 | -3.6 | -0.4 | -1.5 | -5.3 | 4.1 | -0.6 | 0.2 | -3.6 | -4.1 | 3 | -6.9 | -4.5 | -2.3 | 3.7 |
| Business Services 2005 | -1.6 | 4.6 | -4.2 | -4.5 | 3 | 0.1 | -6.3 | -4.7 | -1.3 | 4.1 | -9.5 | -6 | -3.6 | 4.3 |
| Health & Social Work 1970 | -1 | -4.8 | 3.9 | 6.2 | 2.9 | -1.1 | -3.5 | 2.5 | -0.9 | 1.2 | -4.8 | -4.7 | 9.8 | 0.7 |
| Health & Social Work 2005 | 0.6 | 1.4 | 9.2 | 9.4 | 3.4 | 2.2 | -5.3 | 1.7 | -5.3 | 2.6 | -4.7 | -3.8 | 10.9 | -0.8 |
| Education 1970 | 1.3 | 4.1 | 1.8 | 0.1 | -0.1 | 0.3 | -1.1 | 1.5 | -0.8 | -0.7 | -1.1 | -2.7 | 4 | 0.3 |
| Education 2005 | -0.3 | 1.6 | 2.2 | 0.9 | -0.2 | 0.6 | -0.1 | 0.3 | -1.5 | -1.9 | -1.1 | -1.1 | 5.6 | 0.7 |